The
South
Atlantic
Quarterly
Winter 1994
Volume 93
Number 1

The *South Atlantic Quarterly* (ISSN 0038-2876) is published quarterly, at $54.00 for libraries and institutions and $24.00 for individuals, by Duke University Press, 905 W. Main St., 18-B, Durham, NC 27701. Second-class postage paid at Durham, NC. POSTMASTER: Send address changes to *South Atlantic Quarterly*, Box 90660, Duke University, Durham, NC 27708-0660.

Library exchanges and orders for them should be sent to Duke University Library, Gift and Exchange Department, Durham, NC 27708-0180.

The *South Atlantic Quarterly* is indexed in *Abstracts of English Studies*, *Academic Abstracts*, *America: History and Life*, *American Humanities Index*, *Arts and Humanities Citation Index*, *Book Review Index*, *Current Contents*, *Humanities Index*, *Index to Book Reviews in the Humanities*, and *Social Science Source*. This journal is a member of the Council of Editors of Learned Journals.

ISBN 0-8223-6408-5

STATEMENT OF OWNERSHIP AND MANAGEMENT. *The South Atlantic Quarterly* (ISSN 0038-2876) is published four times a year in Winter, Spring, Summer, and Fall by Duke University Press. The Office of Publication and General Business Office are located at 905 W. Main St., 18-B, Durham, NC 27701. The editor is Fredric Jameson at 102 Art Museum, Duke University, Durham, NC 27708-0672. The owner is Duke University Press, Durham, NC 27708-0660. There are no bondholders, mortgagees, or other security holders. EXTENT AND NATURE OF CIRCULATION. *Average number of copies of each issue published during the preceding twelve months:* (A) total number of copies printed, 2,553; (B.1) sales through dealers and carriers, street vendors and counter sales, 0; (B.2) paid mail subscriptions, 1,457; (C) total paid circulation, 1,457; (D) samples, complimentary, and other free copies, 28; (E) total distribution, 1,485; (F.1) office use, left over, unaccounted, spoiled after printing, 1,068; (F.2) returns from news agents, 0; (G) total, 2,553. *Actual number of copies of single issue published nearest to filing date:* (A) total number of copies printed, 2,564; (B.1) sales through dealers and carriers, street vendors and counter sales, 0; (B.2) paid mail subscriptions, 1,549; (C) total paid circulation, 1,549; (D) samples, complimentary, and other free copies, 28; (E) total distribution, 1,577; (F.1) office use, left over, spoiled after printing, 987; (F.2) returns from news agents, 0; (G) total, 2,564.

The Writings of J. M. Coetzee

GUEST EDITOR: MICHAEL VALDEZ MOSES

The
South
Atlantic
Quarterly
Winter 1994
Volume 93
Number 1

J. M. Coetzee

From *The Master of Petersburg*

Good morning. I have come to claim" (he is surprised at how steady his voice is) "some belongings of my son's. My son was involved in an accident last month, and the police took charge of certain items."

He unfolds the receipt and passes it across the counter. Depending on whether Pavel gave up the ghost before or after midnight, it is dated the day after or the day of Pavel's death; it names simply "letters and other papers."

The sergeant inspects the receipt dubiously. "October 7th. That's less than a month ago. The case won't be settled yet."

"How long will it take to settle?"

"Could be two months, could be three months, could be a year. It depends on the circumstances."

"There are no circumstances. There is no crime involved."

Holding the paper at arm's length, the sergeant leaves the room. When he returns, his air is markedly more surly. "You are, sir—?"

The *South Atlantic Quarterly* 93:1, Winter 1994.
Copyright © 1994 by J. M. Coetzee. *The Master of Petersburg* is forthcoming from Viking Penguin, 1994.

"Isaev. The boy's father."

"Yes, Mr. Isaev. If you will take a seat, you will be attended to in a short while."

His heart sinks. He had hoped simply to be handed Pavel's belongings and walk out of this place. What he can least afford is that the police should turn their attention on him.

"I can wait only a short while," he says briskly.

"Yes, sir, I'm sure the investigator in charge will see you soon. Just take a seat and make yourself comfortable."

He consults his watch, sits down on the bench, looks around with pretended impatience. It is early; there is only one other person in the ante-room, a young man in stained housepainter's overalls. Sitting bolt upright, he seems to be asleep. His eyes are closed, his jaw hangs, a soft rattle comes from the back of his throat.

Isaev. Inside him the confusion has not settled. Should he not drop the Isaev story at once, before getting enmired in it? But how can he explain? "Sergeant, there has been a slight mistake. Things are not entirely as they appear to be. In a sense I am not Isaev. The Isaev whose name I have for reasons of my own been using, reasons I won't go into here and now, but perfectly good reasons, has been dead for some years. Nevertheless, I brought up Pavel Isaev as my son and love him as my own flesh and blood. In that sense we bear the same name, or ought to. Those few papers he left behind are precious to me." What if he made this admission unprompted, and all the while they had suspected nothing? What if they had been on the point of giving him the papers, and now pulled up short? "Aha, what is this? Is there more to the case than meets the eye?"

As he sits vacillating between confessing and pressing on with the imposture, as he takes out his watch and glances at it crossly, trying to seem like an impatient *homme d'affaires* in this stuffy room with a stove burning in a corner, he has a premonition of an attack, and in the same movement recognizes that an attack would be a device, and the most childish at that, for extricating himself from a fix, while somewhere to the side falls the nagging shadow of a memory: surely he has been here before, in this very ante-room or one like it, and had an attack or a fainting fit! Why is it that he recollects the episode only so dimly? And what has the recollection to do with the smell of fresh paint?

"This is too much!"

His cry echoes around the room. The dozing housepainter gives a start; the desk-sergeant looks up in surprise. He tries to cover his confusion. "I mean," he says, lowering his voice, "I can't wait any longer, I have an appointment. As I said."

He has already stood up and put on his coat when the sergeant calls him back. "Councillor Maximov will see you now, sir."

In the office into which he is conducted there is no high bench. Save for a huge sofa in imitation leather, it is furnished in nondescript government-issue furniture. Councillor Maximov, the judicial investigator in Pavel's case, is a bald man with the tubby figure of a peasant woman, who fusses over him till he is comfortably seated, then opens the bulky folder before him on the desk and reads at length, murmuring to himself, shaking his head from time to time. "Sad business. . . . Sad business. . . ."

At last he looks up. "My sincere condolences, Mr. Isaev."

Isaev. Time to make up his mind!

"Thank you. I have come to ask for my son's papers to be returned. I am aware that the case has not been closed, but I do not see how private papers can be of any interest to your office or of any relevance to—to your proceedings."

"Yes, of course, of course! As you say, private papers. But tell me: when you talk of papers, what exactly do you mean? What do the papers consist in?"

The man's eyes have a watery gleam; his lashes are pale, like a cat's.

"How can I say? They were removed from my son's room, I haven't seen them yet. Letters, papers. . . ."

"You have not seen them but you believe they can be of no interest to us. I can understand that. I can understand that a father should believe his son's papers are a personal matter, or at least a family matter. Yes, indeed. Nevertheless, there is an investigation in progress— a mere formality, perhaps, but called for by the law, therefore not to be dismissed with a snap of the fingers or a flourish of the hand, and the papers are part of that investigation. So. . . ."

He puts his fingertips together, lowers his head, appears to sink into deep thought. When he looks up again he is no longer smiling, but wears an expression of the utmost determination. "I believe," he says, "yes, I do believe I have a solution that will satisfy both parties. Since the case is not closed—indeed, it has barely been opened—I cannot return the papers to you. But I am going to let you see them. Because I agree, it is unfair, most unfair, to take possession of them in such circumstances and keep them from the family."

With a sudden, startling gesture, like a card-player playing an all-conquering card, he sweeps a single leaf out of the folder and places it before him.

It is a list of names, Russian names written in Roman script, all beginning with the letter A.

"There is some mistake. This is not my son's handwriting."

"Not your son's handwriting? Hm." Maximov takes back the page and studies it. "Then have you any idea whose handwriting this might be, Mr. Isaev?"

"I don't recognize the handwriting, but it is not my son's."

From the bottom of the file Maximov selects another page and advances it across the desk. "And this?"

He does not need to read it. How stupid! he thinks. A flush of dizziness overtakes him. His voice seems to come from far away. "It is a letter from myself. I am not Isaev. I simply took the name—"

Maximov is waving a hand as if to chase away a fly, waving his words away, waving for silence; but he masters the dizziness and completes his declaration.

"I took the name so as not to complicate matters—for no other reason. My name is Fyodor Mikhailovich Dostoevsky. Pavel Aleksandrovich Isaev is my stepson, my late wife's only child. But to me he is my own son. He has no one but me in the world."

Maximov takes the letter from his slack grasp and peruses it again. It is the last letter he wrote from Dresden, a letter in which he chides Pavel for spending too much money. Mortifying to sit here while a stranger reads it! Mortifying ever to have written it! But how is one to know, *how is one to know*, that every day may be the last?

"Your loving father, Fyodor Mikhailovich Dostoevsky," murmurs the magistrate, and looks up. "So let me be clear, you are not Isaev at all, you are Dostoevsky."

"Yes. It has been a deception, a mistake, stupid but harmless, which I regret."

"I understand. Nevertheless, you have come here purporting—but need we use that ugly word? Let us use it gingerly, so to speak, for the time being, for lack of a better—purporting to be the deceased Pavel Aleksandrovich Isaev's father and applying to have his property released to you, while in fact you are not that person at all. It does not look well, does it?"

"It was a mistake, as I say, which I now bitterly regret. But the deceased *is* my son, and I am his guardian in law, properly appointed."

"Hm. I see here he was twenty-one, getting on for twenty-two, at the time of decease. So, strictly speaking, the writ of guardianship had expired. A man of twenty-one is his own master, is he not? A free person, in law."

It is this mockery that finally goads him. He stands up. "I did not come here to discuss my son with strangers," he says, his voice rising. "If you insist on keeping his papers, say so directly, and I will take other steps."

"Insist on keeping the papers? Of course not! My dear sir, please be seated! Of course not! On the contrary, I would very much like you to examine the papers, for your own sake and for ours too. The guidance you could give us would be appreciated, deeply appreciated. To begin with, let us take this item." He lays before him a set of half a dozen leaves written on both sides, the complete list of names of which he has already seen the first page, the A's. "Not your son's handwriting, is it?"

"No."

"No, we know that. Any idea whose handwriting it is?"

"I do not recognize it."

"It belongs to a young woman at present resident abroad. Her name is not relevant here, though if I mentioned it I think you would be surprised. This young woman is a friend and associate of a man named Nechaev, Sergei Gennadevich Nechaev. Does the name mean anything to you?"

"I do not know Nechaev personally, and I doubt very much that my son knew him. Nechaev is a conspirator and an insurrectionist whose designs I repudiate with the utmost force."

"You do not know him personally, as you say. But you have had contact with him."

"No, I have not had contact with him. I attended a public meeting in Switzerland, in Geneva, at which numerous people spoke, Nechaev among them. He and I have been together in the same room—that sums up my acquaintance with him."

"And when was that?"

"It was in the autumn of 1867. The meeting was organized by the League for Peace and Freedom, as the body calls itself. I attended openly, as a patriotic Russian, to hear what might be said about Russia from all sides. The fact that I heard this young man Nechaev speak does not mean that I stand behind him. On the contrary, I repeat, I reject everything he stands for, and have said so many times, in public and in private."

"Including the welfare of the people? Doesn't Nechaev stand for the welfare of the people? Isn't that what he is fighting for?"

"I fail to understand the force of these questions. Nechaev stands only for the immediate overthrow of all the institutions of society, in the name of a principle of equality—equal happiness for all or, if not that, then equal misery for all. It is not a principle that he attempts to justify. In fact he seems to despise all principles as marks of useless intellection. Please don't try to associate me with Nechaev."

"Very well, I accept the reproof. Though I would not have thought of you yourself as a martinet for consistency. But to business. The list of names you see in front of you—do you recognize any of them?"

"I recognize some of them. A handful."

"It is a list of people who are to be assassinated, as soon as the signal is given, in the name of the People's Vengeance, which as you know is the clandestine organization that Nechaev heads. The assassinations are meant to precipitate a general uprising and to lead to the overthrow of the state. If you page to the end, you will come to an appendix which names entire classes of people who are then, in the wake of the overthrow, to suffer summary execution. They include the entire higher judiciary and all officers of the police and officials of the Third Section of the rank of captain and higher. The list was found among your son's papers."

Having delivered this information, Maximov tilts his chair back and smiles amicably.

"And does that mean that my son is an assassin?"

"Of course not! How could he be when no one has been assassinated? What you have there is, so to speak, a draft, a speculative draft. In fact, my opinion—my opinion as a private individual—is that it is a list such as a young man with a grudge against society might concoct in the space of an afternoon, perhaps as a way of showing off to the very young woman to whom he is dictating. Nevertheless, assassination, the plotting of assassination, threats against officialdom—these are serious matters, don't you agree?"

"Very serious. Your duty is clear, you don't need my advice. If and when Nechaev returns to his native country, you must arrest him. As for my son, what can you do? Arrest him too?"

"Ha ha! You will have your joke, Fyodor Mikhailovich! No, we could not arrest him even if we wanted to, for he has gone to a better place. But he has left things behind. He has left papers, more papers than any self-respecting conspirator ought to. He has left behind questions too. Such as: Why did he take his life? Let me ask you: Why do *you* think he took his life?"

The room swims before his eyes. The magistrate's face looms like a huge pink balloon.

"He did not take his life," he whispers. "You understand nothing about him."

"Of course not! Of your stepson and the vicissitudes of his existence I understand not a whit, nor do I pretend to. What I hope to understand in a material, investigative sense, however, is what drove him to his death. Was he threatened, for instance? Did one of his associates threaten to expose him? Did fear of the consequences unsettle him so deeply that he took his life? Or did he perhaps not take his life at all? Is it possible that, for reasons of which we are still ignorant, he was found to be a traitor to the People's Vengeance and murdered in this particularly unpleasant way? These are some of the questions that run through my mind. And that is why I took this lucky opportunity to speak to you, Fyodor Mikhailovich. Because if you do not know him, having been his stepfather and for so long his protector, in the absence of his natural parents, who does?

"Then, as well, there is the question of his drinking. Was he used to heavy drinking, or did he take to it recently, because of the strains of the conspiratorial life?"

"I don't understand. Why are we talking about drinking?"

"Because on the night of his death he had drunk a great deal. Did you not know that?"

He shakes his head dumbly.

"Clearly, Fyodor Mikhailovich, there is a great deal you do not know. Come, let me be candid with you. As soon as I heard you had arrived to claim your stepson's papers, stepping, so to speak, into the lion's den, I was sure, or almost sure, that you had no suspicion of anything untoward. For if you had known of a connection between your stepson and Nechaev's criminal gang, you would surely not have come here. Or at least you would have made it plain from the outset that it was only the letters between yourself and your stepson that you were claiming, nothing else. Do you follow?"

"Yes—"

"And since you are already in possession of your stepson's letters to you, that would have meant you wanted only the letters written by you to him."

"Letters, yes, and everything else of a private nature. What can be the point of hounding him now?"

"What indeed! . . . So tragic. . . . But to return to the matter of the papers: you use the expression 'of a private nature.' It occurs to me that in today's circumstances it is hard to know what 'of a private nature' means. Of course we must respect the deceased, we must defend rights your stepson is no longer in a position to defend, in this case a right to a certain decent privacy. The prospect that after our decease a stranger will sniff through our possessions, opening drawers, breaking seals, reading intimate letters—that would be painful to all of us, I am sure. On the other hand, in certain cases we might actually prefer a disinterested stranger to perform this ugly but necessary business. Would we be easy at the thought of our more intimate affairs being opened up, when emotions are still raw, to the unsuspecting gaze of a wife or a daughter or a sister? Better, in certain respects, that it be done by a stranger, someone who cannot be offended because we are nothing to him, and also because he is hardened, by the nature of his profession, to offense.

"Of course this is, in a sense, idle talk, for in the end it is the law that disposes, the law of succession: the heirs to the estate come into possession of the private papers and everything else. And in a case where one dies without naming an heir, rules of consanguinity take over and determine what needs to be determined.

"So letters between family members, we agree, are private papers, to be treated with the appropriate discretion. While communications from abroad, communications of a seditious nature—lists of people marked down to be murdered, for instance—are clearly not private papers. But here, now, here is a curious case."

He is paging through something in the file, drumming on the desk with his fingernails in an irritating way. "Here's a curious case, *here's* a curious case," he repeats in a murmur. "A story," he announces abruptly—"what shall we say of a story, a work of fiction? Is a story a private matter, would you say?"

"A private matter, an utterly private matter, private to the writer, till it is given to the world."

Maximov casts him a quizzical look, then pushes what he has been reading across the desk. It is a child's exercise book with ruled pages. He recognizes at once the slanted script with its trailing loops and dashes. Orphan writing, he thinks: I will have to learn to love it. He places a protective hand over the page.

"Read it," says his antagonist softly.

He tries to read but he cannot concentrate; the more he tries, the more he sees only details of penmanship. His eyes are blurred with tears too; he dabs with a sleeve to prevent them from falling and blotting the page. "Trackless wastes of snow," he reads, and wants to correct the cliché. Something about a man out in the open, something about the cold. He shakes his head and closes the book.

Ian Glenn

Nadine Gordimer, J. M. Coetzee, and the Politics of Interpretation

Nadine Gordimer and J. M. Coetzee have much in common. Both have condemned apartheid in memorable terms; both have analyzed censorship, promoted black writing, extended the narrow range of South African writing by going beyond a British tradition to draw on Russian and European traditions and writings. They have written generously and with considerable insight about each other.[1] Comparisons between Gordimer and Coetzee have become a staple of literary analysis of South Africa,[2] and these often draw on Gordimer's reaction to Coetzee, with a view to determining his political allegiances and commitment, what one might polemically call his "political correctness."[3]

My reading of Gordimer's and Coetzee's positions is indebted to the work of Pierre Bourdieu on struggles for dominance in intellectual fields, although there are some problems in adapting Bourdieu's French-based and largely homogeneous and monolingual model to a study of South African writing, even of South African writing in English.[4] But the

The *South Atlantic Quarterly* 93:1, Winter 1994.
Copyright © 1994 by Duke University Press.
CCC 0038-2876/94/$1.50.

recent publication of much of Bourdieu's literary criticism in a single volume, *Les Règles de l'art*, the translation into English of many of his major works, and the increasing attention to him in the work of Toril Moi and others should help establish him as the major and most influential figure in recent French thought not to have made a significant impact on Anglo-American literary studies—a situation he addresses indirectly in the preface to the English edition of *Homo Academicus*.

Bourdieu argues that the literary field, like others, is the product of struggles for dominance. In the market of symbolic goods, there is an incessant (if often unrecognized, unadmitted, or unconscious) struggle between an avant-garde that seeks to "make it new," to supplant the models and values in place, and an artistic establishment that uses a variety of strategies to renew and retain its position of predominance. In time, the various figures and the literature constituted by this struggle pass into literary history and the sad, because essentially pointless, eternity of academic debate. Bourdieu's argument (which I have simplified to the point of parody) holds considerable importance for issues such as the debate on what the canon could or should be, but I want here simply to point out some of the immediate issues his analysis highlights, as well as the difficulties one faces in trying to apply it to South African writing.

First, as both critic and novelist, Coetzee represents a serious challenge to Gordimer's preeminence as realist novelist, and to the realist tradition at large. Even though Gordimer won the Nobel Prize in 1991 (in Bourdieu's terms, a sign of a domination so well established that it must be passé) and another South African novelist in the University of Cape Town English Department (André Brink, not Coetzee) was in close contention, Coetzee has overtaken Gordimer as the subject of academic analysis not only in South Africa, but in mainstream academic journals in the United States as well. Second, the artistic field in the English-speaking world is complicated by having at least two major centers in New York and London, and the South African situation is complicated further still by its peripheral and neocolonial status. Although his schema can help deal with the problem, Bourdieu, in his Paris-centric world, rarely has to ask: Which artistic field is the artist playing on? Or, how is the strategy a product of playing on two or more fields at once? Third, the South African political situation, particularly in the era of Cold War contestation before 1990, presented, as a corollary of political revolution or the ascendancy of black political power, a possibility of a radical upheaval rather than simply a continuation of the dominant artistic struggle or game. If, in Bourdieu's view, the field of art is by definition a field of activity of a segment of the dominant class (the dominated segment of the dominant class, but still the dominant class), was his not a pessimistic denial of the potential for a really major change? Was there not the prospect for (if not the historical inevitability of) a radically new kind of art and artist, of intellectual and cultural practice? In what follows we will see how these issues bear on the reception of Gordimer and Coetzee and their self-presentations and creative strategies.

The difficulty of understanding the reception of colonial or provincial or otherwise geographically peripheral writers has been clearly stated by Coetzee. In an American interview, Coetzee says:

> —I seem to have two sorts of critical publics, one of which is in the United States. . . . The other is in South Africa. And the terms in which these two publics operate . . . are rather different. . . . On the one hand, the body of people in the United States read these books in the general terms in which books are read by intelligent, mainly academic type critics in the U.S. Back in South Africa, there is another type of framework in which they are read, which is heavily influenced by Marxism, by general Third World thinking. . . . The primary question . . . is "Where does this book fit into the political struggle?" It is a dominant question there. These are actually the people I live among. I don't want to disparage them at all. . . . They are serious, intelligent people, but they are reading the books in a particular way.[5]

In the decade since this interview, American academic writers have come to feel that they must confront local suspicion of and uneasiness about Coetzee's work. There seems to be a worried assumption that the name "Coetzee" carries an essence of Afrikanerness that is finding expression in his work and that needs to be excused. They want a stamp of approval, a sense that these particular South African goods are legitimate. One is reminded of Gordimer's sardonic and shrewd remark on the international "use" for South African writing, and the kind of collusion by which the white writer might be tempted: "The fiction of white writers also produced the Aristotelian effect—and included in the price of hardback or paperback a catharsis of white guilt, for writer and reader."[6] Coetzee does not easily provide such catharsis; indeed, his work raises questions about the nature of this collusion.

Further complicating Gordimer's and Coetzee's academic reception and consideration in Britain and the United States is the role of South Africans in exile or South African students abroad. Many journals with special interests in the regional or geographical considerations and limitations of writers (*Ariel*, *World Literature Written in English*, *Research in African Literatures*, *Journal of Commonwealth Literature*) have links with expatriates and exiles who, through a variety of strategies and with a divergence of approaches, are undertaking to theorize, explain, contain Gordimer, Coetzee, and others, and to do this in most cases from a position that is linked to but different from theirs. Those who have taken the option of exile, invested the symbolic capital acquired here (out here) abroad (there, the center, the metropolis), have, it could be argued, a particular view of South Africa—are likely, in classic Marxist terms, to suffer a blind spot as to the class distinctions and class interests producing them. Exporting oneself or one's children is one form of preservation of capital, one kind of investment; preparing students for international consumption, one form of local industry. It is not only from South Africa, no doubt, that academics have gone to (or toward) the center, but in our case one does not often find exiled academics reflecting on their interests, grounds, discursive powers, and roles as agents of interchange.[7]

It is perhaps inevitable that colonial theory—whether done by Léopold Senghor, Aimé Cesaire, and Frantz Fanon in Paris, Homi Bhabha in Sussex, Gayatri Spivak in Pittsburgh, Edward Said in New York—is done from the colonizing center, by and for those who have an interest in explaining us, but without (always) explaining what their interest is in being at the center rather than back home. A fuller study would be needed to establish how the interplay of interests and concerns, the network of intellectual and political affiliations, affects the terms of entry of "peripheral" writers into an international mainstream in general and in this case in particular.

═══

A central political issue divides Gordimer and Coetzee. In a review of Coetzee's *Life & Times of Michael K*, Gordimer articulates her sense of where Coetzee's social and artistic vision falls short, differs from hers:

> The white liberal feels *chosen* by the victim of his own society; wasted Michael K becomes the doctor's burden and his only hope of salvation. He believes Michael K can lead him out of history to those "areas that lie between camps and belong to no camp." A revulsion against all political and revolutionary solutions rises with the insistence of the song of cicadas to the climax of this novel.
>
> I don't think the author would deny [that] it is his own revulsion.
>
> And so J. M. Coetzee has written a marvelous work that leaves nothing unsaid—and could not be better said—about what human beings do to fellow human beings in South Africa; but he does not recognize what the victims, seeing themselves as victims no longer, have done, are doing, and believe they must do for themselves. Does this prevent his from being a great novel? My instinct is to say a vehement "No." But the organicism that George Lukács defines as the integral relation between private and social destiny is distorted here more than is allowed for by the subjectivity that is in every writer. The exclusion is a central one that may eat out the heart of the work's unity of art and life.[8]

One of the other most influential attempts to object to Coetzee on such grounds was made by Michael Vaughan, who argued that Coetzee's work showed that he had reached a historical dead end: "He is a Coetzee among Coetzees. He too is subject to an ascribed mode of consciousness, that very one proper to the Northern European Protestant type of colonizer-enslaver of his fiction." And, later: "Coetzee thus casts himself in the role of diagnostician of the malady of Western culture who is unable to propose any cure for this malady."[9]

The problem with most of the attempts like Vaughan's, or with the Lukácsian invocation by Gordimer, is that they are theoretically unsatisfactory as causal explanations, at points almost incoherent. Gordimer moves from an "organicism" (Michael K's? Coetzee's?) that has been distorted by Coetzee's subjectivity to an apparently *willed* exclusion that continues, or returns, in that curious mixed metaphor, to "eat out the heart of the work's unity of art and life." In Vaughan's case, Coetzee remains "a Coetzee" because of what seems to be an insufficient act of will, or intellect, not because he is truly representative but because he is badly so, representing the wrong, historically doomed choice.

The negative judgment about Coetzee needs to be seen against Gordimer's own movement from the claim to serve a subjective artistic vision to her submission to a more clearly social duty and responsibility. Compare two statements—the first from a 1975 passage that precedes a discussion of Sartre's tension between *fidelity* and *contestation* and argues for Turgenev's balanced perspective as exemplary, the second from her 1982 "Living in the Interregnum" speech, in which she signals a change of primary allegiance, an acceptance of a different role and duty:

> What is a writer's freedom?
> To me, it is his right to maintain and publish to the world a deep, intense, private view of the situation in which he finds his society.[10]

> The claim [to have a place in a future South Africa] rests on something else: how to offer *one's self*.
> . . . The white writer has to make the decision whether to remain responsible to the dying white order—and even as dissident, if he goes no further than that position, he remains *negatively* within the white order—or to declare himself positively

as answerable to the order struggling to be born. . . . He has to try to find a way to reconcile the irreconcilable within himself, establish his relation to the culture of a new kind of posited community, non-racial but conceived with and led by blacks.

I have entered into this commitment with trust and a sense of discovering reality, coming alive in a new way—I believe the novels and stories I have written in the last seven or eight years reflect this—for a South Africa in which white middle-class values and mores contradict realities has long become the unreality, to me.[11]

The obvious question is how Gordimer and the critics who criticize Coetzee using her commitment as a standard come to the right, organic, historically sanctioned decision. Are they (consciously? unconsciously?) representing different parts of South African society or speaking on behalf of other sectors? Or are they simply choosing the right (ethical? ascendant?) political commitment? How does Gordimer's aversion to and rejection of her own class, the white South African middle class, make her more organic than Coetzee or other white writers and more representative in a Lukácsian sense?

Coetzee's own pronouncements seem to confirm the diagnosis somewhat, especially when he sounds alienated, uneasy with a categorization of himself as a South African writer: "I sometimes wonder whether it isn't simply that vast and wholly ideological superstructure constituted by publishing, reviewing and criticism that is coercing on me the fate of being a 'South African Novelist.'"[12] Yet it is clear that Coetzee, having considered the demand for commitment from South African writers, explicitly questions the equation of authenticity and artistic health with political commitment:

As someone from South Africa, the question of sincerity in particular occupies me because we are in a social/political situation where, for a white person to say, "Yes, I am for the overthrow of the reigning system," is a peculiar thing. Because the question is, is the motive behind it a desire to climb onto some historical bandwagon? In other words, how does a person know if he is sincere in a situation like that? How does he know that he is speaking the truth?[13]

Coetzee went on to comment that there was a similar pressure on Athol Fugard "to allow the terms of his engagement to be determined for him by the political struggle." It seems to me that Coetzee was also considering Gordimer's and his own choices.

Let us be clear about what is at stake here. Coetzee has written, as critic and creator, of the damaging effects of apartheid on white and black South Africans, but still finds it difficult to project himself in good faith into a politically changed future, to commit himself to a party shaping that future. In moral, artistic, and political terms we are presented, in looking at Gordimer and Coetzee, with choices and strategies and their consequences—not with determining economic or material pressures.

What Coetzee's question about sincerity forces us to consider is that South African dealers in symbolic capital or cultural goods on an international market during the past thirty years increasingly had to have an antiapartheid record, had to have the sanction of black political organizations, and, increasingly, had to face some kind of cultural Sullivan code. The paradoxes in literature, as in South African life more generally, are clear. To oppose apartheid or white rule in South Africa made/makes one acceptable elsewhere; it has been a commitment with benefits abroad. Who controlled that acceptability abroad became one of the major, contested cultural issues of the 1970s and 1980s, and the different choices made by Gordimer and Coetzee on this issue were a major source of their disagreement over the Salman Rushdie incident.

Marxist or neo-Marxist accounts are not able to explain the different choices that Gordimer and Coetzee make on any material grounds. In Gordimer's case, it would seem that her expression of political commitment undoes all formative material conditions, leaving her not organically but existentially representative. Marxist or left-wing criticism of Coetzee (especially in the barely veiled moral forms it has often taken as attacks on his bad bourgeois subjectivity or insufficient ideological effort) appears to be a one-upping intellectual tactic, a way of claiming a legitimate stake in the antiapartheid movement and of denying it to Coetzee. These different judgments on the validity and authenticity of a political commitment for white South Africans challenge us to be more rigorously materialist and to investigate the question of whose choice depended on what position in the struggle for dominance in local and international intellectual and artistic fields—and to track the artistic consequences.

≡≡≡

Bourdieu's work has some affinities with Lucien Goldmann's, which in turn draws on Lukács.[14] Can we find a stronger materialist reading by analyzing the social classes from which Gordimer and Coetzee come—something that would-be materialist critics have signally failed to do—and seeing how their class and social backgrounds influence their themes and inform their political roles? I ask this especially because a Goldmannian ghost fitfully haunts Stephen Clingman's book on Gordimer. Although Clingman considers the hypothesis, he never tries to apply it through an investigation of Gordimer's economic position or her Jewishness.[15] Clingman does not or cannot attempt a Goldmannian analysis for what seem to be reasons of social embarrassment—reasons that inhibit us all.

In Gordimer's case, her Jewishness, although virtually ignored by Clingman and downplayed by Gordimer herself, might be said to place her in a particular segment of white South African society with particular pressures on identity and on the formation of various kinds of international symbolic and intellectual capital. The early, unpublished novel referred to by Clingman seems more suggestive than he allows in indicating how Gordimer uses her Jewish background in developing later themes and attitudes. By way of caution one should note that Gordimer's unusual childhood, marked by her mother's possessive behavior and Anglophile background, and by the Latvian otherness of her father, a childhood clearly translated into, inscribed in, her work, makes it difficult to see her as completely typical.[16] Gordimer's self-analysis of the sense of Jewish alienation and cultural marginalization occurs in *Occasion for Loving*, where Bruno Fuecht, the disliked "European" stepfather, turns out to be the heroine's real father—replacing the family-romance father of British origins.

In Coetzee's case, it should be clear that the explanatory category of Afrikaner is misleading not only conceptually, but also historically.[17] Coetzee is not an Afrikaner, but rather a white South African in the old South African Party sense: someone maintaining or trying to maintain a general identity as a white South African with affiliations to both groups but in no way linked to the National Party. Coetzee's background gives him a distance from Afrikaner as well as English claims and allegiances, while perhaps leaving him responsible for both. What is striking about this consideration is that both Gordimer and Coetzee emerge as outsiders from Afrikaner nationalism and from the obvious alternative for South Africans of British origin in an English identity and refuge. Any attempt to do a Goldmannian reading in detail would need a "thick description" (to invoke Clifford Geertz) in biographical and anthropological terms to consider the sociologies and cultural place of two culturally important groups of white South Africans.

Gordimer's role as an intellectual in South Africa has been shaped from early on by her knowledge of an audience elsewhere, largely in the United States and Britain. Her awareness of the writer's temptation to become a propagandist, to take a party line, to abandon artistic integrity and detachment, marked many of her interviews and early statements. In the increasingly divisive political epoch of the 1980s, her major, international nonliterary statements offered a careful balance among the options of a traditional artistic stance, high Western culture, and a socialist and African-nationalist commitment. Gordimer's rhetoric is worth studying for the ways in which she kept herself from being categorized simply as Marxist or socialist, while making her political commitment, and credentials, clear. Her vehicle for her major statements was the *New York Review of Books*, a medium of high, left Western culture.

In her dominant role in the English-speaking culture of the 1970s and 1980s, Gordimer not only acted as an interpreter of black literature, but reacted to various black political currents, as has been suggested by Stephen Clingman. What Clingman does not consider is that Gordimer's intellectual and artistic strategy of speaking authoritatively to the West on the political and social dilemmas of South Africa necessarily obliged an increasing consideration of the political *tout court* and particularly of black South Africans. This strategy has had both benefits and risks. (I feel impelled to repeat that "strategy" may suggest a conscious, deliberate plot, whereas Bourdieu's point is that Gordimer's espousal of black writers, however generous and heartfelt and uncalculated, was also inevitably a way of reinvesting her symbolic capital and maintaining her prestigious place in the field.) I remember Mike Kirkwood, of Ravan Press, saying that Gordimer's international publishers had not wanted to include the Kafka story in *Something out There* because they felt that it took away from the South African intensity of the collection. Gordimer, in other words, was to keep her artistic place and international preeminence by standing exclusively for the black future in South Africa; it became difficult for her, even had she wanted to, to move away from a South African setting. (Compare Coetzee, who has generally refused, or complicated, a realistic South African setting.)

Gordimer's strategy has been to intensify her focus on black South Africans, and to intensify her commitment to explicitly political themes and major political figures, often thinly disguised versions of historical ones. To draw on Winnie Mandela as strongly as Gordimer seems to do in her portrayal of Marisa Kgosana in *Burger's Daughter* is to benefit from an international set of associations; but it is also to run the risks of the roman à clef, of the "journalistic," or indeed, of sharply changing images of the historical personage.

In the 1980s, Gordimer persistently reenacted in her novels and stories her own gesture of political commitment as the sole, final guarantor of authentic identity. The act of political choice moves the protagonist beyond irony, beyond psychology. The crucial decision of the early *Occasion for Loving*—when Jessie Stilwell moves from the Freudian, familial confrontation with her real father, and what it has done to her attitudes toward her children, to an assertion of politics as the creator of South African identity, and commitment to violent political change as the panacea for all personal ills—is repeated in *Burger's Daughter*, *Sport of Nature*, *My Son's Story*, and many short stories. In the latter cases, however, the political commitment renders the questioning of consciousness—the ironic detail of Gordimer's psychological insight and exploration—pointless, wrongheaded; she moves instead to a more detached or external admiration of epic heroines and heroes, figures whose international renown is signaled by their association with the powerful revolutionary figures of the day.

Gordimer's struggle as an artist has been to continue writing on major themes, such as heterosexual passion, betrayal, and guilt, while asserting the political as sufficient. In the case of Rosa Burger, the commitment is made over time—she flees the political, but her mature decision to return to South Africa deflects us from the critical exploration of her consciousness. She becomes a secret agent, some-one whose political commitment to her father's struggle makes any questioning of her motives, her sexuality (including her sexual snob-bery toward Clare Terblanche), and her relationship to her father some kind of security violation. In the case of *My Son's Story*, the switch is from Sonny, whose extramarital sexual passion becomes a sign of insufficient commitment, to Aila, whose political role makes her, unknown to her family, a secret agent, moving her beyond judg-ment or understanding.

Another way of expressing the change in Gordimer's work is to see how a standard theme is revisited and revised. At the core of her imagination lies a cottage in a garden where illicit lovers find a tem-porary escape from society (*Occasion for Loving*, *Burger's Daughter*, *My Son's Story*, *The Conservationist*, and such short stories as "Crimes of Conscience," "The Life of the Imagination"), but society, in the form of white hostility or political reality, or even black political au-thority, catches up, takes over. In some profound sense, Gordimer needs not only the "little room, an everywhere" (the Donne poem is alluded to specifically in *My Son's Story*), but the watchers outside; she needs to punish the lovers for being there, but also for compro-mising with the watchers. (One of the lovers may be a spy, a watcher in the most obvious form.) The crucial change in Gordimer's work is that while society is blamed for the failure when white authority is outside (*Occasion for Loving*), the lovers are at fault when escape to the cottage might endanger or enfeeble revolutionary commitment (*My Son's Story*).

Another persistent formal and thematic issue in Gordimer's novels is their adaptation of a typically (though not exclusively) female genre, in which the woman's sexual and/or romantic commitment is central, symbolic, and decisive. Gordimer's emphasis is on a symbolic link between politics and sexual behavior. In general sociological terms, the heroines choose either marriage within a limited ethnic group; marriage outside the ethnic group but within the white group; marriage abroad or into exile; or marriage into Africa. Perhaps the most provocative way of putting this is to say that in some sense the offering of *one's self* can be seen as a peculiarly female response in whatever form it takes in Gordimer's novels and that it increasingly takes the form of a commitment to a symbolic mode of marriage with Africa.

Sport of Nature is the novel in which the moral, formal, and political issues involved in Gordimer's choices come to a head, and it may be the most problematic precisely because Gordimer's heroine surrenders at the end to the most traditional notions of male potency and power. At the same time, she, like Gordimer herself, maintains international acceptability, although in her case it is signaled by her bevy of lovers, including a European diplomat, an American politician, an East European theorist, a South African guerrilla leader, and a black African president. When Hillela becomes the president's (senior) wife and a major international political figure, while her daughter by the black guerrilla leader becomes a successful international model, showing that the right sexual-political choice at home leads to splendid rewards abroad, one looks hopefully for signs of irony (which, Clingman has assured me, are there), but, in my case at least, in vain. If anything, it seems a confirmation of Coetzee's suspicion about the wish to jump on a bandwagon and profit from it.

≡≡≡

Coetzee has been a powerful critic and intellectual historian of colonialism and the history of racist thinking, apartheid, and censorship.[18] These critiques are notable for their application of theoretical models and forms of knowledge drawn from the most recent developments in Western thinking. Coetzee's intellectual trajectory is, in other words, that of the dominant mode in contemporary literary studies: American, with strong French influences. Within the literary-intellectual field in South Africa, he has confronted the British-oriented traditions of literary criticism with recent structuralist and poststructuralist theories. His distance from British models and values, his American postgraduate education in the rising field of linguistics, and his residency in the United States during the 1960s gave him a particular set of interests and views on South Africa and literary studies within it, views which have in general—and in no small measure through his impact—become the dominant ones. Coetzee's artistic and intellectual choices have presumed that artistic endeavor and knowledge are international. As with his theoretical models, many of his literary influences (Kafka, Beckett, Joyce, Nabokov, Borges) belong to no single national tradition but to a major, modern, deracinated, and difficult to classify international tradition.

The critical essays collected in *Doubling the Point* make his paradoxical achievement clear. Coetzee is, I think, unusual among twentieth-century writers in being a conventional practicing academic as well as a major novelist. Coetzee has reviewed, translated, and taught creative writing, but he is also a distinguished scholar whose essays have appeared in most South African journals and in many of the major American literary and linguistic ones as well (*Journal of Modern Literature, Critique, Language and Style, Linguistics, MLN, Mosaic, PMLA, Comparative Literature, Semiotica, Journal of Literary Semantics, Representations*, and *Raritan*). He has, in other words, to an extent unmatched by most other major literary figures, submitted to the normal demands of blind, refereed journal submission, played the literary analyst, and treated literature as a diagnostician. If his case is generally rare, does it not say something about the strains of this dual allegiance to creative and critical disciplines, to hunting with the critic-hounds and running with the novelist-hares?

These allegiances have several consequences for Coetzee's work. The first is that his work offers, indeed demands, the kind of critical and theoretical consideration that the major canonical writers in English are accorded, and that its artistic and formal strategies classify him as an international avant-garde writer. As literary artifacts, his novels offer the complexity, the density, that attracts ongoing analysis and consideration. In his attempt to make his novels, like Wallace Stevens's poems, "resist the intelligence almost successfully," Coetzee has chosen the long-term strategy of intellectual investment, playing the literary game as it has been traditionally defined. A second consequence is that Coetzee the critic may be said to have attempted to make his works critic-proof, or at least resistant to available parameters. His novels understand his critics better than the other way around, anticipating their readings and objections. In particular, as a result of Coetzee's double allegiance, his novels consistently demonstrate a sensitivity to the problems of intellectuals, including their relation to power and the difficulties posed by their discursive positions. To come to terms with the autocritiques in his works, literary intellectuals have to be exceptionally wary.

The major political issue confronting the critic of Coetzee's work is precisely the one his critics have failed to reflect on: Why does this linguist make his black characters silent, dumb, Other? How can these mutes be reconciled with Coetzee's meditation on the earth's civilized inheritance?

> [I]f a latter-day ark were ever commissioned to take the best that mankind had to offer and make a fresh start on the farther planets, if it ever came to that, might we not leave Shakespeare's plays and Beethoven's quartets behind to make room for the last speaker of Dyirbal, even though that last speaker might be a fat old woman who scratched herself and smelled bad?[19]

Coetzee's refusal to commit himself to articulating or advancing a future is also a refusal to benefit from the struggle of others, to speak for the Other, to preempt the future of the liberators, to jump on the bandwagon. In one sense, it may even be seen as a challenge—if there is to be a black voice sounding a real change to the artistic field and current assumptions, Coetzee presents it as impossible for him to know.

The cost of Coetzee's strategy has been the charge of "irrelevance" at home and, consequently, international uncertainty as to his role. During the grim, pessimistic 1980s, Coetzee responded to the political crisis in part by becoming increasingly explicit about his political condemnation of white rule, to the point that his most recent protagonist, the retired academic in *Age of Iron*, impotently contemplates immolating herself in protest before Parliament. In formal terms, he was less the Nabokovian innovator, more the liberal humanist he had started out by decrying.

═════

If Coetzee is organically connected to or representative of any class in South Africa, then it must surely be that of professional academics at the traditional English-speaking universities. (I trust that my interests and intellectual strategies here as a colleague of Coetzee's are so transparent as to need no commentary.) In terms of the academic field, it is clear that the University of Cape Town, along with the University of the Witwatersrand, has a place as the university with the strongest international ties, the greatest claim to sharing in international discourse, to attaining top international standards. It has had the greatest interest in proclaiming the international nature of knowledge, in claiming not to be involved in the local applications of apartheid but to adhere to universal notions of academic freedom and disinterested academic inquiry, and in arguing that apartheid is but one manifestation of other issues over which the intellect can triumph.

The University of Cape Town correspondingly faces the charges, from those in different positions in the academic or cultural field, that it is alien, produces students for exile, and does not reflect an African reality. Critics claim that the university's needs-blind admissions policy and affirmative action are simply ways to try to co-opt blacks into an educational system that will reproduce the Anglo-American capitalist values represented by Chancellor Harry Oppenheimer. University academics, it has been charged, are interested only in freedoms and issues that touch them personally, rather than the broad social and political struggles of the masses.

There are crucial differences in South Africa among the Afrikaner *volksuniversiteit* (with its demands that academics serve a racial and linguistic group), the new universities as the "intellectual home of the left" (Jakes Gerwel's phrase defining the University of the Western Cape), and traditional notions of the university. (The differences will be reproduced within universities and departments as well as across them, but the dominant trends are clear.) Some of the strategies and tensions involved in moving from the traditional model of the university to invoke a new position and powers are nicely caught in the following passage by Colin Bundy:

> The ivory tower has already been breached by popular pressures; grappling-irons promise further to scale its walls, and its base of academic autonomy is being undermined. Some of the occupants of the tower, who identify with the struggle against the status quo, welcome the invaders and try to provide them with a scholarship at once committed and intellectually honest.[20]

The strategy of Bundy's article (high/white/left, including traditional Western standards, replete with quotations from *Paradise Lost*, but also modestly proclaimed revolutionary credentials) seems to me close to Gordimer's. From the suspect traditional perspective, one asks whether the tactics half-mischievously invoked (the scholar, disturbed, lifting his head from the book and inviting the barbarians for tea? the fifth-column collaborator attaching the grappling-irons and helping the invaders up?) signal a most unmaterialist abandonment of academic place, privilege, and power, or whether they are intended to ensure the continuation of some kind of intellectual power and intellectual autonomy. Gordimer, in other words, in her commitment to putting herself at the service of a new South Africa, aligns herself with powerful new interests and forces in the intellectual field, forces absent during the heyday of apartheid education when radical oppositional politics were banned.

In South African universities, and in cultural matters more generally, tensions arose during the 1980s between those (notably, in the English-speaking universities) who had traditionally opposed apartheid and thereby maintained an international acceptability and those who claimed that a more explicit political commitment was necessary, that the approval of the African National Congress was essential to validating academic or cultural contacts. In the United States, the role of activists, especially black South Africans in exile, in getting South Africans declared personae non gratae by such organizations as the African Literature and African Studies associations was an obvious form of pressure on white literary intellectuals in South Africa. The rise of largely black writers' organizations such as the Congress of South African Writers and their troubled relationship with traditionally apolitical forums such as P.E.N. were also at issue. The ANC's policy on academic and cultural boycotts, supported by the Anti Apartheid Movement or segments of it and the United Democratic Front, was an attempt to deny academic legitimacy to those who had traditionally claimed to hold it. Gordimer joined the Congress of South African Writers, while Coetzee kept his distance after attending a few meetings.

These issues came to a head, in Cape Town at least, with the Conor Cruise O'Brien and Salman Rushdie affairs, the latter leading to a public confrontation between Coetzee and Gordimer. I want to focus on one aspect of the O'Brien affair, in 1986, when the University of Cape Town bowed to violent, largely black, student pressure in cutting short O'Brien's visit, although several features stand out when we consider this deeply divisive issue from the perspective of the differing intellectual strategies and investments at stake.

Pressure to end O'Brien's visit came largely, at first, from the Anti Apartheid Movement in Ireland, of which O'Brien had been chair. The crucial disagreement between O'Brien and antiapartheid activists was precisely about what kind of boycott should be applied. O'Brien decided that the University of Cape Town had an antiapartheid record, which made it possible for him to visit it, without clearance or apology, to give lectures on nationalism. His position advocated a selective academic boycott of South Africa—to be determined on traditional academic lines, which he felt competent to decide. His quarrel with activists in Dublin, which spilled over into clashes with South African students and led to conflict within the university community afterwards, arose from disputes over who could sanction (in both senses) such a visit. The ANC, the Anti Apartheid Movement, and black American activists (whose positions may increasingly come to differ), although they might have called for a total boycott, in effect argued for a selective boycott on *their* terms and demanded that academics demonstrate a commitment, a loyalty, by asking for approval rather than claiming academic autonomy. The real quarrel, then, was over who controlled academic legitimacy, who selected the terms and grounds of the boycott.

The subsequent Rushdie affair may be seen as emblematic and crucial, as the culmination of the kinds of pressures manifested in the boycotts and the O'Brien affair, and of the opposing artistic strategies of Gordimer and Coetzee. In 1988, Rushdie had been invited to South Africa to talk at the *Weekly Mail* Book Week by the Congress of South African Writers and the *Weekly Mail*. Then the reverberations of *Satanic Verses* were felt. Faxes from Britain, quoting the offensive passages, urged the local Islamic cultural organizations to get the invitation withdrawn, to have Rushdie declared a persona non grata. These local Islamic groups promptly appealed to the government to ban the book, and the government, pleased to show its sensitivity to strong religious feeling, immediately obliged. The Congress of South African Writers, on whose committee Nadine Gordimer served, was placed in a difficult position. There were threats of violence against Rushdie if he came to South Africa (this was before Khomeini issued his death sentence), and pressure on the left alliance from Islamic members to withdraw the invitation. Ultimately, the Congress of South African Writers withdrew the invitation, and Gordimer came to the *Weekly Mail* Book Week panel, on which she had originally been scheduled to appear with Rushdie and Coetzee, to explain and, inevitably, justify the decision.

What followed was one of the most truly momentous public clashes in recent South African culture. It is difficult not to sympathize with Gordimer and the Congress of South African Writers, but the dangers of censorship and the paths down which Gordimer's association with and commitment to a political movement seemed to be leading were clearly perilous.

Coetzee's speech has never been published, and summaries do not do justice to its cutting anger. He pointed out that withdrawing the invitation was an insult, that Rushdie could have been warned of the danger and then left to choose. But much of his criticism was aimed at the ways in which censorship by the mosque was as bad as censorship by the Afrikaner church (with which it could collaborate quite well) and that common to both was their wish to replace all books with one Book, the free play of signification with one final world-view to be imposed by those in power. Coetzee's restatement of some classic academic values may be symptomatic of the limited range of interests of the literary intellectual, but we should read it nonetheless as a defense of a principle vital to the writer, as a warning about the alarming willingness of the new order to follow the practices and logic of the old, as a calculation of the possible costs (though Coetzee never said this directly) of Gordimer's commitment and strategic choices.

After the event, the parties involved apparently changed their minds. Coetzee wrote later: "In retrospect I think Gordimer, in her prudence, was right, I was wrong."[21] Gordimer, in her Nobel Prize speech, spoke of the dangers to the writer represented by the Rushdie case. I could, if pushed, offer a good, Bourdieu-based explanation for this turnaround, but it would take us to the 1990s and the shocks of post–Cold War, of post 2 February 1990, and the shock of the new since then.

Notes

1   Nadine Gordimer, *Conversations with Nadine Gordimer*, ed. Nancy Topping Bazin and Marilyn Dallman Seymour (Jackson, MS, 1990), 189; "The Idea of Gardening," *New York Review of Books*, 2 February 1984, 3, 6; J. M. Coetzee, "The Great South African Novel," *Leadership SA* 2 (1983): 74–79; "Into the Dark Chamber" and "Nadine Gordimer, *The Essential Gesture*," in *Doubling the Point: Essays and Interviews*, ed. David Attwell (Cambridge, MA, 1992), 361–68, 382–88; see also Stephen Watson, "Speaking: J. M. Coetzee," *Speak* (May/June 1978): 23–24.
2   See, for example, Rowland Smith, "Inside and Outside: Nadine Gordimer and the Critics," *Ariel* 19 (1988): 3–9; Kelly Hewson, "Making the 'Revolutionary Gesture': Nadine Gordimer, J. M. Coetzee and Some Variations on the Writer's Responsibility," *Ariel* 19 (1988): 55–72; Richard G. Martin, "Narrative, History, Ideology: A Study of *Waiting for the Barbarians* and *Burger's Daughter*," *Ariel* 17 (1986): 3–21; Michael Vaughan, "Literature and Politics: Currents in South African Writing in the Seventies," *Journal of Southern African Studies* 9 (1982): 118–38.
    The implicit comparison of the writers defines the field as well.
3   A summary of critical uneasinesses is offered by Dick Penner, *Countries of the Mind: The Fiction of J. M. Coetzee* (New York, 1989), 23–28. See also Susan Van-Zanten Gallagher, *A Story of South Africa: J. M. Coetzee's Fiction in Context* (Cambridge, MA, 1991), 10–19. David Attwell shows the most awareness of this issue as well as the greatest degree of movement away from this mode of judgment. See his *J. M. Coetzee and South Africa: Contemporary History and the Politics of Writing* (Berkeley, 1993).
4   Among Bourdieu's many publications that bear heavily on literary sociology, I am particularly indebted to the following three articles: "Flaubert's Point of View"

(trans. P. Parkhurst Ferguson), *Critical Inquiry* 14 (1988): 539–62; "La Production de la croyance: Contribution à une économie des biens symbolique," *Actes de la recherche en sciences sociales*, No. 13 (February 1977): 3–43 ("The Production of Belief: Contribution to an Economy of Symbolic Goods," *Media, Culture and Society* 2/3 [1980]: 261–93); and "L'Invention de la vie d'artiste," *Actes de la recherche en sciences sociales*, No. 2 (1975): 67–94 ("The Invention of the Artist's Life," *Yale French Studies* 73 [1987]: 75–103). Central to my argument is Bourdieu's *Les Règles de l'art: Genèse et structure du champ littéraire* (Paris, 1992), chapter 3 of part 1.

5   Penner, *Countries of the Mind*, 75.

6   Nadine Gordimer, *The Essential Gesture: Writing, Politics and Places*, ed. Stephen Clingman (New York, 1988), 273.

7   The problem of divergent internal and external readings of Gordimer is noted with some concern, but with no reflection on his own position, by Rowland Smith, "Inside and Outside." I hope that my argument makes it clear that my own position as someone who lives in South Africa is subject to similar analysis.

8   Gordimer, "Idea of Gardening," 6.

9   Vaughan, "Literature and Politics," 128, 134.

10   Gordimer, "A Writer's Freedom," in *The Essential Gesture*, 104.

11   Gordimer, "Living in the Interregnum," in *The Essential Gesture*, 264, 278.

12   Tony Morphet, "Two Interviews with J. M. Coetzee, 1983 and 1987," *Triquarterly* 62 (1987): 460.

13   Penner, *Countries of the Mind*, 17.

14   Bourdieu (personal communication) was working with Goldmann on ways to carry forward the latter's work through questionnaires and other sociological techniques just before Goldmann's death.

15   Stephen Clingman, *The Novels of Nadine Gordimer: History from the Inside* (London, 1986), 17 and nn. 37, 38.

16   I use "Latvian" advisedly. Although Gordimer has mentioned Lithuania several times in interviews as her father's country of origin, as does Clingman (*Novels of Nadine Gordimer*, 23), Gordimer has since corrected this and specified that her grandparents worked in Riga. See *Conversations with Nadine Gordimer*, xv, xix, 248.

17   See, for example, Penner, *Countries of the Mind*, 2, 5n. See also Gallagher, *Story of South Africa*, 38–43; and, especially, Coetzee, *Doubling the Point*, 341–42.

18   See, especially, J. M. Coetzee, "Blood, Taint, Flaw, Degeneration: The Novels of Sarah Gertrude Millin," *English Studies in Africa* 23 (1980): 41–58; and "Idleness in South Africa," *Social Dynamics* 8 (1982): 1–13, both of which are reprinted in *White Writing: On the Culture of Letters in South Africa* (New Haven and London, 1988); see also "The Mind of Apartheid: Geoffrey Cronjé (1907–)," *Social Dynamics* 17 (1991): 1–35; and "Into the Dark Chamber," in *Doubling the Point*, 361–68.

19   J. M. Coetzee, "How I Learned about America—and Africa—in Texas," *New York*

Times Book Review, 15 April 1984, 9 (original text restored and reprinted in *Doubling the Point*, 50–53).

20   Colin Bundy, "An Image of Its Own Past? Towards a Comparison of American and South African Historiography," in *History from South Africa*, ed. Joshua Brown et al. (Philadelphia, 1991), 104.

21   Coetzee, *Doubling the Point*, 298.

Rita Barnard

Dream Topographies: J. M. Coetzee and the South African Pastoral

In his recent edition of essays by and interviews with J. M. Coetzee, David Attwell notes that Coetzee's return to South Africa in 1976, and his second novel, *In the Heart of the Country*, marked the emergence of a new concern with *place* in his work. This concern has, in fact, been an enduring one for Coetzee: his criticism and fiction have been profoundly affected by an interest in such geographically or topographically defined genres as the exploration narrative and the pastoral, as well as in such politically significant spaces as the imperial border, the labor camp, and the torture chamber. Even the titles of his first two novels, *Dusklands* and *In the Heart of the Country*, suggest this fascination, referring as they do to strangely elusive and yet symbolically resonant places. It is possible that the structuralist and therefore synchronic orientation of Coetzee's academic training as a linguist might have something to do with his interest in spatial organization; but, as Attwell's observation suggests, this interest also seems to have the experiential and personal

The *South Atlantic Quarterly* 93:1, Winter 1994.
Copyright © 1994 by Duke University Press.
CCC 0038-2876/94/$1.50.

dimension of a skeptically and rigorously examined attachment to the South African landscape: Coetzee once remarked, after all, that people can be in love with only one landscape in their lifetime.[1]

Coetzee's increasing discomfort in recent years with the dominance of the discourse of history (or, more exactly, a Marxian historicism) in South African academic circles may also, in part, be connected to a concern with the spatial. I say "in part" since, in a polemical essay like "The Novel Today," it is clear that Coetzee's impatience with the all-"swallowing" tendency of historical master-narratives comes from his sense of himself specifically as a *novelist*: a sense that in times of political pressure the novel becomes reduced to a mere supplement to or illustration of the discourse of the historical "real."[2] Even so, it seems worth noting that there have been other contemporary social theorists interested in the critical analysis of space who, like Coetzee, have challenged the explanatory privilege of historicism. The geographer Edward Soja, for one, has polemicized vigorously against the marginalization of the spatial by the historical discourse of Western Marxism and has posited that, in contemporary forms of capitalism, spatial relations have become as mystified as the commodity form once seemed to Marx—and thus require renewed attention. This argument urges us to consider, for instance, the degree to which the erasure of the conditions of labor in today's world depends on the geography of late capitalism: the fact that the impoverished workers who produce our glossy commodities live far out of sight, in Mexico, in the Philippines, or in a South African township, and that their invisibility perpetuates the illusion of historical progress in the economic centers. I think that we can say, without falling into a new trap of "swallowing up" Coetzee's novels in the discourse of a critical geography, that this line of thought resonates with certain moments in his writing, both academic and fictional: he is concerned with how people inhabit, how they imagine, and how they represent the physical terrain that surrounds them.

The literary possibilities of a critical geography are suggested in an intriguing passage by John Berger (which Soja cites in his opening chapter):

> Prophecy now involves a geographical rather than historical projection; it is space and not time that hides consequences from

us. To prophesy today it is only necessary to know men [and women] as they are throughout the whole world in all their in-equality. Any contemporary narrative which ignores the urgency of this dimension is incomplete and acquires the oversimplified character of a fable.[3]

The notion that it is space that hides inequalities from us, in particu-lar, calls to mind Coetzee's comments on the political geography of South Africa:

If people are starving, let them starve far away in the bush, where their thin bodies will not be a reproach. If they have no work, if they migrate to the cities, let there be roadblocks, let there be curfews, let there be laws against vagrancy, begging, and squat-ting, and let offenders be locked away so that no one has to hear or see them. If the black townships are in flames, let cameras be banned from them. . . . Certainly there are many lands where prisons are used as dumping-places for people who smell wrong and look unsightly and do not have the decency to hide them-selves away. In South Africa the law sees to it as far as it can that not only such people but also the prisons in which they are held become invisible.[4]

These ideas have significant implications for those who strive to understand (and change) the inequality of South African men and women. Apartheid, as Coetzee so clearly understands, operates from day to day as a means of distributing people in space and, in the process, of controlling the way they see the world. The system per-petuates itself by decreeing that certain spaces be invisible: home-lands, prisons, torture chambers, and black cities are deliberately hidden, removed from view. The beneficiaries of apartheid are, after all, not particularly sadistic; they (we) would simply rather not see the "consequences" of which Berger speaks. The ideal—and in some sense actual—social topography for those in power would be the one described by a vagrant in Coetzee's *Life & Times of Michael K*: a workers' camp placed hundreds of miles away, "in the middle of the Koup" or some such arid waste, from which they could "come on tiptoe in the middle of the night like fairies and do their work, dig their gardens, wash their pots, and be gone in the morning leaving everything nice and clean."[5]

I would suggest that in moments like these his writing offers us something of that demystifying "geographical projection" or even "prophecy" (though Coetzee would certainly balk at this term) of which Berger speaks. In such instances, Coetzee renders visible the places that the system would rather keep out of sight and mind. Elsewhere, his examination of the spatial seems more literary, as in his implicit critique of the reiterative codes that have shaped descriptions of South African landscapes: the descriptive catalogue, for instance, in which "the Karoo has been done to death in a century of writing and overwriting (drab bushes, stunted trees, heat-stunned flats, shrilling of cicadas, and so forth)."[6] Perhaps most importantly, he forces us to examine our automatic responses to "place" (for example, white South Africans' passionate and often proclaimed love of the country's vast landscapes): to ask what political and imaginative *failure* such a passion might conceal.[7]

‗‗‗‗‗

The notion of place has not been completely ignored by South African literary critics: Stephen Gray, for one, has suggested that the notion of a "sense of place" could be used as a crude but serviceable means of mapping the successive phases of a South African (and a more generally postcolonial) literary historiography. In the first phase, the colony offers what Richard Rive has called a "Scenic Special": the exotic appeal of a distant place. Its landscape is presented to readers in the centers of power as *different*, a novel entertainment for the armchair traveler back "home." It offers a kind of verbal safari, entirely Eurocentric in its assumptions. Although its historical origins (as Gray points out) lie in the Renaissance, this kind of literature remains enormously influential: it is still evident in writers like Lawrence Durrell, in TV documentaries, and, I would add, in such profitable exports as Jamie Uys's film *The Gods Must Be Crazy*. (The Disney film *A Far-Off Place*, based on the work of Laurens van der Post, is perhaps the genre's most recent avatar.)

The second phase is more distinctively and assertively "colonial" and emerges with such exceptional figures as Olive Schreiner. (Miles Franklin, the author of *My Brilliant Career*, would be her Australian counterpart.) In such isolated and singular texts as Schreiner's *Story of an African Farm*, "phase two" literature reacts to the cultural tourism of the first phase by asserting an inescapable rootedness in the landscape and the emotional horizon of the colony; in Schreiner's case that setting is, of course, the vast and stony desert of the Great Karoo, which has become (perhaps because of her novel) the archetypal South African landscape. It is ironic, as Gray points out, that this literature was received in the metropolitan center (where Schreiner had to find her readers) as indistinct from "phase one" writing: *The Story of an African Farm* was largely seen as bringing an entertainingly novel and fresh "sense of place" to English literature, and Schreiner's critique, from her forbidding marginal vantage point in the South African desert, of the aridity of European ideas and values was readily overlooked.

In its third phase South African writing becomes, for Gray, much less vulnerable to such Eurocentric misreading, since it is associated not only with a full-fledged sense of national identity, but with the emergence of a cultural nexus that supports a national literature: a publishing industry, a community of local readers and critics, and a self-referring use of language, norms, and values. Place remains, or so the argument goes, a defining feature, but it is no longer—as it was with "phase two" writers—a cultural battlefield on which the rights to an indigenous identity must be fought. It becomes, in Gray's view, more of a shared and felt milieu, a familiar backdrop from which writers as different as Athol Fugard, for instance, writing from his home in the Eastern Cape, or Sipho Sepamla, writing from the vantage point of the explosive Soweto scene, can stage their distinct literary projects.[8]

There are clearly a number of theoretical problems with this outline. It is, for instance, open to the objection that it defines place as the "single variable" that generates the distinctiveness of South African writing: "The elements of plot, character, action, use of dialogue, rhythm, and all the other techniques of making literature, remain the same" as in the great tradition of the British canon.[9] This presupposition surely minimizes the thematic and stylistic inventiveness of postcolonial writing and ignores the effects of political determinants on literary forms and genres. But the most important weakness vexing Gray's schema is the fact that he relies on an all too empirically conceived notion of "place" (which is used interchangeably with "setting"); the implicit notion of artistic representation, consequently, is straightforwardly mimetic and bears the implication that South African literature must represent the South African land.[10] It is no accident, then, that Gray makes no reference to the work of J. M. Coetzee: the first part of *Dusklands* and *Waiting for the Barbarians* (*Foe* had not yet appeared by then) are not set in South Africa at all. But the exclusion is also symptomatic: Gray's historiographic schema could not accommodate Coetzee's treatment of place, which in effect swallows up and explodes all of its categories. Coetzee's work, as Stephen Watson has observed, seems to "float free of time and place, even in the act of alluding to a time and place which is specifically South African."[11] What is at stake for him is not place or landscape as an object of mimesis, but the discursive and generic and political codes that inform our understanding and knowledge of place. There is a deliberate analytical unsettledness in Coetzee, which deconstructs, rather than assimilates to, any South African literary tradition, or any South African "sense of place."

This tendency is emphasized by Teresa Dovey (the author of the first full-length study of Coetzee's novels) when she deftly selects, as one of the keywords of her study, Roland Barthes's notion of "atopia": *drifting habitation*.[12] The word evokes, in appropriately spatial (or perhaps antispatial) terms, the deconstructive and "writerly" quality of Coetzee's texts: his formal shiftiness, the fact that his novels, like hermit crabs, inhabit, but only to abandon, the shells of various fictional genres, such as the narrative of exploration, the pastoral, and so forth.[13] "Atopia," in short, identifies Coetzee's project as one of displacement. It is a refusal to settle in a space that is conventionally and ideologically given, a critical gesture which Dovey explains (in the Lacanian terminology she privileges) as "a constant deferral of the position available to the subject in language." While I shall eventually take issue with Dovey's readings, the idea of "atopia" provides a useful rubric under which we may briefly consider one way that

Coetzee problematizes the notion of a "sense of place": the metafictional aspects of his novelistic topographies.

≡≡≡

The idea of "drifting habitation" is perhaps most applicable to *In the Heart of the Country* and is most readily illustrated in those instances where the text seems to offer a scenic description. This is, of course, a novel whose problematic temporality strikes us immediately: we are never allowed to be certain about *when* the events take place (the narrator is never sure if she is in a time of donkey carts or bicycles or airplanes), nor are we sure what "really happens"— the sequence and effects of events are always in doubt. The same is true about the novel's ostensible setting—despite the realistic details of stone, the whitewashed homestead, the gravelly yard, the chickens, the dust, and the gleaming copperware. The title itself initiates a kind of ironic instability: it appears to allude to a symbolically resonant location, but the narrative, with its rapid succession of often self-cancelling segments, seems really to have nothing at its "heart." The text continually reminds us that the farm is entirely fictive, that there is, properly speaking, no "setting," no "stone desert," but only "stony monologue." Magda, the narrator of this monologue, repeatedly, and regretfully, insists that the panorama before her depends entirely upon her consciousness, her words:

> Seated here I hold the goats and stones, the entire farm and even its environs, as far as I know them, suspended in this cool, alienating medium of mine, exchanging them item by item for my word-counters. A hot gust lifts and drops a flap of ochre dust. The landscape recomposes itself and settles.

Yet it would also be incorrect—and too safe—to think of this consciousness as in any way settled or "central"; Magda thinks of herself as a void, a hole, and frequently seems on the verge of dissolving into a complete insubstantiality: "a ghost or a vapour," she muses, "floating at the intersection of a certain latitude and a certain longitude," an intersection that remains a purely hypothetical location. The farm is not just set in the proverbial "middle of nowhere" (such remoteness would accord with the realist notion of the vastness of the Karoo range): it *is* nowhere, "on the road from no A to no B in the world, if such a fate is topologically possible"; it is configured almost as a kind of antispace: "a turbulence, a vortex, a black hole," a swallowing up of any presence.[14]

Considering all this, what seems curious is the extent to which the novel remains so visual in its effect, how much it remains concerned with description. Even the highly self-reflexive passage cited above seems just for a moment, when a gust of wind raising the dust appears to disturb the "suspended" verbal landscape, to flirt with a more conventional realism. And there are certainly moments when the narrative offers, albeit ironically, a conventional South African "sense of place"—a rural "scenic special" of sorts. We might think, for instance, of the evocation of the impoverished settlement, Armoede, where the servant, Hendrik, goes to fetch his bride. The description is offered in the form of a list, the slightly weary tone of which emphasizes the familiarity and typicality of the details (once again the reader who knows the code, or so the very form suggests, can extend the catalogue): "the bleak windswept hill, the iron shanties with hessian in the doorways, the chickens, doomed, scratching in the dust, the cold snot-nosed children toiling back from the dam with buckets of water, the same chickens scattering now before the donkey-cart." But despite the vividness of detail, the context does not permit this scene of "local color" to attain a lasting mimetic effect. The narrator merely imagines this scene, admitting that she has never been to Armoede. (Indeed, she "seem[s] never to have been anywhere": a confession that explains the curiously improvisational quality of even her descriptions of her own home—her ignorance, for instance, of whether or not she happens to have any neighbors.) The place name "Armoede" also seems to work in a complicated and contradictory way, debunking, as it were, its own suggestion of referentiality, its own South Africanness. To anyone familiar with the country, the name Armoede (Poverty) could seem "realistically" typical, calling to mind any number of those curiously morbid place names that dot the South African map: Weenen (Weeping), Lydenburg (Town of Suffering), Put-Sonder-Water (Waterless Well), or Misgund (Begrudged). But this reality effect is undercut, one feels, by the all too perfect, too allegorical, match between the name and the scene; the appellation seems to bear the mark of the literary, or at least to draw attention to the linguistic label: it is all, as Magda laments, a matter of "names, names, names."[15]

In the absence of any resistance to this process of naming, and of the linguistic reciprocity of which Magda dreams, all becomes solipsistic, improvisational: the landscape is a figment of Magda's narratorial consciousness, her "speculative . . . geography," one might say; but her consciousness seems equally determined by this fictive, composed land. Her "speculative bias," her radical, though somehow insubstantial freedom, has its origin, Magda tells us, in the vast distances of the land into which she must stare. "I make it all up in order that it shall make me up": such are the unstable, shifting operations, the "lapidary paradoxes," that make up this fiction.[16]

It is easy to see why this novel in particular has provided grounds for the Lacanian reading offered by Dovey: her association of the narrating self with the hermit crab, scuttling from shell to shell, or code to code, or signifier to signifier, is in many ways compelling and accurate. But it seems to me that in the matter of genre, which is central to Dovey's understanding of Coetzee's "fiction-as-criticism," the purely deconstructive reading reveals certain limitations.[17] It is true, of course, that a generic instability and self-consciousness is perhaps the most telling characteristic of self-reflexive fiction. Coetzee himself notes that what clearly distinguishes the postmodern text from the realist novels of, say, Defoe or Hardy, is that Moll Flanders and Jude never pause to ponder what kind of text they seem to be inhabiting.[18] And *In the Heart of the Country* is no exception: Magda is constantly questioning what kind of action or event might justify her insubstantial presence in the elusive heart of that country: not Greek tragedy, despite the imagined axe-murder and the surrounding "theatre of stone"; nor gothic romance, despite her brief fantasy of waiting for "a castle [to] crumble into a tarn"; nor even the colonial idyll, with its dreary possibilities of marriage to a neighbor's second son or dalliance with an itinerant schoolmaster.[19] Yet the seductions of the more lyric aspects of the pastoral are ever present in the novel and are, I think, not so easily dismissed.[20] When Magda asserts that she would not be herself if she did not "feel the seductions of the cool stone house, the comfortable old ways, the antique feudal language," it is still possible to take the remark as just another momentary, self-cancelling speculation. But by the end of the novel, the tone seems to have shifted. The monologue concludes on a note which suggests that Coetzee's fictional strategies are perhaps not fully explained by an "atopian" reading. This lyrical finale, however self-consciously announced as "closing plangencies," expresses a desire that seems rather more specific, rather more local than the universal linguistic condition of desire and deferral that is figured for Dovey by the hermit crab:

> There are poems, I am sure, about the heart that aches for Verlore Vlakte, about the melancholy of the sunset over the koppies, the sheep beginning to huddle against the first evening chill, the faraway boom of the windmill, the first chirrup of the first cricket, the last twitterings of the birds in the thorn-trees, the stones of the farmhouse wall still holding the sun's warmth, the kitchen lamp glowing steady. They are poems I could write myself. It takes generations of life in the cities to drive that nostalgia for country ways from the heart. I will never live it down, nor do I want to. I am corrupted to the bone with the beauty of this forsaken world. . . . I have chosen at every moment my own destiny, which is to die here in the petrified garden, behind locked gates, near my father's bones, in a space echoing with hymns I could have written but did not because (I thought) it was too easy.[21]

As Peter Strauss has argued, those nostalgic poems on Verlore Vlakte (Lost Valley), which are remembered but not parodied in these lyrical lines, preserve a certain pastoral possibility, which the reader is allowed—barely—to discern, but in which the narrative voice never fully indulges. While it would be reductive to ascribe the passion of these lines to the author, there is surely in the passage a kind of unison—or at least a kind of homology—between narrator and author. (And I shall resist speculating on an intriguing comment in the final interview of *Doubling the Point*, where Coetzee notes, in describing the person he was as an adolescent, that "for a variety of reasons" he ceased visiting the family farm, "the place on earth he has defined, imagined, constructed, as his place of origin."[22]) In the same way that Magda has up to this point scrupulously resisted, and still resists, the pastoral possibility, Coetzee's work resists the easy option of creating a fictional dwelling place, a fictional utopia—"that heady expansion into the as-if," as Magda calls it. Coetzee's work in general suggests a reluctant abnegation of certain artistic forms, a gesture that is also evident in his uncharacteristically revealing comments (again, in *Doubling the Point*) on the situation of the contemporary author. He speaks of "the pathos—in a humdrum sense of the word—of our position: like children shut in the playroom, the room of textual play, looking out wistfully through the bars at the enticing world of the grownups, one that we have been instructed to think of as the mere phantasmal world of *realism* but that we stubbornly can't help thinking of as the *real*."[23] Coetzee is, in short, anything but enamored of the antimimetic and deconstructive techniques that he himself deploys: he speaks of the "impasse" of "anti-illusionism" while recognizing—almost regretfully—the necessity for such techniques. In the history of the novel, he argues, metafiction is a "marking of time." It is surely no coincidence that this condition of marking time, of waiting, is the same morbid condition so often associated with white South Africans, living in the uncertain age of what Nadine Gordimer (following Gramsci) has called the "interregnum."[24] It seems to me, therefore, that we must, while acknowledging the paradoxical nature of such a move, situate and *localize* his atopian strategies; we must also recognize not only a historical but an ethical impulse behind Coetzee's anti-illusionism. For it is specifically as a white South African that Coetzee feels he must refrain from the pastoral, and it is as a novelist writing within a certain troubling historical configuration that he must avoid producing what he calls, in an essay on Beckett, "the daydream gratification of fiction."

The problem with Teresa Dovey's determinedly deconstructive reading of Coetzee's work is that it is not balanced by a consciousness of the contingency and historicity of cultural forms. Most notably, there is no sense that the Western psychoanalytic and deconstructive theories she deploys may themselves be destabilized, slipping into different nuances and creating different meanings and allegiances when they are invoked in different contexts, deployed at some remove from their original source.[25] This critique has been suggested in general terms by David Attwell, who notes that in Dovey's discussion of *In the*

Heart of the Country the Hegelian master/slave dialectic is entirely stripped of its historical-political aspect, that is, of the implication that such goals as freedom and self-realization are attainable only *in a just society*.[26] The problem becomes even clearer if one looks closely at some of Dovey's curiously reductive readings of passages from Coetzee's work. A characteristic instance occurs when she glosses a key moment in *Life & Times of Michael K*, a passage in which the starving Michael K meditates on the minimal and ahistorical way he would like to live on the land—refusing to be a settler:

> I am not building a house out here by the dam to pass on to other generations. What I make ought to be careless, makeshift, a shelter to be abandoned without a tugging at the heartstrings. . . . The worst mistake, he told himself, would be to try to found a new house, a rival line, on his small beginnings out at the dam.

Dovey's reading of this rather touching passage renders it almost mechanically self-referential. Michael K's improvised dwelling place becomes nothing but an allegory for the operations of this novel: "This text in particular [i.e., *Life & Times of Michael K*] must not be too closely bound to Coetzee's own meanings; he must be able to abandon it, without a tugging at the heartstrings, to the successive meanings which each new reading will generate." For all its apparent openness, this is precisely the kind of comment that makes one hesitate to offer a more specific interpretation. But even if we take K's invisible, traceless, self-erasing mode of living on the land as a figure for a mode of writing, we must remember that K himself (not the quickest mind around) sadly recognizes that it is the context of war, the *times* of Michael K, if you will, that demands this strategy:

> What a pity that to live in times like these a man must be ready to live like a beast. A man who wants to live cannot live in a house with lights in the window. He must live in a hole and hide by day. A man must live so that he leaves no trace of his living. That is what it has come to.

"Drifting habitation" as a literary strategy must likewise be seen as a historical condition.[27]

A similar point can be made in relation to Dovey's reading of

another important meditation in *Michael K*, when, after a vicious
assault on the Jakkalsdrif labor camp, K ponders the relationship between parasite and host:

> Parasite was the word the police captain had used: the camp at
> Jakkalsdrif, a nest of parasites hanging from the neat sunlit town,
> eating its substance, giving no nourishment back. Yet to K lying
> idle in his bed, thinking without passion (What is it to me, after
> all? he thought), it was no longer obvious which was host and
> which parasite, camp or town. . . . What if the hosts were far out-
> numbered by the parasites, the parasites of idleness and the other
> secret parasites in the army and the police force and the schools
> and factories and offices, the parasites of the heart? Could the
> parasites then still be called parasites? Parasites too had flesh and
> substance; parasites too could be preyed upon. Perhaps in truth
> whether the camp was declared a parasite on the town or the
> town a parasite on the camp depended on no more than on who
> made his voice heard loudest.

Dovey relates this passage, as we could surely have predicted, to
J. Hillis Miller's argument in "The Critic as Host": "[T]he term 'parasite,' " she ventures, "comes to signify as a locus of substitution, and
refers to the way in which Coetzee's novel, which is parasitic in relation to the previous texts which it deconstructs, will in turn become
the host to successive parasitic readings."[28] While it is certainly possible to understand the relationship of host and parasite in terms of
acts of reading and interpretation (acts that are thematized in section 2 of the novel, where the medical officer creates rather than
"reads" the story of Michael K), I find myself wanting to insist that
the atopian reading, the punning etymology which turns the "parasite" into a (dare I say mere?) "locus of substitution," misses something. It universalizes, and in so doing flattens out the operations of
a text that seems to ask questions with urgent ethical implications
for South Africa in particular: Who eats whom? Who lives off whom?
Who lives in the town and who in the camp? Who lives in the city
and who in Soweto?[29] In other words, the host/parasite opposition
carries a certain local potency: the atopian slippage, the "endlessness
of textuality," as Attwell puts it, is halted by "the brute facticity of

power."[30] And that power manifests itself in a certain socially and materially constructed topography.

≡≡≡

I would like, then, to move from the keyword "atopia" to the phrase "dream topography": an idea that can enable us to give the ethical and political dimensions of Coetzee's novels their due, without recourse to any kind of naive empiricism. The term emerges from Coetzee's discussion of the South African pastoral in *White Writing*, where the notion of genre becomes not so much a metafictional strategy— a temporary home for the writerly hermit crab—but a kind of social dreamwork, expressing desires and maintaining silences that are profoundly political in origin. The idea of the generic and ideological topography offers us a spatial concept that is more stable and historical than "drifting habitation": not a "sense of place," but a sense of discursive and cultural maps.

The essays in *White Writing* are mainly concerned with two rival "dream topographies," both of which are aspects of the pastoral: they are the maps and the ideological blueprints that this genre has projected on the land. Both of these projections are sketched out in Coetzee's 1977 review of Ross Devenish and Athol Fugard's film, *The Guest* (the plot of which is based on an incident in the life of the Afrikaans poet Eugène Marais—an almost life-long morphine addict— who is sent to go cold turkey on a Transvaal farm). To the dismay of the well-meaning director, Coetzee observed that the film's representations of the white man's relation to the land were patched together from flattering myths designed—however unconsciously— to keep certain unresolvable inconsistencies from view.[31] The Afrikaner family is presented via a visually seductive mise-en-scène of "whitewashed walls, . . . dark verticals of doors and windowframes," a dinner table in the glow of lamplight: interiors reminiscent, or so Coetzee claims, "of the classic Dutch painters," settings that gleam "with Rembrandt browns and golds." The compelling visual image, he points out, suggests that the Meyers are "not rootless colonials" but, simultaneously, "rude children of the African earth and heirs to a venerable European tradition." The limited contexts in which we see the family also make it difficult to raise certain troubling questions about the running of this African farm. Coetzee spells out some of these: "If the Meyers run a cattle farm, why do they never talk about cattle? . . . Where do the African farm laborers who materialize out of nowhere for a single fifteen-second sequence live? How do the Meyer men spend their time when they are not eating?" The film confines itself to the terrain permitted by the ideological horizons of the South African pastoral, within which the Meyers and their farm, Steenkampskraal, stand as emblems of simplicity and permanence. As far as the film's presentation of the poet goes, Coetzee argues, another myth applies: that of the Genius in Africa, the man for whom consciousness is pain, and for whom the African landscape is "a murderous mother-goddess," silently rejecting the alienated poet-supplicant who tragically adores her stony bosom. This glamorously dystopian relationship with the land is no less ideologically fraught than the rough-hewn arcadia of the (non-genius) Boers. The essay raises for the first time an idea that will become a major theme of *White Writing*: that is, to the majority in South Africa, for whom "Africa is a mother who has nourished them and their forebears for millions of years," this stoic lyricism would make no sense at all. "South Africa, mother of pain, can have meaning only to people who can find it meaningful to ascribe their 'pain' ('alienation' is here a better word) to the failure of Africa to love them enough."[32] An apparently aesthetic preoccupation with the land can mask a resistance to thinking about South Africa in social terms.

In *White Writing*, the two ideological positions discovered earlier, in *The Guest*, are described in more elaborate and more generally (generically) applicable terms. Coetzee maps out the first "dream topography" as follows: "[A] network of boundaries crisscrossing the surface of the land, marking off thousands of farms, each a separate kingdom ruled over by a benign patriarch with, beneath him, a pyramid of contented and industrious children, grandchildren, and serfs." In this map of the land, the farm—the soil—characteristically becomes a kind of wife to the father and sons who all merge into a single mythic husband/man. With the notable exception of the English writer Pauline Smith, it is fair to identify this "dream topography" with the more nostalgic and romantic aspects of the Afrikaner *volkskultuur*. It is the mythic space not only of novelists like Van Bruggen or Van den Heever (whom Coetzee discusses), but also of countless movies, stories from popular magazines like *Huisgenoot*, and old soaps from Springbok Radio. I can recall such titles as *Uit Juffrou se Dagboek* (From the Schoolmistress's Diary), *Die Du Ploois van Soetmelksvlei* (The Du Ploois of Sweetmilk Valley), or *Die Geheim van Nantes* (The Secret of Nantes)—"Nantes" and "Soetmelksvlei" are, to an Afrikaans speaker, immediately recognizable toponyms: the names of family farms. While Coetzee does not mention these subliterary examples of the genre in *White Writing*, they confirm its thoroughly ideological status. Key to Coetzee's approach, however, is the understanding that this topography is a mode of writing, that it is not only of a literary or a mass-cultural sort, but also of a material one: the furrows of the plow, in this social text, assume the character of a signature, a deed of ownership, a title to the land.[33] The pastoral activities of digging, building, fence-making—even the construction of those Cape Dutch houses in the classic shape of the letter H—are acts of ideological inscription.

The second and rival "dream topography" is South Africa

> as a vast, empty, silent space, older than man, older than the dinosaurs whose bones lie bedded in its rocks, and destined to be vast, empty, and unchanged long after man has passed from its face. Under such a conception of Africa—"Africa, oldest of the continents"—the task of the human imagination is to conceive not a social order capable of domesticating the landscape, but any kind of relation at all that consciousness can have with it.

This stoic and defeatist lyricism—this poetry of empty space—originates with the antipastoral of Schreiner's *Story of an African Farm* and is continued by a succession of English-language poets (Sidney Clouts stands, for Coetzee, at the end of this line). Although the key trope here is absence, silence, the failure of language, it is again imperative that this naturalistic topography of desolation should also be apprehended as writing: it does not inscribe the land, as in the Afrikaans pastoral, with the obvious signatures of culture and cultivation, but rather projects a kind of blankness onto the land. In that blankness—the same blankness that Marlow discovers on the map of Africa in *Heart of Darkness*, that imposed emptiness which so fascinated him as a boy—Coetzee reads a certain "historical will to see as silent and empty, a land that has been, if not full of human figures, not empty of them either; that is arid and inflexible, perhaps, but not inhospitable to human life, and certainly not uninhabited."[34] Erasure is also an act of writing—and not simply its binary opposite. Indeed, the message of silence that the lone poet encounters in the empty landscape bears an uncomfortable resemblance, or so Coetzee concludes, to the "writing" of those official historiographers who claimed that the land settled by the Voortrekker pioneers in the nineteenth century was open, empty, and unpeopled.

The critical point is that in both dream topographies the black man, whether as the farmer of an earlier age, or the agricultural worker, or even just as human presence, is obscured. As in his review of *The Guest*, Coetzee's analysis in *White Writing* leads to a series of profoundly uncomfortable questions—questions that strike at the heart of the South African political system and that these apparently pacific ideological landscapes are designed to avoid. Does the poet's inevitable failure to hear the language of the stones "stand for, or stand in the place of, another failure, by no means inevitable: a failure to imagine a peopled landscape, . . . to conceive a society in South Africa in which there is a place for the self?" Or even more pointedly: "Was there no time before the time of the forefathers, and whose was the land then? Do white hands truly pick the fruit, reap the grain, milk the cows, shear the sheep in these bucolic retreats? Who truly creates wealth?" *White Writing* illuminates the crucial, embarrassing blindness implicit in the white man's dream about the land: its necessary "blindness to the colour black." It also reveals a characteristic and consistent critical procedure: an effort on Coetzee's part not to read the "writing," but to ask what it occludes, and to find the truth not in the utterance, but in the evasions and omissions. It is a method of demystification, of revealing the textual and cultural unconscious.[35]

The themes and methods of *White Writing* are also evident in Coetzee's fiction.[36] *Life & Times of Michael K*, for instance, is at least in part a meditation on the ideological function of the pastoral and an example of the critical strategy of subverting the dominant—of listening to silences. That there should be connections between these

two texts is hardly surprising since the novel was written concur-
rently with some of the essays in *White Writing*. Even the lines from
Ovid's *Metamorphoses* that serve as the epigraph to *White Writing* indicate certain overlapping concerns. They symbolically capture the
conditions that beset the life of Michael K, the gardener, and that
have historically beset South Africa, the troubled garden colony.
(The settlement at the Cape of Good Hope was originally intended
as a garden and a supply station for the ships of the Dutch East India
Company.)

> Pressing his lips to foreign soil, greeting the unfamiliar moun-
> tains and plains, Cadmus gave thanks. . . . Descending from
> above, Pallas told him to plow and sow the earth with the ser-
> pent's teeth, which would grow into a future nation.

From the beginning, the epigraph suggests, the settler's pastoral
efforts have been productive of, and indeed synonymous with, war
and strife. The context in which K finds himself likewise conflates
the ideas of gardening and war, or at least forces them into an uncomfortable oxymoronic embrace: in the novel people dig to plant mines,
or march in prison camps with spades over their shoulders.[37]

   Michael K sets out with a desire to escape the war and capture a
pastoral dream: "a whitewashed cottage in the broad veld with smoke
curling from its chimney." But his experience soon teaches him that
the land is mapped and gridlocked in such a way that the pastoral
fantasy, let alone an idyllic rural life, is proscribed for a person who is
officially classed as "coloured": "CM–40–NFA–Unemployed." He can
live freely in this terrain only by being simultaneously a trespasser
and an escapee. Coetzee's use of a black protagonist is essential to
the novel's demystificatory operations. The perspective of one like
K allows Coetzee to reveal the dystopian dimensions of the Afrikaner's dream topography of beloved farms and fences—those enclo-
sures by which the Visagies of the novel (like the real-life Van der
Merwes, Bothas, Coetzees, Malherbes, and Barnards) have staked out
their "miles and miles of silence . . . to bequeath . . . to their children
and grandchildren in perpetuity." The novel's allegorical strategies
represent this landscape in a photographic negative, showing its exact
homology with the Foucauldian "carceral archipelago." K's South

Africa is a place where one can only dream of "forgotten corners and angles and corridors between the fences, land that belonged to no one yet." What one actually experiences, however, is a proliferation of "camps":

> camps for children whose parents run away, camps for people who kick and foam at the mouth, camps for people with big heads and people with little heads, camps for people with no visible means of support, camps for people chased off the land, camps for people they find living in storm-water drains.[38]

For those outside, and, indeed, for those inside the landed clans, the map of the Afrikaner's pastoral merges with the map of a vast prison comprising innumerable cells—a society in which everybody is either fenced in or guarding a gate. The scandalous force of this image can be grasped only if one recalls the repeated and utterly conventional association of the vast South African landscape with notions of freedom, a commonplace of innumerable patriotic songs, such as "Die Lied van Jong Suid-Afrika" (The Song of Young South Africa):

> Die hoogland is ons woning, die land van son en veld,
> Waar woeste vryheidswinde waai oor graf van menig held.
> Die ruimtes het ons siel gevoed, ons kan geen slawe wees,
> Want vryer as die arendsvlug is die vlugte van ons gees.
>
> (The highland is our dwelling place, the land of sun and veld,
> Where wild winds of freedom blow over the graves of many
>   heroes.
> The open space has fed our souls, we cannot ever be slaves,
> For freer than the eagle's flight are the flights of our spirit.)

One of Magda's more profound insights from *In the Heart of the Country* comes to mind here: one can be imprisoned just as readily in a large place "as in a small."[39] And, as Coetzee points out in his Jerusalem Prize acceptance speech, liberty "comes in a package" with equality and fraternity; and in a land without that fraternity, it is therefore inevitable that a "literature of vastness" should carry undertones—the undertones that Coetzee turns into the dominant tones of this novel—of "feelings of entrapment, entrapment in infinitudes."[40]

In the light of this discussion, it seems all the more significant that we should discover in Coetzee's fictional meditations on the South African pastoral the one scene which must, above all, remain hidden if the Afrikaner's dream topography is to be sustained (sustained, that is, in its mythical virtue). This scene appears in Magda's "speculative history"—or "speculative geography":

> Hendrik's [the servant's] forebears in the olden days crisscrossed the desert with their flocks and their chattels, heading from A to B or from X to Y, sniffing for water, abandoning stragglers, making forced marches. Then one day fences began to go up . . . men on horseback rode up and from shadowed faces issued invitations to stop and settle that might also have been orders and might have been threats, one does not know, and so one became a herdsman, and one's children after one, and one's women took in washing.[41]

The erased presence of those earlier nomads represents a challenge to the birthright of the "Boer." The lines remind us vividly that the history of agricultural enclosure, as Raymond Williams demonstrates so well in *The Country and the City*, is not just a history of settlement, but one of *displacement*: the first herder-farmers became temporary sojourners, or, like Robert in *Life & Times of Michael K*, persons of "no fixed abode." This displacement is the secret historical precondition of the Afrikaner's idyllic map of rural homesteading: the old tracings "from A to B" are the submerged and erased text that challenges the settlers' elaborately inscribed title to the land.

The logic of the pastoral topography imposed on this originary scene requires that the black man's inscriptive acts of digging and plowing should leave no trace—should be legally and culturally invisible. This idea is, I would argue, played upon throughout *Life & Times of Michael K*. It is perhaps most powerfully and frighteningly expressed in a passage where K imagines that all the dispossessed might be sent off to dig precisely in order to erase themselves: to scoop out a mass grave into which they can then be thrown, by means of which their presence becomes not just obscured, but permanently deleted.[42]

The brilliance of Michael K's own strategy is that he finds a way

to reclaim displacement, invisibility, tracklessness as a form of freedom. He turns the social condition prescribed for him—to work the
land without owning it, without having a story—into something else,
something to be desired. The significance of his solution is prefigured
in a memory he retains from his school days:

> One of the teachers used to make the class sit with their hands
> on their heads, their lips pressed tightly together and their eyes
> closed, while he patrolled the rows with his long ruler. In time,
> to K, the posture grew to lose its meaning as punishment and
> became an avenue of reverie.

K's mode of farming rewrites (despite *and* because of its invisibility)
the rules of the game of the South African pastoral. He keeps alive
"the idea of gardening" almost by its negation: the idea of plenty
through starvation, the idea of self-affirmation in self-erasure, the
idea of rural dwelling and settlement in "drifting habitation." [43]

The same can be said of Coetzee's artistic practice. The capacity
for changing the rules of the game is precisely what he values most
in a work of art.[44] One might say, moreover, that he too proceeds by
negation and, if need be, invisibly. This connection with K is deli-
cately suggested, I think, in one of the interviews from *Doubling
the Point*, where Attwell and Coetzee discuss a quotation from Rilke
which Coetzee had cited in a 1974 essay on Nabokov: "It is our task
to imprint this provisional, perishable earth so deeply, so patiently
and passionately in ourselves that its reality shall arise in us again
invisibly. *We are the bees of the invisible.*"[45] The impulse here is strikingly lyrical; but Coetzee responds to it cautiously, commenting on
the nostalgic qualities of Nabokov's desire for the past, and observing
that one must look at the past with a cruel enough eye to see what
made that joy and that innocence possible. The observation clearly
applies not just to the past, but also to the pastoral, and to the poetry
of empty space that celebrates South Africa's vast landscapes. Coetzee's position in this regard is, one might say, dialectical. As he has
indicated both in *White Writing* and in his Jerusalem Prize acceptance
speech, it is no longer possible to love the land in unreflective "sincerity": white South Africans have claimed all too often that they
love the mountains, the earth, the trees and flowers—all those things

that cannot return love. This kind of poetry can no longer be written. And yet it seems that one must, secretly and invisibly, continue to "imprint" the "provisional, perishable earth" in oneself, in the manner suggested by Rilke, so that, as Michael K says in one of his naively wise meditations, the thread that binds man to the earth should not be entirely broken.

It is appropriate, then, that such critics as Neil Lazarus and (at times) David Attwell should have associated Coetzee's work not so much with that of other postmodern fabulists as with the modernist critical theory of Theodor Adorno; Coetzee's works, in the words of Adorno's essay on commitment, "point to a practice from which they abstain: the creation of a just life."[46] This connection raises the following question: If Coetzee's fiction is in the main antipastoral and dystopian, then isn't our task as critics (following his own example) to read dialectically, to subvert the dominant, to discover in his work the utopian possibility, the pastoral impulse which cannot be written directly? One of the most remarkable and virtuosic passages in *White Writing* suggests that this approach is exactly what is called for. Here, Coetzee seems to address his fellow critics directly: "Our craft," he says, "is all in reading *the other*: gaps, inverses, undersides; the veiled; the dark, the buried, the feminine; alterities." But then he poses the following question: "Is it a version of utopianism (or pastoralism) to look forward (or backward) to the day when the truth will be (or was) what is said, not what is not said, when we will hear (or heard) music as sound upon silence, not silence between sounds?"[47] These surprisingly wistful lines in many ways resemble the lyrical conclusion to *In the Heart of the Country*; one detects, in both instances, a regretful, minimalist lyricism, a yearning to come right out and sing "the beauty of this forsaken world."[48] But we should not underestimate the cautiousness of Coetzee's language—a language that is, as Strauss puts it, "forever on guard against itself."[49] The *White Writing* passage admits only in the form of a rhetorical question to a desire for the pastoral (utopian) possibility and indicates a strong awareness of the untimeliness, indeed the scandalousness, of this desire. It asserts, in a way that certainly does recall Adorno, the necessarily negative stance of the contemporary work of art, the refusal of easy "day-dream gratification," so that the utopian impulse may be preserved for a later, less bleak time.[50]

It is therefore not only possible, but necessary, to read the outlines of this utopian desire in Coetzee's fiction and in his criticism. Like the Magistrate of *Waiting for the Barbarians*, who in a dream urges the barbarian girl to put people in the empty city she builds out of snow, Coetzee's texts ask, especially in their silences, for a landscape full of people, a society of reciprocity and fraternity. A more explicit moment can be found in the essay "Into the Dark Chamber," where Coetzee notes that Rosa Burger (in Gordimer's novel *Burger's Daughter*) "suffers and waits for . . . a time when humanity will be restored across the face of society, and therefore when all human acts, including the flogging of an animal, will be returned to the ambit of moral judgment." In such a space and in such a time, Coetzee notes, the novel would once again be able to "take as its province the whole of life," and only under such circumstances could the ultimately dystopian, the ultimately secretive space of the torture chamber, "be accorded a place in the design."[51] We could easily extend this logic and say that at such a place and in such a time the novel could again invoke, not ironically but lyrically, the "country ways" of the pastoral: the "whole of life," which, after all, includes digging, includes planting, includes the cultivation of one's garden.

Notes

This essay is for two of my uncles: Simon Malherbe, farmer at Franschhoek, and W. S. Barnard, Professor of Geography at Stellenbosch.

1 J. M. Coetzee, *Doubling the Point: Essays and Interviews*, ed. David Attwell (Cambridge, MA, 1992), 6; and "Interview with Folke Rhedin," *Kunapipi* 6 (1984): 10.

2 J. M. Coetzee, "The Novel Today," *Upstream* 6 (Summer 1988): 2.

3 Edward W. Soja, *Postmodern Geographies: The Reassertion of Space in Critical Social Theory* (New York, 1989), 22.

4 Coetzee, *Doubling the Point*, 361–62.

5 J. M. Coetzee, *Life & Times of Michael K* (New York, 1985 [1983]), 82.

6 Coetzee, *Doubling the Point*, 142.

7 Coetzee's insistence that the land must not be imagined as an empty panorama but as a place inhabited, however sparsely, with human beings is evident in *White Writing: On the Culture of Letters in South Africa* (New Haven, 1988) and is also

implied in the discussion of the importance of reciprocity and fraternity in his Jerusalem Prize acceptance speech (1987).

8 Stephen Gray, "A Sense of Place in the New Literatures in English, Particularly South African," in *A Sense of Place in the New Literatures in English*, ed. Peggy Nightingale (London, 1986), 5–12. Gray also projects, somewhat vaguely, a fourth phase of a kind of postnational, multicultural, and critically potent marginality; he cites only the Australian writer David Malouf as a possible example—no South Africans (11–12).

9 Ibid., 7.

10 If our analysis is to be truly critical, it is important to emphasize that a place, or a "setting," is by no means inertly material, but that it is socially and discursively produced. A concept like "landscape" makes the point particularly well: the word, as John Barrell has pointed out, was used in the realm of aesthetic representation (to describe a kind of painting) well before landscapes came to be observed in the "real world," before the word began to refer to a given tract of land; moreover, aesthetic and social concepts have continued to materially modify the very shape of the land. Landscapes are always forms of a "second nature"; "place" and "setting" are never empirical, never separate from forms of writing. See John Barrell, *The Idea of Landscape and the Sense of Place, 1730–1840: An Approach to the Poetry of John Clare* (Cambridge, 1972), esp. chapter 1.

11 Stephen Watson, "Colonialism in the Novels of J. M. Coetzee," *Research in African Literatures* 17 (1986): 374.

12 Teresa Dovey, *The Novels of J. M. Coetzee: Lacanian Allegories* (Johannesburg, 1988), 52.

13 Dovey uses this image of the hermit crab as the central metaphor of her Lacanian reading of Coetzee, citing as an epigraph a passage from *In the Heart of the Country* (New York, 1982 [1977]), 43–44. The passage from Barthes to which she alludes appears in *Roland Barthes by Roland Barthes*, trans. Richard Howard (New York, 1977), 49. It is interesting that while for Dovey the word "atopia" means something similar to Derrida's "différance," in Barthes's text it actually has a political meaning (and one that is particularly pressing in the South African context): it addresses the problems of the class position/allegiance of the intellectual.

14 J. M. Coetzee, *Heart of the Country*, 12, 26, 41, 17, 19, 39.

15 Ibid., 17.

16 Ibid., 101, 19, 20, 73, 8.

17 Dovey, *Lacanian Allegories*, 9.

18 Coetzee, *Doubling the Point*, 62–63.

19 Coetzee, *Heart of the Country*, 3, 17.

20 This point is also addressed by Peter Strauss, "Coetzee's Idylls: The Ending of *In the Heart of the Country*," in *Momentum: On Recent South African Writing*, ed. M. J. Daymond, J. U. Jacobs, and Margaret Lenta (Pietermaritzburg, 1984), 121–28—the best essay to date on the pastoral impulse in Coetzee's work.

21 Coetzee, *Heart of the Country*, 138–39.

22 Coetzee, *Doubling the Point*, 393–94.

23 Ibid., 63.

24 Ibid., 27. See the epigraph to Gordimer's *July's People* (New York, 1981): "The old is dying and the new cannot be born; in this interregnum there arises a great diversity of morbid symptoms." Coetzee's interest in this condition is evident in the title of *Waiting for the Barbarians* (1980). See also J. M. Coetzee, "Listening to the Afrikaners—Waiting," a review of Vincent Crapanzano's *Waiting: The Whites in South Africa, New York Times Book Review*, 14 April 1985, 3, 28; and Coetzee, *Michael K*, 158.

25 Richard Begam's essay in this issue of *SAQ* is an excellent example of a critique that avoids this rigidity, that is fully conscious of the condition that Edward Said has called "traveling theory."

26 David Attwell, "The Problem of History in the Fiction of J. M. Coetzee," in *Rendering Things Visible: Essays on South African Literary Culture*, ed. Martin Trump (Athens, OH, 1990), 113.

27 Coetzee, *Michael K*, 101, 104; Dovey, *Lacanian Allegories*, 288; Coetzee, *Michael K*, 99.

28 Coetzee, *Michael K*, 116; Dovey, *Lacanian Allegories*, 292.

29 This topographical representation of a social parasitism is evident not only in Michael K's thoughts regarding the town and the camp, but elsewhere in South African literature as well; the same metaphorical logic underpins Mongane Serote's poem "City Johannesburg," for example, in which the city is figured as a parasitic plant growing off the vitality of the black township. At rush hour it inhales or exhales the black workers as its very breath; its power is rooted in their weakness.

30 Coetzee, *Doubling the Point*, 11.

31 Ibid., 115–20. Devenish's response is appended to the original review. See J. M. Coetzee, "The White Man's Burden," *Speak* 1 (1977): 4–7.

32 Coetzee, *Doubling the Point*, 118, 117.

33 Coetzee, *White Writing*, 6–7, 85.

34 Ibid., 7, 177.

35 Ibid., 9, 11, 5. In *Doubling the Point*, Coetzee has appeared to question the value of demystificatory readings on the interesting grounds that they in fact privilege mystification. He describes himself as having become "suspicious of such suspiciousness" (106). Even so, I still think this kind of practice is essential to his thinking—as is perhaps only confirmed by his suspicions.

36 We must, I think, read the strange scenes at the end of *In the Heart of the Country*, where Magda tries to spell out her enigmatic messages in painted stone for the benefit of mysterious Spaniards who seem to pass overhead in an airplane, as a kind of literalization of the romantic notion that to represent Africa one needs to speak a language that is indigenous to and at one with the land. Magda's signifiers are literally and absurdly of the land—the stones, the very earth. Coetzee discusses this kind of "poetry" in *Doubling the Point*, 377.

37 There is a kind of pastoral burlesque in the idea of Michael K's leaving the war-torn city not like the epic hero of old, with his father on his shoulders, but with his mother in a wheelbarrow.

38   Coetzee, *Michael K*, 9, 70, 97, 47, 182.

39   Coetzee, *Heart of the Country*, 122.

40   Coetzee, *Doubling the Point*, 97–98.

41   Coetzee, *Heart of the Country*, 18–19.

42   Coetzee, *Michael K*, 94.

43   Ibid., 68, 109.

44   Attwell, in his introduction to *Doubling the Point*, describes one of the presuppositions on which Coetzee's fiction is based: "[I]f authority *is* ultimately a function of power, then it ought to be possible, through the rediscovery of fiction's capacity to reconfigure the rules of discourse, to find a position *outside* current power relations from which to speak. This is the sense in which Coetzee speaks . . . of the imperative to 'imagine the unimaginable' " (11).

45   Coetzee, *Doubling the Point*, 27.

46   Theodor Adorno, "Commitment," in Ernst Bloch et al., *Aesthetics and Politics*, ed. and trans. Ronald Taylor (London, 1977), 194; quoted in *Doubling the Point*, 12.

47   Coetzee, *White Writing*, 81. The connection with Adorno seems all the more appropriate if one considers that these remarks develop from the idea that we have become accustomed to the kind of modern music Adorno favored; Coetzee's example is the "substantial silence structured by tracings of sound" created by Webern.

48   Coetzee, *Heart of the Country*, 139.

49   Strauss, "Coetzee's Idylls," 128.

50   The response by South African critics to the *Life & Times of Michael K* suggests that Coetzee's cautiousness with regard to what can be said in the present is well-founded. Stephen Clingman ("Revolution and Reality: South African Fiction in the 1980s," in Trump, ed., *Rendering Things Visible*) has dismissively noted that Coetzee seems to leave us, by the end of *Michael K*, with the moral learned by Candide: "Il faut cultiver notre jardin." "Is Coetzee," Clingman asks, "simply returning us to this Voltairean dictum without any sense of irony?" (48). The sense of scandal in Clingman's question is of course shaped by the immediate association of the cultivation of a garden with an individualistic escape from "what would normally count as political." But it seems to me that Coetzee wants us to question this kind of knee-jerk antipastoralism. We should at least be allowed to ask why an interest in the pastoral can no longer be possible, and why the values traditionally associated with the pastoral (Raymond Williams cited, among these values, the idea of a natural way of life: of peace, innocence, simple virtue) should no longer, apparently, be desired.

51   Coetzee, *Doubling the Point*, 368.

Derek Attridge

Trusting the Other: Ethics and Politics in J. M. Coetzee's *Age of Iron*

To read J. M. Coetzee's *Age of Iron* is to read, or overread, a strange kind of letter, written in 1986 by a dying woman in Cape Town to her married daughter in the United States.[1] This, at least, is the fictional contract we enter into, although we are given little in the way of realistic reinforcement that might enable us to imagine the words appearing on paper at the end of a pen. Even the highly implausible epistolary activity of a Clarissa Harlowe or a Saint-Preux is conducted with occasional nods to the mechanical requirements of letter writing, but here the novelist places no constraints on the verbal creativity of his character. Yet in one sense Mrs. Curren's words are more fully imbued with what might be regarded as the spirit of epistolarity than most fictional letters (or, for that matter, nonfictional ones): that is, in their utter dependence on and directedness toward a single, absent other, whose absence is the force that brings the words into being while rendering their task—of communication, above all, the communication of love (whatever that

The *South Atlantic Quarterly* 93:1, Winter 1994.
Copyright © 1994 by Duke University Press.
CCC 0038-2876/94/$1.50.

means)—impossible. Mrs. Curren's daughter is the living being she is closest to, the one she most easily trusts, the one she turns to as soon as she hears the news—which sets in progress the letter and therefore the novel—that the cancer she is suffering from is terminal.

The intensification of love brought about by the news is expressed without embarrassment (one of the habitual human reactions the novel seeks to move beyond) in an early passage describing Mrs. Curren's feelings when she enters the empty house on her return from the doctor, one of many passages that could be quoted to show the powerful other-directedness of the writing:

> So: how I longed for you! How I longed to be able to go upstairs to you, to sit on your bed, run my fingers through your hair, whisper in your ear as I did on school mornings, "Time to get up!" And then, when you turned over, your body blood-warm, your breath milky, to take you in my arms in what we called "giving Mommy a big hug," the secret meaning of which, the meaning never spoken, was that Mommy should not be sad, for she would not die but live on in you.[2]

Living on in her daughter is a matter of bequeathing what she has learned, not as a body of doctrine or information, but by way of sharing the learning experience itself—an experience in which unlearning is as important as learning. Hence the long letter, which moves between recountings of the extraordinary events of these last weeks and difficult reassessments of values and habits built up over a lifetime, all produced as a loving gift for a daughter who will not receive it until the donor is dead—except that, if the gift is truly received, the mother will live on in the daughter. As she puts it later in the letter: "These words, as you read them, if you read them, enter you and draw breath again. They are, if you like, my way of living on. Once upon a time you lived in me as once upon a time I lived in my mother; as she still lives in me, as I grow toward her, may I live in you."[3]

It is hard to know what to call the gift, the message; words like "insight," "knowledge," "wisdom," and "understanding" all belong too irredeemably to the discourse from which Mrs. Curren is achieving a difficult escape, the discourse of knowledge as content and inheritable property rather than as always contextualized responsiveness, activity, and self-questioning. "I may seem to understand what I say, but, believe me, I do not," she admits at one point; and just before the end, she calls hers "a death without illumination."[4] The gift is, of course, the text of the whole novel, or rather the opportunity to read that text; it is J. M. Coetzee's as well as Mrs. Curren's gift (even though we must keep distinct the operations of posthumous letter and published fiction), and there is no possibility of summing up its moral or political "lesson." It's not even clear that something positive is being bequeathed, and I therefore prefer the term "understanding" over other alternatives in that it may be taken in a verbal sense, in the sense, that is, of an activity that need not correspond to a noun. The gift that the letter represents can be offered and received only as an act.

To describe *Age of Iron* in this manner is to emphasize its staging of a personal struggle, but it is also significant that this struggle is born out of and conducted within a highly specific historical situation, which produces a radical reinterpretation, and in some ways a critique, of the age-old motif of wisdom achieved in the shadow of death. Indeed, it is the history of South Africa and, more specifically, the policies of Afrikaner nationalism which have determined that the gift of a mother's love will take the form of a letter, since they are the direct cause of the daughter's decision to leave the country. (She has vowed not to return until the people responsible for these policies are "hanging by their heels from the lampposts," when she will "throw stones at their bodies and dance in the streets."[5]) This is not to say that the daughter's presence would have made the giving, and the living on that is its potential outcome, easier. The longing for unmediated communication, for a physical bond to seal and perfect what is thought of as merely verbal transmission, is driven by a fantasy of total union that cannot, in fact, exist between individuals;[6] and there is even a sense in which the distance and the necessity of written correspondence make possible for Mrs. Curren a fullness of giving, and hence of love and of living on, in that it enables the gift to be posthumous, without thought of return.[7]

But the gift, the love, the narrated experience must be *received*; this, as far as Mrs. Curren is concerned, is its raison d'être. What arises, therefore, is the crucial question of the agent or messenger: Mrs. Curren must trust someone to get the letter to her daughter after her death. It is not just a matter of engaging someone to carry out a commission that can be checked on and, if necessary, rectified; Mrs. Curren has to rely on another person to perform a task that, by its very nature, she cannot verify. Hence there is something absolute about the trust that is called for, as there is about the gift of understanding that it makes possible.

The person to whom Mrs. Curren entrusts the letter is someone who has entered her life as if in response to the intense longing I have already described, a homeless man who chooses, for no satisfactorily explained reason, to take up residence in her backyard on the very day that she receives the fatal medical prognosis. Through this coincidence, he takes the place of the absent daughter, although one could hardly imagine a less likely individual for this office. Mr. Vercueil, as Mrs. Curren comes to call him (without being sure of the spelling or indeed the pronunciation—" 'His name is Mr. Vercueil,' I said. 'Vercueil, Verkuil, Verskuil' "[8]), is a survivor on the fringes of South African society, living on the streets, alcohol-dependent, unaffected by the obligations of human relationship or community; a man so removed from the structures of social and political life that he even appears to have escaped the grid of racial classification on which apartheid rests. (His race, at least, seems to be an issue of no significance to the other characters, whereas their own lives, as the novel graphically demonstrates, are largely determined by the positions in which their racial categorizations place them.) He has shown himself to be outside any of the normal codes that govern interpersonal relations (which is also to say, outside the codes of the realist novel); his unpredictability and unreadability, his imperviousness to the logic of an economy of labor and reward, service and indebtedness, often exasperating to Mrs. Curren, would seem to render him the least appropriate repository for anyone's trust.[9] But it has been clear from the opening of the novel that Vercueil will play a central role in Mrs. Curren's revision of her selfhood and her values: it is with his arrival that the letter begins, and he is from the start associated both with the daughter and with Mrs. Curren herself: "Why do I give this man food? . . . For the same reason I gave you my breast. . . . When I write about him I write about myself."[10]

It is worth following the text closely as it presents the act of entrusting, since it goes to the heart of the strange relationship between the old lady and the derelict, and, as I've suggested, the entire project of the letter depends on it. Mrs. Curren has had very little experience of Vercueil when she decides to make him responsible for posting the letter, a decision that seems to be unusually pure: it appears not to be the product of a calculation and is not explicable in terms of any rational scheme.[11] The process whereby she comes to her decision is not articulated; the request to Vercueil is cited in the letter without preparation or explanation: "There is something I would like you to do for me if I die. There are some papers I want to send to my daughter. But after the event. That is the important part. That is why I cannot send them myself."[12] There is a startling lucidity about Mrs. Curren's insistence that she can convey what she wants to convey only after her death; her daughter must read this letter in the knowledge that its writer is not there to be questioned or negotiated with, that its claimed authority—from the vantage of approaching death—has been justified, and that it is not, for all its expression of longing and love, a plea for sympathy and comfort: "I tell you this story not so that you will feel for me but so that you will learn how things are." The letter will thus function more like literature than most letters, since the work of literature, too, casts itself off from its author and renders questioning problematic—something that Coetzee, when questioned about his fiction, frequently insists upon.[13]

Mrs. Curren emphasizes that the task is, as an action, about as undemanding as any task could be:

> "All you will have to do will be to hand the parcel over the counter at the post office. Will you do that for me?"
>
> He shifted uncomfortably.
>
> "It is not a favor I would ask if I could help it. But there is no other way. I will not be here."
>
> "Can't you ask someone else?" he said.

To make a promise, to accept someone's trust, is something Vercueil cannot or will not do; he lives his life without commitments, without reference to the future (and with references to the past that hardly have the ring of truth).[14] His attempt to shift the burden (a negligible burden in itself, but one whose weightiness simply *as a promise* is accurately perceived by Vercueil) is typical of his behavior. But Mrs. Curren is convinced, against all logic, that he is the man for the job: "Yes, I can. But I am asking you. These are private papers, private letters. They are my daughter's inheritance. They are all I can give her, all she will accept, coming from this country." And Vercueil continues to be evasive and ill at ease.

> "I don't know," said the man, the messenger, playing with his spoon.
>
> He will make no promise. And even if he promises, he will do, finally, what he likes.[15]

"Never mind," says Mrs. Curren, and a little later, as if in response to being let off the hook, Vercueil makes his unreliable commitment: " 'I'll post your parcel for you,' he said." Mrs. Curren or Coetzee (does it make sense to ask which?) ends the first section of the text on this sentence.

Much later in her letter, Mrs. Curren returns to this future act upon which her project depends.

> If Vercueil does not send these writings on, you will never read them. You will never even know they existed. A certain body of truth will never take on flesh: my truth: how I lived in these times, in this place.
>
> What is the wager, then, that I am making with Vercueil, on Vercueil?
>
> It is a wager on trust. So little to ask, to take a package to the post office and pass it over the counter. So little that it is almost nothing. Between taking the package and not taking it the difference is as light as a feather. If there is the slightest breath of trust, obligation, piety left behind when I am gone, he will surely take it.
>
> And if not?
>
> If not, there is no trust and we deserve no better, all of us, than to fall into a hole and vanish.
>
> Because I cannot trust Vercueil I must trust him.[16]

Trust is a relation to the future that is based on no rational grounds; to entrust a task to someone in the certainty that it will be done is not to trust, but merely to act on the basis of advance knowledge; trust, like a pure decision, is born of uncertainty and uncertainty alone. It fully emerges only in the case of someone who, like Vercueil, cannot be trusted even to carry out the most trivial of tasks. The very triviality of the task thus makes this the supreme act of trust, upon which the entire judgment of the future rests—the future of South Africa, the future of humanity, "all of us." [17] A little further on, Mrs. Curren reiterates the magnitude and the counterlogic of her act: "I give my life to Vercueil to carry over. I trust Vercueil because I do not trust Vercueil. I love him because I do not love him. Because he is the weak reed I lean upon him." [18]

Another way of putting this is that there is only one kind of trust that truly deserves the name: trust in the other. I have elsewhere discussed Vercueil as a manifestation of otherness in Mrs. Curren's life and in the novel; the two points I want to stress here are that otherness is always *perspectival* and that it is always *produced*. [19] First, there is no transcendent other (except in certain kinds of religious discourse); there is only an other that presents itself to a specific subject in a particular place and time; otherness is always otherness *to* someone (who inevitably, and by virtue of the existence of the other, is put in the position of the self and the same). And, second, the other does not come from elsewhere, but is a product of the identical constituting act that has produced the self/same. Vercueil comes, then, as the other who challenges Mrs. Curren's daily habits of orderliness, cleanliness, and thrift just as much as he challenges her principles of moral responsibility, obligation, and charity, and his otherness arises from everything that she (or rather, her inherited culture) has rejected in developing those habits and erecting those standards.

Mrs. Curren is right to trust Vercueil, for doing so is itself a crucial aspect of the understanding that she is bequeathing in the act of composing this letter. If her daughter reads the letter, she will read the words quoted above and will know that her mother's apparently imprudent choice was in fact a good one; she will experience (and not merely learn as a lesson) what trust is, the kind of trust that the future of the South Africa she left behind, in what might be regarded as a failure of trust, desperately needs. If she doesn't get the letter, of course, her mother's trust and the understanding that it implies will have been discredited, removing the very reason for reading it.

Yet there is a sense in which, for the reader, the question of whether

Vercueil does or does not post the parcel is irrelevant (it remains in any case unknowable, entirely outside the boundaries of the novel); it is Mrs. Curren's unprogrammed and complete act of trust that saves "all of us." Trust in the other and in the future is at the ethical heart of a situation such as that which prevailed in South Africa in 1986, or that which prevails today.[20] This is not a *political* prescription, since it does not contain any program indicating when, where, and how such trust should operate; nor is it a vague liberal-humanist truism, urging individuals to behave justly toward others. Through its staging of an encounter (to be read neither as a realistic exemplar nor as a universal allegory, but as a uniquely configured enactment of a general truth that exists only in such unique enactments), the novel offers a precise *understanding* of trust, and of its relation to the vital questions of the other and the future, involving an apprehension that is no less intellectual (perhaps all the more so) for being irreducible to programmatic rules. It is an understanding that can be conveyed only in such a novel, or such a letter, or such a life.[21] Whether or not it reaches the daughter is, to Coetzee, to us, immaterial (as is the question of whether the daughter understands what she has received or is disgusted or horrified by it)—and even Mrs. Curren recognizes early on that she writes, as she says to her daughter, "to you but not to you; to me; to you in me." Writing is that which lives on because its addressee is always multiple and divided; and to write is therefore to trust the other who will read—other because unknowable and unfixable in advance.

If I say that Mrs. Curren's relationship with Vercueil in this novel is a staging of a fundamental ethical understanding, I may give the impression of a text that is highly generalized in its procedures. But the sense in which I am using "ethics" grounds it in the specific, the singular, the historical, the contingent. "One must love what is to hand," Mrs. Curren explains to her daughter.[22] It is in the *details* of the relationship, often comic, never predictable, that the Vercueil sections of the novel have their force, the absurdity of the old lady's cossetings and conversations (often one-sided), the pathos of her moments of dependence, the triumph of collaborative actions; and it is in these details that the ethical is played out, as Mrs. Curren learns to overcome a lifetime's habits of thought and action. But hers is not the story of a saint: Mrs. Curren's acceptance of the other has limits, as when Vercueil brings a woman into the house—when we perhaps witness unacknowledged sexual jealousy as well—or when she faces the white South Africans she detests, on television or in person.[23] Only in her unique relationship with Vercueil do we find a continuous generosity and openness, running under the spasms of irritation and exasperation that Mrs. Curren experiences.

Of course, the relationship as we see it is entirely constructed by Mrs. Curren; we have no access to Vercueil's motives or attitudes, and for all we know he feels no reciprocal warmth or commitment. (The contrast with another Coetzeean survivor in inauspicious times, Michael K, is striking, since his thoughts are for the most part made available to us.) Quite early in the letter, Mrs. Curren describes how she played a recording of the Goldberg Variations while Vercueil smoked a cigarette outside the house: "Together we listened. At this moment, I thought, I know how he feels as surely as if he and I were making love."[24] It is a moment of startling intimacy, although neither Mrs. Curren nor the reader can know if Vercueil is even listening to the music. In a different novel, Vercueil's otherness would dissolve, bit by bit, and some shared terrain would emerge where, remade by the relationship, they would achieve communication. But Coetzee is writing of an otherness that is not to be conjured away; Vercueil remains unknowable to the end, and in that end fuses—or is fused in Mrs. Curren's mind—with the equally irreducible otherness of death.

One of the most extraordinary qualities of Mrs. Curren's response to Vercueil is that, although it transgresses so many of her values, it is achieved without a great struggle; the code of "proper behavior" rapidly loses its relevance. The man is allowed to stay in the backyard, brought coffee the next morning (which he spits out at her feet when she begins to lecture him), and is invited to sleep in the house, eventually in her bed. (It is her readers—including, one imagines, her daughter—who must struggle to comprehend and sympathize with her growing closeness to and dependence upon the dirty, foul-smelling alcoholic at the same time that she is cutting herself off from all "normal" sources of help.) Her early condemnation of him gives way to a willingness to learn from him, and to learn from the fact of his utter difference from herself.[25]

Insofar as we read this behavior "realistically," we can understand it only as a sign of the psychological effect of approaching death, which deprives conventional mores of their relevance and encourages a certain "allegorical" reading of reality. Thus at several points Mrs. Curren plays with an allegorization of Vercueil, both believing in his otherworldliness and making fun of herself for doing so: he is "the messenger"; early on, his appearance is called an "annunciation"; but then he is "[n]ot an angel, certainly" (after this thought she reads Tolstoy's "story of the angel who takes up residence with the shoemaker"). Later, he is "[n]o Odysseus, no Hermes, perhaps not even a messenger." Toward the end, she describes how he carried her through the streets and she asked herself (jokingly? seriously?), "When would the time come when the jacket fell away and great wings sprouted from his shoulders?" Soon after this she admits to him that when he first arrived she wondered if he were "an angel come to show me the way," and continues, "Of course you were not, are not, cannot be—I see that. But that is only half the story, isn't it? We half-perceive but we also half-create."[26]

The fact that the central character so self-consciously plays with allegorizations of her own experience (she even raises the obvious link between her condition and that of the country as a whole, and at one point she observes, "It was like living in an allegory") prevents us from straightforwardly reading Coetzee's narrative as an allegory.[27] Vercueil is readable at a perfectly literal level, a historical rather than a metaphorical sign of the breakdown of social order during the late phase of apartheid (evident also in the marauding bands of children), a scavenger seeing an opportunity in a helpless and increasingly crazy old lady, eagerly joining in her plans to commit suicide, although finally lacking the skill and sobriety to take full advantage of her— until, in one possible reading of the ending, he finally murders her.

At the same time, we cannot ignore the allegorical quality of the story of the old woman's illness and the unaccountable visitor, especially as we read it in conjunction with, and in contrast to, the more historically plausible story of Mrs. Curren's maid and her family. Although he comes as a derelict in need of shelter and not as an annunciating angel, Vercueil's arrival and subsequent behavior, and Mrs. Curren's increasingly intimate relationship with him, do not yield wholly to the interpretive canons of the realistic novel. (Readers of Coetzee's fiction will recognize this oscillation between verisimilitude and its undermining; the figures of Jacobus Coetzee, Magda, and Michael K are earlier instances.) To take one striking example, the final sentence of *Age of Iron* fulfills the goal enunciated by Mrs. Curren near the beginning ("To embrace death as my own, mine alone") in a climactic use of the angel motif: "He took me in his arms and held me with mighty force, so that the breath went out of me in a rush. From that embrace there was no warmth to be had." Yet we cannot be sure whose allegory this is, Mrs. Curren's in a letter to her daughter or Coetzee's in a sentence that abandons the conceit of the continuously written letter, nor exactly what is being allegorized in the final, hardly triumphant coldness.[28]

So Mrs. Curren's response to the other in the form of Vercueil can be read as a kind of heightened staging of the very issue of otherness, a story that is continuous with attempts by such "philosophical" writers as Levinas, Blanchot, and Derrida to find ways of engaging this issue. The idiosyncratic and inconsistent reality of Vercueil and the fully realized persona of Mrs. Curren do not distance the novel from these more discursive attempts; on the contrary, the philosophical argument requires concrete instances, since to apprehend the other as a general phenomenon is to take away its otherness. (At the same time, of course, no concrete instance can exhaust the issue.) As in these writers, the other is not sought, but impinges on a life without notice, without discernible reason: "I did not choose him. He chose me. Or perhaps he merely chose the one house without a dog." The other appears in the form of the *arrivant*: "I didn't choose you, but you are the one who is here, and that will have to do. You arrived. It's like having a child. You can't choose the child. It just arrives."[29] We are *already* obligated to the other; we find ourselves responsible for it/him/her/them, and responsible in an absolute way; it is not a matter of calculating a certain degree of responsibility and then acting upon it. Of course, we can refuse this responsibility, and most often we do; but this is a story of what happens to someone who accepts it, without calculation, without forethought—or better, accepts it on the far side of calculation and forethought, at the end of a long life lived according to the rules (and as a classicist, Mrs. Curren is deeply aware of the long history of those rules). The fullest acceptance of responsibility to and for the other may indeed be to trust the other, since this is to put the relationship to the other under the rubric of the future, and only in a willingness not to preprogram the future can the other—whose impact upon our lives remains incalculable and unforeseeable—be accepted.[30]

Crucial, too, is the way that Mrs. Curren allows herself to be changed by the other. On the second day of Vercueil's residence in her backyard she chides him for wasting his life, and comments, "It is true: I do not understand it. Something in me revolts at the lassitude, the letting go, the welcoming of dissolution." Much later, we find her writing to her daughter: "Letting go of myself, letting go of you, letting go of a house still alive with memories: a hard task, but I am learning."[31] With an unconscious echo of Heidegger's *Gelassenheit*, she charts her altering apprehension of the task that confronts her in her dying days in a convulsed society.

≡≡≡≡≡

In the interviews with David Attwell in *Doubling the Point*, Coetzee takes it for granted that there is an opposition between the "ethical" and the "political." Although he remarks that "the last thing I want to do is to *defiantly* embrace the ethical as against the political," his emphasis (together with the context of this comment) indicates that he feels himself aligned with the former, albeit not in a way that, as he says, would contribute "toward marking the ethical as the pole with the lack." And later, when he comments, "I think you will find the contest of interpretations I have sketched here—the political versus the ethical—played out again and again in my novels," it is evident that it is the political that is to be corrected by the ethical, and not vice versa.[32]

My discussion of trust, otherness, and the future in *Age of Iron* will have suggested ways in which we might understand the two terms: the ethical involves an always contextualized responsiveness and responsibility to the other (as unique) and to the future (as unknowable), while the political is the realm of generalizations, programs, and predictions. It's worth noting the reversal that this implies in the way these terms are often used: here it is the ethical, not the political, which is concerned with concrete acts and persons, and the political which deals in general rules. My argument is that in the political arena we often think we are engaging with the concrete when we are imposing generalities and that the generalities on which philosophical ethics has usually rested are evasions of the genuinely ethical, which can be thought through only in relation to the singular and the contingent.

It would be a mistake, however, to think that ethics and politics are separate domains and that Coetzee engages only with the former. A politics worth espousing is surely a politics that both incorporates the ethical and is incorporated in it, while acknowledging the inescapable tension and continual revaluation that this mutual incorporation implies. All of Coetzee's novels enact this tension, the necessary conflict of programs and persons, of a desire to know and order and a willingness to accept otherness and contingency. The story of Mrs. Curren, her absent daughter, and Mr. Vercueil has its roots in the politics of modern South Africa; but in itself, it does not deal directly with the imperatives of the political. The other main narrative thread in *Age of Iron*, which weaves through and constantly impinges upon the story of the central relationship, is directly concerned with the demands and difficulties of politics—especially in its relation to ethics—in a situation of extreme oppression and forceful resistance.

Here too the question of otherness is central; Mrs. Curren again and again finds herself faced with members of the black community whose values and actions she finds it difficult to comprehend: her maid, whom she knows as "Florence," her maid's cousin or brother, Mr. Thabane, her son, Bheki, and above all Bheki's friend, whom we know only by his unconvincing *nom de guerre*, "John," and by the name the police have for him, "Johannes."[33] (The policemen whom she encounters at various points in the novel also affront her values, but with the effect of reinforcing, not shaking, them.) Their otherness is very different from Vercueil's, however; indeed, the difference is dramatized in the hostility between the township people and Vercueil. Florence can see him only as "rubbish" and as "good for nothing," and the boys despise him perhaps even more strongly. (It is, incidentally, in their treatment of him that we have the strongest suggestion that he would be placed by the apartheid system in the category "non-white," since they appear to regard his alcoholism as a capitulation to white domination: "They are making you into a dog!"[34])

Bheki, Florence's fifteen-year-old son, has come to stay with his mother and sisters in Mrs. Curren's backyard because of the increasing violence in Guguletu, the township where he normally lives, and his friend soon joins him. John's first, highly characteristic act is to take Vercueil's brandy away from him. As this act suggests, Bheki's friend is the most strongly delineated exemplar of the new role which the children of the township have found, leading their elders in a revolutionary struggle that has displaced the normal concerns of childhood and reversed traditional parent-child relationships: " 'I cannot tell these children what to do,' said Florence. 'It is all changed today. There are no more mothers and fathers.' " Mrs. Curren sees this as a manifestation of the age of iron in which she is living, damaging the very future that children traditionally represent: " 'And when they grow up one day,' I said softly, 'do you think the cruelty will leave them? What kind of parents will they become who were taught that the time of parents is over?' "[35]

Although she implicitly acknowledges an affinity between these children and her own daughter—they are "children of iron"; her daughter is "like iron"—she insists, at great personal cost, on preserving the one-way passage of mother-to-daughter inheritance and love: hence her determination that the letter will reach her daughter only after her own death. She explains to Vercueil: "[T]hat is something one should never ask of a child, . . . to enfold one, comfort one, save one. The comfort, the love should flow forward, not backward. That is a rule, another of the iron rules."[36] Of course, iron rules are just what Mrs. Curren distrusts, but her insistence is her way of living in the times; in another age, she would telephone her daughter (as Vercueil, pragmatic as ever, urges her to do), who would fly back to South Africa to comfort her dying mother. Mrs. Curren's hope, however, is that instead of taking, she can give, and in that way project her own best existence into the future; her fear, of course, is that her child will be like the township children, hardened by the circumstances of her South African upbringing and incapable of the receptivity needed to understand and, in turn, pass on the gift.

Mrs. Curren's response to the otherness of John is of a different order than to that of Vercueil; we are not tempted into allegorical readings, but made to feel the acute difficulty of establishing any relations across the divide between bourgeois white liberal and committed black revolutionary. In her early encounters with the boys Mrs. Curren vents her helpless anger at their flouting of the codes of propriety, and she experiences a particular dislike for John: "The boy stopped speaking to Bheki and regarded me. I did not like that look: arrogant, combative." Then there occurs the incident in which Mrs. Curren sees a police van force the boys, who are riding together on a bicycle, to collide with a parked truck; John is badly injured, and Mrs. Curren, deserted by both Vercueil and Florence, stays with him, trying to staunch the flow of blood from his gashed forehead until an ambulance finally arrives. But this act does not establish a reciprocal bond; when they next meet, in the hospital where Mrs. Curren eventually tracks John down, he resists her solicitude and her admonitions. "My words fell off him like dead leaves the moment they were uttered. The words of a woman, therefore negligible; of an old woman, therefore doubly negligible; but above all of a white."[37]

For Mrs. Curren, John represents absolute political commitment, which means an absolute privileging of the political over the ethical; as she sees it, his single-minded assault on white power involves sexism, ageism, racism, and deafness to any subtleties or any qualifications of his classifications and prescriptions. It is an attitude that has no place whatever for Vercueil (the only major character in the novel who is never described by means of the metaphor of iron). In the hospital she lectures John on the importance of allowing for exceptions to general rules (even while she half-acknowledges that the times do not allow for "all that close listening, all those exceptions, all that mercy"), while on a later occasion she inveighs against his masculine, black-and-white, iron understanding of the world and argues in favor of "everything indefinite, everything that gives when you press it."[38]

Mrs. Curren's opposition to John's political beliefs is not distinct from her dislike of him as a person. She portrays him as entirely unattractive, a portrayal all the more striking in that it emphasizes that he is still a child:

> I did not like him. I do not like him. I look into my heart and no-where do I find any trace of feeling for him. As there are people to whom one spontaneously warms, so there are people to whom one is, from the first, cold. That is all. . . . A simplified person, simplified in every way: swifter, nimbler, more tireless than real people, without doubts or scruples, without humor, ruth-less, innocent. While he lay in the street, while I thought he was dying, I did what I could for him. But, to be candid, I would rather I had spent myself on someone else.[39]

Yet she does not dismiss him; as with Vercueil, his very otherness seems to exert a strong pull on her, as if her special situation renders her exceptionally willing to allow her inherited values to be tested to the limit. She pushes her sick body into an exhausting search for him in hospital, gives up, and then returns when she learns from Florence where he is. Without making a choice, she finds herself responsible to and for him.

Later, one night, he appears at her house, a refugee, his injuries unhealed, and Mrs. Curren ministers to him. The event produces an extraordinary "confession" to her daughter, in which she struggles to find an appropriate, we might say ethical, response to the boy.

> I do not love this child, the child sleeping in Florence's bed. I love you but I do not love him. There is no ache in me toward him, not the slightest.
>
> Yes, you reply, he is not lovable. But did you not have a part in making him unlovable?
>
> I do not deny that. But at the same time I do not believe it. My heart does not accept him as mine: it is as simple as that.

The recognition that the otherness to which she is struggling to open herself has been produced by the very values in whose name she claims to be acting is one that she can accept rationally but not emo-tionally. And this leads her to question her capacity to love: "Not wanting to love him, how true can I say my love is for you? For love is not like hunger. Love is never sated, stilled. When one loves, one loves more. The more I love you, the more I ought to love him."[40] Her struggle is a struggle to redefine love—the love that is the origin and driving force of the entire letter—in such a way as to include that which is most resistant to it (more resistant even than Vercueil, whom she finds "hard to love" for his physical repulsiveness, but to whom she does, in a strange way, warm spontaneously). It is a love that is not defined, as love usually is, in opposition to duty, but one that flows directly from duty.

When the police kill John in her backyard, Mrs. Curren—now defying all propriety for the sake of her difficult love—attempts to climb into the ambulance with the body. Prevented from doing so, she walks away from the house and into the most horrifying of her degradations, as a group of children force a stick into her mouth, prying it open in search of gold fillings, while she lies beneath an overpass, too ill to resist. Her reaction reveals how far she has traveled from the moral truisms that once nourished her: ridiculing her momentary urge to beg for mercy, she chides herself, "What nonsense. Why should there be mercy in the world?" Vercueil finds her and carries her to a wooded space to sleep on a flattened cardboard box, and there she makes another "confession"—to Vercueil (who may not be awake for all of it), but also to herself and to her daughter—in which she articulates as fully as she can her new understanding of the political struggle she is caught up in. While insisting that she still detests "these calls for sacrifice that end with young men bleeding to death in the mud," she nevertheless acknowledges the inadequacy of the concepts she has hitherto been guided by—"honor," "shame," and "goodness" ("What I had not calculated on was that more might be called for than to be good")—and the necessity for what she calls "heroism": a word that, having come to mean something different from what it did in her classical education, perhaps helped her to love the unlovable John, or at least to acknowledge his independence and worth as an other.[41] This implies a new understanding of the political necessity and inevitability of the children's activism and attitudes, and therefore of a conflict—the conflict between the ethical and the political, which is also a conflict *within* both the ethical and the political—that cannot be resolved in the present by a feat of analysis that seizes the future, but that has to be worked through, stage by stage, painful detail by painful detail.[42] The understanding we glimpse here is not entirely new, however; it has been implicit, for instance, in her urge to *record* the black voices that have so implacably opposed hers, and to transfer them to her daughter as part of what she bequeaths to her.

It is an age of iron, the worst of times, and its particular deformations of the human spirit call for a response that is neither moralizing nor cynical. Mrs. Curren has to acknowledge that nothing she can say will detract from the heroic self-sacrifice of the township children, made vivid to her in the deaths first of Bheki and then of John; theirs is a situation in which the only possible ethic is an ethic of comradeship, single-mindedness, and blind courage.[43] For Mrs. Curren, and by implication for J. M. Coetzee and the majority of his readers, who are in a markedly different situation, the ethical appears in another guise: as the difficult task of responding with full justice to the moment, with a trust in the other and the future that is ultimately beyond measure. In understanding the nature of this task, the test posed and the example presented by Vercueil are of the utmost importance. An ethical response on the part of privileged South African whites to the violent and dehumanizing campaign of the townships would be one that is neither condemnation nor approval, neither detachment nor immersion, but a *living-through* (in concrete action as well as in thought and emotion) of the torsions it produces in shared value systems. What is enacted in this novel is the acute ethico-political trauma of the postcolonial world, where no general rule applies, where a conflict of values is endemic, and where every code of moral conduct has to be tested and justified afresh in terms of the specific context in which it is being invoked. But this is not a lesson to be learned, a conclusion to be reached. Mrs. Curren's new understanding is not something she has achieved; it exists in, and cannot be separated from, the negotiations and questionings she has experienced. Although in these extreme times the political and the ethical may seem absolutely opposed, they are not. The ethical cannot be reduced to the moral injunctions about the individual and the exception enshrined in Mrs. Curren's inherited creed; it is a process of constant reappraisal and self-redefinition through which those injunctions are tested, reaffirmed, or remade. The political cannot be reduced to the need for solidarity and simplification, for fixed readings of the past and the future, which is the guise that it must sometimes wear; it is always subject to the demands of the ethical.

The peculiar importance of literature as a cultural practice lies in its capacity to play out these issues, in a process that is not measured in terms of its meaning or its result. Reading a work of literature entails opening oneself up to the unpredictable, the future, the other, and thereby accepting the responsibility imposed by the work's singularity and difference. There is also abundant evidence that *writing* a literary work is often a similar experience.[44] In a sense, the "literary" *is* the ethical. Literary criticism, however, can seldom make the same claim. What I have given is only a crude sketch of the rich working through of questions of trust, love, alterity, politics, and ethics in *Age of Iron*; I have necessarily schematized and simplified where the novel remains fluid and even self-contradictory. Its power lies not in any hagiographic object lesson—the uniqueness of Mrs. Curren's personality and predicament precludes that—but in its enactment, in charged, exploratory, sometimes consciously self-indulgent language, of a number of interrelated struggles in which the reader is invited to participate with sympathy but also with critical judgment.

It is characteristic of Coetzee that he should risk building a politically engaged novel on such overworked concepts as "trust" and "love," and one might predict that his having done so will be frequently misunderstood (both by those who want to exclude the political and by those who want to emphasize it). Only by paying close attention to the penetrating and lucid way in which such terms are questioned in his fiction—operating always as fiction and not as disguised treatise or tract, operating, that is, in response to the contingent, the unpredictable, the other—can we do justice to Coetzee's work, which does not hesitate to engage the dominating legacy of Western thought and culture and to stage, with remarkable results, the transformation that it undergoes, in a curious and conflicted living-on, in our postcolonial world.

Notes

1   J. M. Coetzee, *Age of Iron* (New York, 1990).
2   Ibid., 5–6.
3   Ibid., 131.

4 Ibid., 131, 195.

5 Ibid., 75.

6 Mrs. Curren contemplates this image of union, half-blaming her historical location for its impossibility, but half-recognizing it as a fantasy: "In another world
I would not need words. I would appear on your doorstep. 'I have come for a
visit,' I would say, and that would be the end of words: I would embrace you
and be embraced. But in this world, in this time, I must reach out to you in
words" (9). Mrs. Curren's refusal to use the telephone to communicate the news
of her condition to her daughter can be understood as a rejection of a medium
that offers neither presence nor the possibility of a posthumous verbal gift. We
learn of one unsatisfactory phone call some time after the event—"not words, not
living breath passing between us, but the ideas of words, the idea of breath"—
which may have conveyed "love but not truth"; in this letter, however, are "truth
and love together" (129). The novel suggests that it is finally only in conveying
truth—not a transcendent content, not "the" truth, but a historical, contingent
experience, what Mrs. Curren calls "my truth: how I lived in these times, in this
place"—that love is transmitted (130).

7 As this paragraph will have begun to indicate, my engagement with *Age of Iron*
has been informed by a number of theoretical writings. (It is likely that Coetzee
is familiar with many of these, although this is not part of my argument.) Most
important, perhaps, are several texts by Jacques Derrida, including *Given Time: 1.
Counterfeit Money*, trans. Peggy Kamuf (Chicago, 1992); "Living On/Borderlines,"
in Harold Bloom et al., *Deconstruction and Criticism* (New York, 1979), 75–176;
"Force of Law: The 'Mystical Foundation of Authority,' " in *Deconstruction and the
Possibility of Justice*, ed. Drucilla Cornell, Michel Rosenfeld, and David Gray Carl-
son (New York, 1992), 3–67; and "Psyche: Invention of the Other," in *Acts of Literature*, ed. Derek Attridge (New York, 1992), 310–43. Some aspects of Emmanuel
Levinas's many discussions of the Other have also been important, most obviously,
Totality and Infinity: An Essay on Exteriority, trans. Alphonso Lingis (Pittsburgh,
1969), as has the work of Jean-François Lyotard, notably, *The Differend: Phrases
in Dispute*, trans. Georges Van Den Abbeele (Minneapolis, 1988); and Maurice
Blanchot, *The Writing of the Disaster*, trans. Ann Smock (Lincoln, NE, 1986). As
far as the burgeoning field of Coetzee criticism is concerned, I have found especially useful the work of David Attwell (most recently, *J. M. Coetzee and South
Africa: Contemporary History and the Politics of Writing* [Berkeley and Cape Town,
1993]); Benita Parry (for example, "The Holes in Coetzee's Narratives," in *Critical
Perspectives on J. M. Coetzee*, ed. Graham Huggan and Stephen Watson [London,
forthcoming]); Gayatri Chakravorty Spivak, "Theory in the Margin: Coetzee's
Foe Reading Defoe's *Crusoe/Roxana*," in *Consequences of Theory: Selected Papers
from the English Institute, 1987–88*, ed. Jonathan Arac and Barbara Johnson (Baltimore, 1991), 154–80; and Stephen Watson, "Colonialism and the Novels of J. M.
Coetzee," *Research in African Literatures* 17 (1986): 370–92.

8 Coetzee, *Age of Iron*, 37. The subject of names in Coetzee's work is worth an essay
in itself, which would point out the repeated undermining of their supposed simple

referentiality and the making evident of the power relations within which they function. It might begin with Coetzee's decision to withhold his own forenames, which has given rise to an uncertainty rather like Mrs. Curren's over "Vercueil": thus while Ian Ousby's *Cambridge Guide to Literature in English* (Cambridge, 1988) and D. L. Kirkpatrick's *Contemporary Novelists* (4th ed., New York, 1986) both confidently give his name as "John Michael Coetzee," Dick Penner's *Countries of the Mind: The Fiction of J. M. Coetzee* (New York, 1989) and Kevin Goddard and John Read's *J. M. Coetzee: A Bibliography* (Grahamstown, 1990), with equal assurance, give "John Maxwell Coetzee." *Le Nouvel observateur* presents him as "Jean-Marie Coetzee" (interview with Claude Wauthier, 28 June 1985, 54), and Linda Hutcheon calls him just "Michael Coetzee" (*A Poetics of Postmodernism: History, Theory, Fiction* [New York, 1988], 77, 107, 198). The entry in *Contemporary Literary Criticism* (vol. 66), contrary to its usual practice but perhaps wisely, settles for "John M. Coetzee" as his "full name."

An analogous ambiguity occurs with respect to the name of the letter writer in *Age of Iron*. She is unnamed at first, but we eventually learn that her married name is "Curren" and that her initials are "E. C." However, both Coetzee himself, in the interviews in *Doubling the Point: Essays and Interviews*, ed. David Attwell (Cambridge, MA, 1992), 250, 340, and some critics—presumably following the author's extratextual comments—refer to her as "Elizabeth Curren" (as critics sometimes provide a surname for another "E. C.," the Emma of Joyce's *Portrait of the Artist as a Young Man*, transferring the name "Clery" from the surviving fragment of *Stephen Hero*). This is even shortened to "Elizabeth" (out of the same unconscious sexism that makes critics speak of "Susan"—but not "Robinson" or "Daniel"—in *Foe*), a familiarity at which we can imagine Mrs. Curren—who always addresses and usually speaks of Vercueil as "Mr. Vercueil"—wincing sharply.

Coetzee's fiction also repeatedly presents us with nameless characters—the barbarian girl, the medical officer—or characters whose names are in one way or another problematic—Michael K (who is consistently called "Michaels" by the medical officer), Friday, and Mrs. Curren's servant and her family. The question of naming is, of course, central to any question of the relation to, and the resistance of, the other.

9   Tony Morphet, in his appreciative review of the novel, "The Inside Story," *Southern African Literary Review* 1 (April 1991): 1–3, gives an excellent description of Vercueil's imperviousness to comprehension.

10 Coetzee, *Age of Iron*, 7, 9.

11 Carl Schmitt's discussion of what he calls "the decision in absolute purity," constituted by a moment which is not derivable from any preexisting norms, is relevant here (see his *Political Theology: Four Chapters on the Concept of Sovereignty*, trans. George Schwab [Cambridge, MA, 1985], 13) and in part underlies Derrida's exploration of the issue of deciding in such texts as "Afterword: Toward an Ethic of Discussion," in *Limited Inc.*, ed. Gerald Graff (Evanston, IL, 1988), 111–60, and "Force of Law." The question of the decision is related to the questions of justice, of the gift (see Derrida's *Given Time*), and, as in this novel, of trust.

12 Coetzee, *Age of Iron*, 31.

13 Ibid., 103. One of the many instances is the following, from *Doubling the Point*: "I am immensely uncomfortable with questions—like this one—that call on me to *answer for* (in two senses) my novels, and my responses are often taken as evasive. . . . What I say is marginal to the book, not because I as author and authority so proclaim, but on the contrary because it would be said from a position peripheral, posterior to the forever unreclaimable position from which the book was written" (205–6).

14 Coetzee, *Age of Iron*, 31. Nietzsche's account (see *The Genealogy of Morals*, trans. Walter Kaufmann and R. J. Hollingdale [New York, 1967]) of humanity's reaching the stage of being able to promise is helpful in understanding Vercueil's reluctance; as Nietzsche puts it, "Man himself must first of all have become *calculable, regular, necessary*, even in his own image of himself, if he is to be able to stand security for *his own future*, which is what one who promises does!" (58). But we should not be too quick to assume that Vercueil is some sort of innocent primitive or noble savage, ignorant of the basic ties of human community; seeing him through Mrs. Curren's eyes alone, we have no way of knowing what ingredients of calculation or cynicism are at work in him (just as we cannot fathom what complexities underlie the silence of the barbarian girl in *Waiting for the Barbarians* or of Friday in *Foe*). It is important that we, like Mrs. Curren, not know this, since this is what makes her trust so remarkable.

15 Coetzee, *Age of Iron*, 31–32.

16 Ibid., 130.

17 Both Levinas and Derrida associate the future with crucial questions of ethics, responsibility, and alterity. For Levinas, "[t]he future is what is not grasped, what befalls us and lays hold of us. The other is the future." See "Time and the Other," in *The Levinas Reader*, ed. Sean Hand (Oxford, 1989), 44. Derrida's thinking has always shown an acute awareness of the question of the future, emerging most obviously in, for instance, his considerations of chance, of deferral, of iterability, of the promise, of the date, and of friendship.

18 Coetzee, *Age of Iron*, 131.

19 Derek Attridge, "Literary Form and the Demands of Politics: Otherness in J. M. Coetzee's *Age of Iron*," in *Ideology and Aesthetics*, ed. George Levine (New Brunswick, in press).

20 Neil Lazarus stresses the significance and necessity of pure trust in the specific case of the white South African writer: a trust that is "sacrificial—or at least potentially sacrificial, for its outcome cannot be known in advance." See "Modernism and Modernity: T. W. Adorno and Contemporary White South African Literature," *Cultural Critique* 5 (Winter 1986–87): 150.

21 This is to point to the crucial importance of what has traditionally been called "form": the unique staging of human meanings that constitutes a work of literature (which need not be confined to the traditional category so named) and its reading. For further discussion, see my "Literary Form and the Demands of Politics."

22 Coetzee, *Age of Iron*, 190.

23 See, for example, the episode in the picnic spot above Hout Bay (ibid., 127).

24 Ibid., 30.

25 Mrs. Curren's response to Vercueil can be understood as a further exploration of the issues discussed in Coetzee's essay "Idleness in South Africa," in *White Writing: On the Culture of Letters in South Africa* (New Haven, 1988), 12–35; while the essay traces the repeated condemnation of the "Hottentots" at the Cape as "idle," the novel enacts a principled refusal to impose preexisting moral codes on those who do not acknowledge them.

26 Coetzee, *Age of Iron*, 32, 5, 14, 140, 160–61, 168.

27 Ibid., 65, 90.

28 Ibid., 6, 198. The ending has been read as a wholly positive conclusion, but this may be as much a product of the desire for positive conclusions as of attentive readings. Coetzee himself disagrees with Attwell's suggestion that it represents a final absolution for Mrs. Curren, making a comment on his own novel with his usual distance and caution: "The end of the novel seems to me more troubled (in the sense that the sea can be troubled) than you imply. But here I am stepping onto precarious ground, or precarious water; I had better stop" (*Doubling the Point*, 250).

29 Coetzee, *Age of Iron*, 12, 71.

30 The relationship between Mrs. Curren and Vercueil is clearly a rewriting of the relationship between Susan Barton and Friday in *Foe*, Coetzee's previous novel. (Mrs. Curren's letter, like Barton's narrative, is an attempt to constitute a self, partly through storytelling, in a situation that could not have been predicted.) Barton, too, finds herself responsible for someone who is wholly other to her and is baffled by the task this responsibility imposes, the task of doing justice to the other; but there is no equivalent in *Foe* to Mrs. Curren's future-directed act of entrusting. For more on the difficulty of responding to the other without denying its otherness, see my essay "Oppressive Silence: J. M. Coetzee's *Foe* and the Politics of the Canon," in *Decolonizing Tradition: New Views of 20th-Century "British" Literature*, ed. Karen Lawrence (Urbana, 1991), 212–38.

31 Coetzee, *Age of Iron*, 8, 130.

32 Coetzee, *Doubling the Point*, 200, 338.

33 Once again, the other eludes the will-to-name of the power that dominates it. Mrs. Curren is learning that the English names by which she has known her servant's family are not "true" names: Florence's son—"once I knew him as Digby, now he is Bheki" (36); her daughters—"the elder, whose name, says Florence, is Hope (she does not entrust me with the real name)" (37); her husband— "William—not his true name but the name by which he is known in the world of his work" (43); Florence herself—"Perhaps I alone in all the world called her Florence. Called her by an alias. Now I was on ground where people were revealed in their true names" (101). We might note, too, that, as so often, Coetzee weaves one of his own names—John—into the text in an unsettling reminder of the fictionality of this world.

34 Coetzee, *Age of Iron*, 47, 45.

35 Ibid., 39, 49.

36 Ibid., 50, 75, 73.

37 Ibid., 47, 79.

38 Ibid., 81, 146.

39 Ibid., 78–79.

40 Ibid., 136, 137.

41 Ibid., 159, 163, 165.

42 Attwell's admirable reading of this novel in *J. M. Coetzee* seems nevertheless to underestimate the effect of Mrs. Curren's continuing attempt to revise and re-articulate her response to the political conditions of her time and place; he refers to her "direct and unsubtle" judgment of the white nationalists and to her "condemnation of the new forms of puritanism and militarism evident in the township youth" (122), without acknowledging that both these positions are later questioned.

43 I have not discussed the effect upon Mrs. Curren of her traumatic experience in the township and squatters' camp, especially as evidenced by the long address to her daughter (109–12) and the equally long speech to Vercueil (124–26), both prompted by Bheki's death; such a discussion would have to be part of a fuller attempt to account for her ethical growth. However, this episode is reminiscent of the traditional narrative of the South African white whose eyes are opened to the horrors of the system he or she lives in and benefits from, an essentially political narrative that Coetzee is seeking to force into new territory (the territory I am calling the ethical). Mrs. Curren's meditation on her return from the township, moving and deeply felt though it is, is framed by two glimpses of a scene that reminds us of the less easily categorizable learning process she is undergoing: Vercueil asleep on her toilet. It is also worth noting that, in spite of the overwhelming effect on her of Bheki's killing, she admits toward the end that John, imagined waiting with his pistol for the moment of death, is with her "more clearly, more piercingly than Bheki has ever been" (175).

44 Coetzee is one of those who has testified to this experience: "The *feel* of writing fiction is one of freedom, of irresponsibility, or better, of responsibility toward something that has not yet emerged, that lies somewhere at the end of the road. When I write criticism, on the other hand, I am always aware of a responsibility toward a goal that has been set for me not only by the argument, not only by the whole philosophical tradition into which I am implicitly inserting myself, but also by the rather tight discourse of criticism itself" (*Doubling the Point*, 246). Or again: "First you give yourself to (or throw yourself into) the writing, and go where it takes you. Then you step back and ask yourself where you are, whether you really want to be there" ("Thematizing," in *The Return of Thematic Criticism*, ed. Werner Sollors [Cambridge, MA, 1993], 289).

Paul A. Cantor

Happy Days in the Veld: Beckett and Coetzee's *In the Heart of the Country*

If I had been set down by fate in the middle of the veld in the middle of nowhere, buried to my waist and commanded to live a life, I could not have done it.
—*In the Heart of the Country*

Let us go on as if I were the only one in the world, whereas I'm the only one absent from it.
—*The Unnamable*

As one of the leading authors of his nation, J. M. Coetzee is usually discussed in a South African context. His works are understandably viewed as contributions to the passionate debate raised by the racial policies of the South African government. More generally, critics treat Coetzee's impressive body of work as an example of what is often called postcolonial literature, analyzing how his fiction explores the manifold problems of decolonization, national liberation, and ethnic identity. By contrast, I want to read Coetzee in a broader literary context; his works take on added meaning if we see them in re-

The *South Atlantic Quarterly* 93:1, Winter 1994.
Copyright © 1994 by Duke University Press.
CCC 0038-2876/94/$1.50.

lation to the European literary tradition he evidently has in mind whenever he writes. He is an unusually learned, even scholarly, novelist, and although he has written extensively on African literature, he has also published essays on canonical European authors, such as Kafka and Beckett. His books are filled with allusions to and quotations from European literature. The title *Waiting for the Barbarians*, for example, is taken from a poem by C. P. Cavafy, and perhaps the most important precursor text for this novel is Kafka's "In the Penal Colony."

The way Coetzee explicitly and self-consciously positions himself in relation to the European literary tradition seems to place him in the camp of postmodernism. In his fiction he is constantly struggling with prior texts, calling their view of reality into question and sometimes actively rewriting them, most notably in *Foe*, his postmodern exercise in recreating *Robinson Crusoe*. Despite some misgivings about the use of the term, I want to pursue the question of Coetzee's postmodernism. Although I initially present the postmodernist view of Coetzee as an alternative to the postcolonial, I also hope to use this opportunity to explore the relation of postmodernism and postcolonialism. These movements are arguably the two most important currents in contemporary literature, but their relationship to each other is a vexed question.[1] Some critics see them as similar and even intertwined, citing Salman Rushdie, for example, as a writer who is both postcolonial and postmodernist.[2] But others view the two as opposed; some, for example, contrasting the sterility of postmodernism as a kind of academic exercise with the vitality of postcolonialism as a form of literature that is genuinely engaged with important ethical, social, and political concerns.

To explore the relation of postmodernism and postcolonialism in Coetzee, I have chosen his second novel, *In the Heart of the Country* (1977). Set on a remote farm in the veld, this book is filled with peculiarly South African concerns. Dealing with white/black, master/slave, and male/female relationships, it raises important issues of race, class, and gender. Moreover, it needs to be read in the context of the South African literary tradition. As several critics have noted, *In the Heart of the Country* deconstructs the traditional myth of the South African Boer farm as it came to be embodied in a whole series of farm novels.[3] Indeed, Coetzee's discussion of the South African farm novel in his critical study *White Writing* reads like a commentary on *In the Heart of the Country*. In particular, his analysis of Olive Schreiner's *The Story of an African Farm* as a "critique of colonial culture" that follows the farm myth "only negatively" provides a point-by-point blueprint for *In the Heart of the Country* as a kind of anti-farm novel.[4] But even as it is saturated with South African concerns, *In the Heart of the Country* also contains a number of buried quotations from William Blake.[5] Furthermore, the insects that infest the landscape of the novel are appropriate to the South African setting, according to a formula that Coetzee again derives from Schreiner, but they also call to mind Kafka, especially when the narrator imagines herself as a "thin black beetle" or talks of her "metamorphosis." Above all, Samuel Beckett looms over *In the Heart of the Country*, from the moment when the narrator talks about "pebbles to permute," recalling the famous passage on sucking-stones in *Molloy*, to the moment (captured in my title and my epigraph from Coetzee) when he implicitly compares his narrator to Beckett's Winnie in *Happy Days*.[6] Beckett is arguably the single greatest literary influence on Coetzee, and, of all his novels, *In the Heart of the Country* comes closest to Beckett in style and substance.

≡≡≡≡≡

In the Heart of the Country tells such a powerful story that the temptation to plunge right into analyzing what happens is almost overwhelming. A tale of incest, parricide, miscegenation, and rape, *In the Heart of the Country* might be billed as "Faulkner in the veld." The story is narrated by a lonely spinster named Magda, who lives in isolation on a sheep farm. At the beginning, her father brings home a new bride to replace Magda's mother, who has evidently died. Magda resents this intrusion into the intense relationship she has with her father, and soon kills both him and her stepmother. But at this point, the story seems to begin afresh. This time, a black servant on the farm, Hendrik, is the one who brings home a new bride, called Klein-Anna. Magda's father quickly becomes attracted to this young woman and begins a sexual relationship with her. Once again, Magda resents this development and ends up killing her father, although this time it may be something of an accident. But because of Magda's guilt, Hendrik gains a hold over her, reversing their master/servant relationship and eventually raping her. Magda tries to hide the death of her father from the increasingly intrusive authorities. Abandoned in the end by everyone, she goes crazy, and we last see her pictured with her imagined father, perhaps even with his disinterred body.

This is at least an attempt to give a coherent account of what takes place in *In the Heart of the Country*. The narrator, Magda, is a superbly realized character, a creature of overwhelming frustration whose suffering and humiliation affect us deeply. The story is told so completely from her point of view that it is difficult not to identify with her, sharing her concerns and taking her side. But however tempting this approach may be, it has problems. Magda is not a reliable narrator; she is clearly insane by the end of the story, and may well be so long before then. To be sure, her insanity is one way for Coetzee to document how oppressed she is. But however much it may add to our sympathy for her, it does not do much for our faith in the accuracy of her account. The narrative of *In the Heart of the Country* is not easy to sort out, and determining where Coetzee's sympathies lie is no less difficult.[7] The story is told from Magda's point of view, but it frequently invites us to ask what her father or Hendrik or Klein-Anna thinks of these events. Thus, even if we are primarily interested in issues of race, class, and gender in Coetzee's novel, we must also analyze its technical aspects. We cannot simply look at the story that seems to be told; we have to look at how it is told. That is one of the ways in which the novel is postmodern—it tells a story, but at the same time it raises fundamental doubts about that story, about what really happens.

The postmodern method of *In the Heart of the Country* is prefigured in the opening paragraph:

> Today my father brought home his new bride. They came clip-clop across the flats in a dog-cart drawn by a horse with an ostrich-plume waving on its forehead, dusty after the long haul. Or perhaps they were drawn by two plumed donkeys, that is also possible. My father wore his black swallowtail coat and stove-pipe hat, his bride a wide-brimmed sunhat and a white dress

tight at waist and throat. More detail I cannot give unless I begin to embroider, for I was not watching. I was in my room . . . reading a book or, more likely, supine with a damp towel over my eyes fighting a migraine.

This seems at first to be a straightforward realistic narrative. Notice the authenticating effect of the quaint details in the second sentence, almost a textbook example of good descriptive writing. But we are brought up abruptly by the "or perhaps" at the beginning of the third sentence. Suddenly we are given the sense of an alternate reality: the cart may have been drawn by two donkeys instead of a horse. Either case would be perfectly realistic and firmly anchor us in a novelistic world. But when we are given two narrative possibilities, with no basis for preferring one to the other, it undermines our sense of the reality of what we are viewing. Magda goes on to give more authenticating details, but then undermines her own credibility. She admits that she did not actually witness the event she is narrating, leaving us to wonder about the source of her information. From the very start, then, we are faced with an unreliable narrator. When Magda talks of embroidering, she calls our attention to the fictionality of her narrative. Evidently, this story is being made up by someone who spends her afternoons reading books, that is, caught up in a fictional world rather than the real one. Magda's final claim, that she was "more likely" to have been "fighting a migraine" than reading, is even more disturbing. It is one thing for her to claim to be unsure about events she did not witness, but now she reveals that her uncertainty extends even to her own experience. Moreover, the way she describes herself, with a towel over her eyes, is ominous: in Coetzee's first image of his narrator she is willfully blinding herself to reality.[8]

The opening paragraph of *In the Heart of the Country* is typical of what happens throughout the novel. Coetzee knows how to tell a gripping story, but at the same time he works to undermine its reality.[9] Anyone familiar with Beckett will recognize that Coetzee derives these narrative techniques and strategies from him, especially from his trilogy.[10] In his narratives, Beckett is constantly suggesting alternate possibilities and raising doubts about the reliability of his narrators, even about their existence in the strange case of *The Un-*

namable. One way of formulating the postmodernism of *In the Heart of the Country* is to say that it abjures the use of a master-narrative and instead accepts a pure play of fabulation.[11] A typical modernist novel, say, *The Sound and the Fury*, tells a complicated story, perhaps from several different perspectives, perhaps with many chronological shifts and leaps. But with some effort, we can work out the narrative line of a modernist novel and can usually even construct a coherent chronology. But the case is different in a postmodern narrative, in which different, mutually exclusive versions of the story are presented as equally possible. In reading *In the Heart of the Country*, we do not first get the impression that Magda killed her father because he brought home a new bride and only later learn that she killed him because he was having sex with a black servant girl. One could imagine a Faulkner novel along those lines, in which the racial issue would gradually emerge as more important than the sexual. But that is not how *In the Heart of the Country* works. Coetzee offers no way for us to decide which account of Magda's murder of her father is true. If anything, the juxtaposition of the two accounts suggests the fictionality of both.

Indeed Coetzee has his narrator oscillate between certifying and decertifying her own narrative. Presenting another narrative possibility as more likely, Magda is quick to start spinning a new yarn, only to have it soon sound no more plausible than the last one. She raises doubts about even the most fundamental facts in the story: "Or perhaps I have been mistaken all the time, perhaps my father is not dead after all."[12] In a subtle touch, Coetzee has Magda begin one of her new narratives with words that echo an earlier one:

> Six months ago Hendrik brought home his new bride. They came clip-clop across the flats in the donkey-cart, dusty after the long haul. . . . Hendrik wore the black suit passed on to him by my father with an old wide-brimmed felt hat and a shirt buttoned to the throat. His bride sat by his side clutching her shawl, exposed and apprehensive.

If we compare this passage to the opening paragraph of the novel, we get an uncanny sense of sameness and difference. Noting the verbal parallels, we realize that Magda has a narrative schema ready at hand: describe the new couple riding in a cart (horse or donkey optional), then describe the man in terms of his clothes, finally describe the woman (make sure that somebody has a wide-brimmed hat). Thus Coetzee brings out the literariness of these moments: this is not how things really happened, but how Magda begins a story. Coetzee is calling our attention to the act of fabulation, as we get the distinct impression that the narrator is making up the story according to literary patterns that have become habitual to her.[13]

Speculating about her siblings, like any good author Magda decides to focus our attention and make one example come to life for us. Thus she begins to invent the glorious Arthur:

> But of all my stepbrothers and stepsisters it was Arthur I loved most. If Arthur had thrashed me I would have squirmed with pleasure. . . . But alas, golden Arthur never noticed me, occupied as he was with winning the race and catching the ball and reciting the six times table. The day that Arthur left I hid in the . . . wagonhouse vowing that never another morsel of food would pass my lips. As the years went by and Arthur did not return I thrust his memory farther and farther from me, till today it recurs to me with all the remoteness of a fairy-tale. End of story. There are inconsistencies in it, but I have not the time to track down and abolish them.[14]

Subtle touches like "alas," "golden Arthur," and "never another morsel" alert us to the clichéd nature of this passage. Coetzee introduces just enough overwriting to make the passage stand out in the texture of *In the Heart of the Country*, with the result that we sense that Magda is making it up. Even she comes to that realization by the end of the passage, recognizing its "fairy-tale" character and all but admitting its fictionality. Perhaps Magda's father and Hendrik are merely better realized characters than Arthur, but no less fictional.

But the postmodern effect of *In the Heart of the Country* goes deeper. We do not simply get a sense of Magda as creating fictions; that, after all, might at least leave us with a stable sense of a narrator. But in Coetzee's novel even the narrator herself is finally revealed to be a fiction. Coetzee draws upon another strategy he learned from Beckett as his narrator begins to become aware of the fact that she is merely a figure in a novel. Most fictional characters never question their strange existence within the covers of a book: that is, they act and speak as if they were real live human beings and not figments of an author's imagination. For much of *In the Heart of the Country* Magda behaves in this way, convinced of her own reality. But she has moments when she is puzzled by her ontological status, sensing the artificiality of the conventions according to which she is constructed:

> A day must have intervened here. Where there is a blank there must have been a day during which my father sickened irre-coverably, and during which Hendrik and Klein-Anna made their peace, for thenceforth they were as before. . . . It must have been a day which I passed somehow. Perhaps I spent it asleep.[15]

Here Magda is becoming aware of the novelistic convention of ellipsis. We have become so used to this convention that we often fail to notice how many gaps we are left with in the lives of even the most fully realized characters. But in postmodern fashion, Coetzee calls attention to the artificiality of the narrative convention of ellipsis. Magda at first tries to explain away the gaps in her life, but then begins to admit that something is strangely absent in her existence:

> But, to tell the truth, I am wary of all these suppositions. I sus-pect that the day the day was missing I was not there; and if that is so I shall never know how the day was filled. For I seem to exist more and more intermittently. Whole hours, whole afternoons go missing.

Like Beckett, Coetzee asks us to imagine what the convention of ellipsis "feels" like to a character within a novel, how jolting it must be to be whisked from a Monday to a Thursday with no glimpse of the intermediary days, perhaps as a result of a heartless editor's blue pencil.[16] Coetzee emphasizes the elliptical quality of the novel by dividing *In the Heart of the Country* into 266 numbered sections, separated by spaces. Instead of trying to create the illusion of a seam-less web of narrative, he forces us to see that any story is built up out of discrete blocks. Magda's tendency to make false starts and abrupt reversals in her narrative reinforces our sense of a story that does not cohere. Finally Magda comes to realize that ellipsis is a function of the narrator's power: "All at once it is morning. It seems to lie in my power to skip over whole days or nights as if they did not happen." [17]

Magda's self-awareness as a character in a novel accounts for many of the more peculiar features of *In the Heart of the Country*. For example, it explains why she keeps trying to reassure herself that she really exists: "A phantom, I am no phantom. I stoop. I touch this skin and it is warm, I pinch this flesh and it hurts. What more proof could I want? I am I." But Magda also has moments when she senses something peculiarly inauthentic and literary about her existence: "My learning has the reek of print, not the resonance of the full human voice telling its stories." This kind of moment, when a character senses what is lacking in his existence and begins to feel unreal, happens throughout *The Unnamable*:

> Help, help, if I could only describe this place, I who am so good at describing places, walls, ceilings, floors, they are my specialty, doors, windows, what haven't I imagined in the way of windows in the course of my career. . . . [I]f I could describe this place, portray it, I've tried, I feel no place, no place around me, there's no end to me, I don't know what it is, it isn't flesh, it doesn't end, it's like air.

In a passage that sounds as if it came straight out of *The Unnamable*, Magda senses that her existence is strangely disembodied, insubstantial, and attenuated:

> I have never seen Armoede, I seem never to have been anywhere, I seem to know nothing for sure, perhaps I am simply a ghost or a vapour floating . . . suspended here by an unimaginable tribunal until a certain act is committed. . . . I have never been to Armoede, but with no effort at all, this is one of my faculties, I can bring to life the bleak windswept hill. [18]

As a mere character in a book, Magda has, of course, never actually been anywhere. Everything that seems real to her is in fact imagined; in that sense, the fullness of her existence is an illusion and hence a kind of emptiness.

Midway through the novel, Magda has a Beckettian epiphany during which, in a "meditation on unattached existence," she puzzles over her artificial life on the page:

> And is it not remarkable how at one moment I can be walking away from a scene of crisis, from gunfire and screaming and interrupted pleasures, my shoes scuffling the pebbles, . . . and at the next moment I can be lost to things and back in the gabble of words? Am I, I wonder, a thing among things, a body propelled along a track by sinews and bony levers, or am I a monologue moving through time, approximately five feet above the ground, if the ground does not turn out to be just another word, in which case I am indeed lost? Whatever the case, I am plainly not myself in as clear a way as I might wish.

Here Coetzee challenges the myth of presence, in particular the famous Cartesian certainty of the ego, the idea that, however much the world may be in doubt, the self is perspicuous to itself. Magda virtually admits that she is not a real person but only a stream of words on page after page in a novel.[19] Throughout section 122, Magda ponders the motivations for her actions, hoping that she has some psychological depth as a character, that she has a psychic interior from which her actions flow and which she herself can come to understand. But what she keeps coming back to is what we might call her postmodern flatness; as a character in a novel, she acts the way she does not because she has her own reasons or motives, but because that is the way her story is written. Magda hopes that she has a real self, "the true deepdown I beyond words." But despite her illusion of self-consciousness, her sense that she has immediate access to her self, her existence is in fact profoundly mediated; she exists only in the medium of words.[20]

Magda's becoming aware of herself as a character in a novel culminates in a passage late in the book:

> [T]he words must have gone on (for where would I be if they stopped?) but gone on without trace, without memory. Or perhaps there is no time, perhaps I am deceived when I think of my medium as time, perhaps there is only space, and I a dot

of light moving erratically from one point in space to another, skipping years in a flash, now a frightened child in the corner of a schoolroom, now an old woman with knobbly fingers, that is also possible, my mind is open, and it would explain some of the tentativeness with which I hold my memories.

This is once again a brilliant attempt to give a sense of how weird it would feel to live within the elliptical world of a novel. In some sense, characters in novels do exist in space, not in time. Once a novel is published, the fate of its characters is sealed, their lives are no longer in process, their whole story is laid out over the course of the pages.[21] It is only an illusion produced by the way we read novels, page by page, that the story of the characters appears to unfold over time. In fact, page 697 of a long Russian novel exists at the same time as page 1, even though it may take readers real days, and the characters fictional years, to get from one to the other. Characters in traditional novels are prisoners of the narrative conventions according to which they are constructed. At the chronological beginning of their life stories, they may think of themselves as young; at the chronological end, as old. But Coetzee occasionally allows Magda to see through the smokescreen of these conventions; she realizes that space (pages), not time (years), separates the moments of her artificial life. Like the replicants in the film *Blade Runner*, Magda verges on grasping that the memories on which her sense of identity is based are not real, but manufactured for her by her author.[22] That is why she wants to go searching through the loft for mementos, to "find evidence of a credible past." In this respect, she resembles Beckett's two most famous characters in *Waiting for Godot*: "We always find something, eh Didi, to give us the impression we exist?" Magda comes to inhabit the same twilight realm in which Vladimir and Estragon dwell, a strangely attenuated existence in which she hovers between reality and fiction.

Since Magda is the narrator of *In the Heart of the Country*, any doubts about her reality quickly extend to the whole world of the book:

> Why is it left to me to give life not only to myself, minute after surly minute, but to everyone else on the farm, and the farm

itself, every stick and stone of it? . . . How can I afford to sleep? If for one moment I were to lose my grip on the world, it would fall apart: Hendrik and his shy bride would dissolve to dust in each other's arms . . . my father would float like a black cloud and be sucked into the lair inside my head. . . . All that would remain would be me, lying for that fatal instant in a posture of sleep on an immaterial bed above an immaterial earth before everything vanished. I make it all up in order that it shall make me up. I cannot stop now.

This passage explains why Magda shares the logorrhea of Beckett's characters. She is afraid to stop speaking because, if she consists merely of a stream of words, to stop speaking would be literally to cease to exist: "What I lack is the courage to stop talking, to die back into the silence I came from." But speech is no solution for Magda, since she feels that it alienates her from her true self and its deep desires:

Words alienate. Language is no medium for desire. Desire is rapture, not exchange. It is only by alienating the desired that language masters it.

Longing for "a life unmediated by words," Magda constantly feels speech drawing her into an inauthentic and fictional realm, unlike the paradise of immediacy that natural beings such as flowers enjoy:

I am forever not they, and they not I, . . . I can never be the rapture of pure self that they are but am alas forever set off from them by the babble of words within me that fabricate and re-fabricate me as something else, something else. . . . Would that I had never learned to read.[23]

Magda's perception of her literariness leads to her rejection of her literacy. Even as she comes to realize that she consists of nothing but words, she loses her faith in the power of words to capture reality. Thus Coetzee's narrative in effect deconstructs itself.

Thus far we have seen how *In the Heart of the Country* destabilizes our sense of reality, working to efface any clear and absolute distinction between the real and the fictional, and in particular to undermine the sense of the self as a fixed reference point or bedrock of reality. By portraying a fictional character who becomes aware of her own fictionality, Coetzee suggests that the self itself may be a fiction. Rather than existing as an independent reality, prior to any act of representation, the self is constituted precisely in the act of representation and hence according to the conventions of representation: "I create myself in the words that create me."[24] In the idiom of poststructuralism, Magda does not write her story; her story writes her.[25] More generally, Coetzee portrays a postmodern world in which language does not represent a preexistent, self-subsisting, and independent reality; rather, language constitutes reality in the act of representation: *"It is a world of words that creates a world of things."* In overall conception and in a wealth of detail, *In the Heart of the Country* reflects the influence of Beckett as well as that of such poststructuralist philosophers as Derrida and Foucault.[26] Magda may live in the veld, but it seems that her life was scripted in Paris.

Is *In the Heart of the Country* thus to be understood as postmodern rather than postcolonial? Is Coetzee more properly classified with Beckett than with Achebe or Ngugi? That Coetzee can be shown to have one foot in Europe does not mean that he does not still have one foot in Africa. And perhaps it is precisely Coetzee's position between two cultures that accounts for both his postmodernism and his postcolonialism; his postmodernism must be understood in the larger context of his postcolonialism. *In the Heart of the Country* raises doubts about the representability of reality, but it does not do so in an abstract or universal context. Coetzee portrays a South African woman of European extraction living on a farm, and the way she loses touch with reality clearly follows from those particular circumstances. She thus illustrates the issue with which Coetzee grapples throughout *White Writing*. For Coetzee *the* question to be posed in analyzing South African literature is: How can categories that were developed to deal with European experience be used to understand Africa and distinctively African experience? In particular, how can languages with roots in Europe be transposed to describe and narrate African experience?[27] In *White Writing*, Coetzee is interested in those cases where the slipperiness of representation can be traced to a political source: the attempt to transfer epistemological categories from one realm to another that results from the imperialist ventures of Europe.

For example, *White Writing* contains a fascinating analysis of the problem of landscape painting for Europeans in South Africa. Coetzee starts from the geological (and meteorological) fact that the landscape of South Africa is very different from anything in northern Europe. A number of factors, above all, the lack of rain, conspire to create an arid landscape in South Africa, thus precluding the lush green prospects that have long delighted European painters. Hence, Coetzee points out, European painters who came to South Africa brought the wrong palettes. They could not use all of the wonderful shades of green they had developed to paint their landscapes back home in Europe; at the same time, they lacked the various "fawns, browns, and greys" needed to capture the distinctive shades of the veld.[28] European painters were simply not equipped to paint the South African landscape. Notice that Coetzee's point is not about the paintability of landscape as such. His assumption seems to be that European artists had in fact learned how to paint the European landscape reasonably well. As he sees it, the problem comes only when artists try to transfer the means of representation from one kind of landscape to another. Presumably, Coetzee believes that the South African landscape can be properly painted, once artists develop a suitable palette. Whatever problems Coetzee raises about representation in landscape painting are thus specific to the colonial situation. When people impose their rule on an alien country, they try to impose their categories of representation as well. That is when the mismatch between means of representation and reality occurs.

Throughout *White Writing* Coetzee draws parallels between political and epistemological concepts. Taking possession of something, making it your property, colonizing it is akin to naming it, categorizing it, capturing it in artistic form, or, as Magda declares, "To the spur of desire we have only one response: to capture, to enclose, to hold." This will-to-power characterizes even something as innocent looking as landscape poetry. Coetzee criticizes European Romantic poetry for its "imperial eye—the eye that by seeing names and dominates."[29] He sees something imperialistic in the way that the Romantic poet tries to impose his ego on nature, and thus he views Wordsworth as the prototype of the colonial poet and his artistic appropriation of landscape.[30] Troubled by this use of literature, Coetzee searches for an alternative form, one that would not be possessive. He turns to the example of the South African poet Sydney Clouts, who in Coetzee's view deliberately avoids using poetry to take possession of an alien landscape:

> Clouts provides the most radical response as yet to the burden assumed by the South African poet of European culture: the burden of finding a home in Africa for a consciousness formed in and by a language whose history lies on another continent. To the charge that the poet show what position must be taken in order to see Africa as it really is . . . Clouts responds by taking no position, or by taking all possible positions, thus denying the primacy [of] the prospect position itself . . . and proposing instead an unsettled habitation *in* the landscape.[31]

The poetic strategy Coetzee defines here is exactly what we have been talking about in postmodern fiction, namely, the renunciation of a master-narrative. The presentation of multiple realities is the narrative equivalent of "taking no position, or taking all possible positions."

Coetzee's analysis of Clouts's poetry provides an important clue to his own procedure as a novelist. Coetzee takes the metaphor embodied in the idea of a master-narrative seriously, and *master* is always a loaded word in a South African context. A narrative may be an attempt to master reality, to impose a set of alien categories on it. The only way for Coetzee to resist that tendency is to show the failure of any master-narrative, to show that no one perspective or viewpoint can fully convey or capture the truth about South Africa. Coetzee cites a resonant line from Clouts's poem "Residuum": "I am the method of the speck and fleck." In a strange way, this line perfectly characterizes the technique of *In the Heart of the Country*. By giving us only specks and flecks of narrative, Coetzee keeps the novel from settling into a coherent story line. The unsettled character of the narrative reflects the unsettled character of Magda and by extension all Europeans in South Africa; they cannot come to rest in an alien landscape as long as they try to impose categories from the home country upon it. Coetzee describes Clouts's "Residuum" as

> a kind of flickering of poetic force from object to object, the poem refusing to settle, since as soon as it settled it would be absorbed into the object. The life of the poem is thus, as it were, in the spaces between the lines.

Similarly, one might say that the life of *In the Heart of the Country* lies in the spaces between the numbered sections.

Coetzee's fascination with blank spaces reflects his postmodern sense that presence always points to absence. The postmodern artist is acutely sensitive to the fact that whenever anything is presented, something else must be correspondingly omitted. Coetzee focuses on these gaps as moments of silence, which he regards as the key to contemporary art:

> Our ears today are finely attuned to modes of silence. We have been brought up on the music of Webern: substantial silence structured by tracings of sound. Our craft is all in reading *the other*: gaps, inverses, undersides; the veiled; the dark, the buried, the feminine; alterities. To a pastoral novel like *The Beadle* we give an antipastoral reading like the present one, alert to the spaces in the text (Where is God? Where is Africa?). Only part of the truth, such a reading asserts, resides in what writing says of the hitherto unsaid; for the rest, its truth lies in what it dare not say for the sake of its own safety, or in what it does not know about itself: in its silences.[32]

Here the postmodern concept of silence modulates into the postcolonial concept of silencing. When we detect a silence in a work, we must trace it to the fact that a particular voice has been silenced, the voice of a threatening other, perhaps a feminine voice in a masculine literature, or a black voice in a white literature. For Coetzee, postmodernism has alerted us to the limitations of representation, suggesting that it always involves some kind of distortion, some kind of bias. He stresses the political aspect of this process; the bias he dwells on is the bias of a dominant group—males over females, whites over blacks—the kind of dominance endemic to colonial situations.

The postmodern enterprise—exploring the absences, the omissions, the blank spaces, the silences in art—becomes the postcolonial enterprise of exposing political acts of silencing, the imposition of an alien regime on a recalcitrant people. This confluence of postmodernism and postcolonialism in Coetzee is clearest in *Foe*, a novel in which he takes a classic of European literature, Defoe's *Robinson Crusoe*, and shows how the dissident voices of women and blacks have been suppressed in the narrative. In Coetzee's version, Defoe steals the story of Crusoe from a woman named Susan Barton and writes her out of the narrative, while Friday has lost his tongue, leaving his thoughts and desires opaque to all the Europeans who seek to understand him. Postmodern in its technique, *Foe* is postcolonial in its underlying conception.

The confluence of postmodernism and postcolonialism in Coetzee derives from the poststructuralist idea that all relations, epistemological as well as political, are structured as relations of power. The relation of subject to object, of representation to reality, of word to thing—all are attempts at mastery.[33] Trained in linguistics and knowing his Saussure, Coetzee sees conflict going on at all levels of language, even at the most basic one of the phoneme, where one meaningful sound can be defined only in opposition to another. Magda reflects on the struggle involved in the articulation of speech:

> I am exhausted by obedience to this law . . . whose mark lies on me in the spaces between the words, the spaces or the pauses, and in the articulations that set up the war of sounds, the *b* against the *d*, the *m* against the *n*.[34]

What Coetzee has in mind here is Saussure's fundamental insight that there are no pure or absolute phonemes. We perceive a voiced plosive (*b*), for example, only in contrast to an unvoiced plosive (*p*). That is the only way we can hear the difference between the sounds *bat* and *pat* and thus use them to represent different things. But for Coetzee the principle of binary opposition at work in phonemes is not restricted to the realm of language. *In the Heart of the Country* portrays a world shot through with binary oppositions: master/slave, white/black, man/woman, old/young, father/child, European/native, human/animal, god/human, and so on. In each case the first term defines itself in opposition to the second, in particular by asserting its superiority over the other. Magda intuits this point in analyzing the sexual desirability of Klein-Anna for her father:

> What can they have to say to each other? The truth is that he needs our opposition, our several oppositions, to hold the girl away from him, to confirm his desire for her, as much as he needs our opposition to be powerless against that desire. . . . There is a level, we both know, at which Klein-Anna is a pawn and the real game lies between the two of us.

Magda sees that Klein-Anna is not intrinsically desirable to her father. He is attracted to her because she is Hendrik's wife, and thus he can prove his power over his servant by taking her away from him. Klein-Anna is also attractive to Magda's father because she is black; in possessing her he can violate a taboo in his daughter's mind and simultaneously assert his superiority to her.[35] Klein-Anna takes on meaning for Magda's father only in the context of a web of social relations in which he is seeking to define his role, a role of mastery. Coetzee is evidently aware of the way that Lévi-Strauss extended Saussure's principles of structural linguistics into anthropology, showing that the world of kinship relations is structured like the world of phonemes, with each unit taking its meaning only as a result of its place in an overall system of binary oppositions.

As Magda repeatedly sees, language is a realm of power, of structured hierarchical relations:

> I was born into a language of hierarchy, of distance and perspective. It was my father-tongue. I do not say it is the language my heart wants to speak, I feel too much the pathos of its distances, but it is all we have.

The buried quotation from Nietzsche in this passage shows how important the master/slave dialectic is in Coetzee's novel.[36] Referring to Hegel as well on the topic in section 250, Coetzee portrays the self-defeating character of the process of enslaving. The master defines himself in binary opposition to his slave, that is, he derives his sense of his worth from someone he regards as beneath his contempt. Seeking respect from a human being he himself does not respect, the master finds his triumph to be hollow. Or, as Magda puts it: "Was my father crucified on the paradox the voices expound: that from people who bent like reeds to his whims he was asking, in his way, for an affirmation of his truth in and for himself?"[37] Here Coetzee identifies the tragedy of all colonialism, and specifically of the apartheid regime in South Africa: ultimately, people can achieve recognition of their dignity only from their equals, not from people they have enslaved. Hence Magda is always seeking to find an equal she can speak to, which explains her attempts to bring Hendrik and Klein-Anna into her household. Magda yearns for some kind of pure language, perhaps the language of lovers, a language that could be spoken among equals. But the only language she knows is shot through with indications of hierarchy. In *White Writing* Coetzee points out that Afrikaans is unusually sensitive as a language to issues of hierarchy; in its traditional form, some nouns are used only of blacks and some only of whites.[38] The mastery of whites over blacks was thus encoded even in the language of South Africa.

Any attempt to subvert that rule would have to attack language itself. The postmodern paradoxes of language Coetzee explores ultimately take us to the heart of the postcolonial dilemma. Magda's deepest frustration arises from the fact that she has to use language to undo the work of language. Her bizarre encounter with the superior beings of the flying machines somehow gives her the hope that she might learn to transcend the divisions of her hierarchical world:

> Why will no one speak to me in the true language of the heart? The medium, the median—that is what I wanted to be! Neither master nor slave, neither parent nor child, but the bridge between, so that in me the contraries should be reconciled!

The aliens who seem to invade Magda's world, perhaps with the intent of colonizing her, at first hold out the hope of a language of "pure meanings," a language of "universal meanings," the kind of language that could bring people together rather than, like colonial English, tearing them apart. But the language of these aliens turns out to be Spanish, simply another one of the great colonial languages, or a variant of Esperanto, a supposedly universal language that was in fact forged largely out of Western European roots and thus a good example of the false universalism of European culture, a kind of imperialism in language. Magda would like to use language to break out of the social categories that have been imposed on her, but she keeps finding that language is a profoundly socialized phenomenon: "It is not speech that makes man man but the speech of others."[39] In her frustration at trying to use language to escape the prison of language, we may be getting a glimpse of her author's own dilemma as a writer.

The effort to destabilize and deconstruct epistemological categories takes on a new and urgent meaning in a postcolonial context. The way the identity of the self dissolves into a fiction in *In the Heart of the Country* is not an empty postmodernist gesture; we are witnessing the identity of the colonial oppressor in the process of dissolution. When Coetzee shows the falseness of representation in *In the Heart of the Country*, it is not merely a sophisticated epistemological exercise; he is suggesting how African reality is distorted when imperial masters try to impose their European categories on it.[41] In *In the Heart of the Country*, the floating, disembodied, decentered ego of Beckett's *The Unnamable* becomes the displaced, alienated, and rootless self of the European imperialist in the land he has conquered. What at first appears to be metaphysical isolation turns out to be a form of political isolation: the waste land is the land laid waste by imperialism.

≡≡≡

To highlight the postmodernism in Coetzee by examining his relationship to Beckett does not in the end detract from his significance as a postcolonial author. In fact, it leaves us with a better sense of how deep Coetzee's postcolonial critique runs, encompassing an analysis of how even the epistemological categories of Europe are complicit in the colonial enterprise. And after analyzing Coetzee in the light of Beckett, we might consider analyzing Beckett in the light of Coetzee. Perhaps even the postmodernism of Beckett needs to be understood in a postcolonial context. Beckett, after all, has a good deal in common with Coetzee. Both come from countries with complicated colonial histories. Like Coetzee, Beckett spent some time teaching abroad and lived a good part of his life in foreign lands. Just as Coetzee moves between the two languages of English and Afrikaans, Beckett moved between English and French.[42] Perhaps Beckett's own sense of the slipperiness of representation can be traced to his experience of being caught between different cultures, and thus coming to understand the arbitrariness of the categories that can be imposed on the world. As some critics are beginning to suggest, the great Irish writers of the twentieth century, including Joyce and Beckett, take on new meaning when understood as in some sense postcolonial.[43] The conjunction of Beckett and Coetzee suggests that postmodernism and postcolonialism may be more closely intertwined as literary phenomena in the twentieth century than at first appears. It may turn out that postcolonialism is the more fundamental phenomenon and that we will succeed in tracing many of the features of literature that we now label "postmodern" to the postcolonial situation of so many authors in this century, including some Europeans.

Worrying over whether postmodernism or postcolonialism is the more fundamental phenomenon may seem like a typically empty academic exercise. But a serious issue is at stake in this debate. When postmodernists call into question the representability of reality, they tend to do so in a purely negative way, undermining our belief that anything can ever be true. That is why many critics speak of the sterility of postmodernism and wonder whether authors are losing sight of any useful function for literature. As we have seen, *In the Heart of the Country* is an extremely complicated text, with much of the convoluted and even involuted quality of postmodern fiction. But the novel seems to be energized by a seriousness and an intensity that come from its subject matter, not from its technique. For the purposes of creating a purely postmodern effect, Coetzee could have portrayed a character who becomes aware of her fictionality in all sorts of circumstances, but he chose to make her a Boer woman on a South African farm, with all the implications that such a subject has for a South African writer. Like *Foe, In the Heart of the Country* seems to be more concerned with correcting false representations of reality than with suggesting the unrepresentability of reality as such.[44] We come away from *Foe* feeling not just that there are many ways of telling a story, but that Defoe got this particular story wrong, and that by omitting the perspectives of the woman and the black in the narrative, he distorted reality. Similarly, *In the Heart of the Country* conveys the sense that it is the mismatch between the colonial consciousness and the native landscape that produces the problems in representation, not a basic gap between language and the world.

At times, then, Coetzee shows signs of diverging from "standard" postmodernism. Recall that in his discussion of landscape painting, he is willing to invoke the very unpostmodern concept of nature. The question he keeps asking is whether the painter's palette is suited to the nature of the landscape that he wishes to paint. In comparing English, South African, and American landscape painting, Coetzee traces the differences to what sound like real, objective features in the landscape. To be sure, Coetzee has read enough Derrida and Foucault to feel uncomfortable talking about nature:

> It is impossible to say whether American landscape emerges so dramatically on canvas because the topography "is" dramatic, or whether features of landscape are emphasized that invite dramatic treatment, just as it is futile to ask whether the South African landscape is so often represented as monotonous because it "is" monotonous, or because a preconception reigns that Africa is static, sunk in aeons of slumber, or . . . because an eye trained in Europe sees no variety in the veld.[45]

It is the postmodern side of Coetzee that makes him put the word *is* in quotation marks. He cannot quite bring himself to talk about the way the world really is, and yet his whole discussion of landscape is premised on the idea that some forms of painting *mis*represent nature, thus implying that some forms represent it correctly, or at least more correctly than others. When Coetzee raises the issue of whether a landscape is "dramatic" or "monotonous," he is correct to regard this as a subjective issue, but when he talks about whether a landscape is green or brown, he knows how to open his eyes, look at the world, and decide the truth of the case.

In the end Coetzee's postmodernism remains in tension with his postcolonialism. As a postmodern writer, all he can claim is that every representation involves distortion, and he can offer no reason for preferring one representation over another. But as a postcolonial writer, he wishes to champion one mode of representation over another, or at least to reject what he firmly believes to be false modes of representation. Deeply concerned that European forms of representation have distorted our view of Africa, he seeks distinctively African modes of representing African experience more faithfully. In short, his postcolonialism demands that he reopen the question of truth and consider whether we need some standard of objective reality or nature by which to judge the biases and distortions introduced by the "imperial eye."[46] Coetzee cannot logically speak of misrepresentation by European categories if he does not allow for the possibility of some mode of true representation, or at least of truer representation.

If *In the Heart of the Country* moves us as deeply as I believe it does, the reason is not to be found in its postmodern techniques, which it shares with much European and American fiction, but in its evocation of a South African setting, with all the human tragedy that involves. Although I have been guilty of deflecting attention from the story that the novel tells in order to explore the complexities of how it tells it, in the end I fully sympathize with those readers and critics who find themselves in the grip of Magda's tale. The novel has many ugly moments, but it has many tender ones as well, and none more tender than the moment when Magda, like the Magistrate in *Waiting for the Barbarians*, tries to reach out and communicate with someone she finds alien, Klein-Anna:

> I lean over her, I caress her arms, I hold her limp hands in mine. That is what she gets from me, colonial philosophy, words with no history behind them, homespun, when she wants stories. I can imagine a woman who would make this child happy, filling her with tales from a past that really happened, how grandfather ran away from the bees and lost his hat and never found it again, why the moon waxes and wanes, how the hare tricked the jackal. But these words of mine come from nowhere and go nowhere, they have no past or future, they whistle across the flats in a desolate eternal present, feeding no one.[47]

This passage gives us one last glimpse of the crosscurrents of postmodernism and postcolonialism in Coetzee. The image of words whistling across a desolate plain calls to mind Beckett. However, the problem with Magda's words is not the failure of words as such, but the failure of words that have "no history behind them." Magda's words have

not arisen naturally from this landscape; they result from a great dis-
location, the imperial enterprise in South Africa that includes the
imposition of European languages on African reality.

But as unsuited as Magda's words are to the landscape, she can
imagine an alternative that would be nourishing: "tales from a past
that really happened." Here Magda contemplates the prospect of
pleasing Klein-Anna with the kind of stories that are native to Africa,
stories that grew, as it were, out of the landscape—folktales and
myths that embody the wisdom of a native community, the kind of
stories that one finds, for example, in the writing of Amos Tutuola.
Early in her narrative, Magda looks back nostalgically to the days
when she shared a language with the children of the servants on the
farm, a language by means of which she could participate in a form
of storytelling that made a unity of her world:

> I sat at the feet of their blind old grandfather while he whittled
> clothes-pegs and told his stories of bygone days when men and
> beasts migrated and lived together on the trail. At the feet of
> an old man I have drunk in a myth of a past when beast and
> man and master lived a common life as innocent as the stars in
> the sky.[48]

Giving her glimpses of an Edenic relation to nature, these simple
stories made childhood a kind of paradise for Magda.[49] In the middle
of a sophisticated novel, a virtual showcase of postmodern narrative
techniques, Coetzee evokes the literary alternative: the naive storytelling of a native tradition. He may dazzle us with the postmodern
fabulation of *In the Heart of the Country*, but at the same time he
reminds us of the power of a simple fable to move us and teach us
the truth, and thus of why we, too, like Klein-Anna and Magda, first
came to cherish stories in our lives.

Notes

1 For an insightful discussion of this issue, see Kwame Anthony Appiah's essay
"The Postcolonial and the Postmodern," in his *In My Father's House: Africa in the
Philosophy of Culture* (New York, 1992), 137–57.

2 See, for example, Mark Edmundson, "Prophet of a New Postmodernism: The

Greater Challenge of Salman Rushdie," *Harper's Magazine* (December 1989): 62–71.

3 See, for example, Dick Penner, *Countries of the Mind: The Fiction of J. M. Coetzee* (New York, 1989), 58; and Susan VanZanten Gallagher, *A Story of South Africa: J. M. Coetzee's Fiction in Context* (Cambridge, MA, 1991), 97, 99, 105–6.

4 J. M. Coetzee, *White Writing: On the Culture of Letters in South Africa* (New Haven, 1988), 66.

5 Word-for-word quotations from Blake, which can be found in sections 50, 203, and 259, come from *There Is No Natural Religion* and *The Marriage of Heaven and Hell*.

6 J. M. Coetzee, *In the Heart of the Country* (Harmondsworth, 1982 [1977]), 18, 92, 120.

7 That it is necessary to make this point is shown by Gallagher's claim, which I can only characterize as wishful thinking, that "Magda's narrative ends with questions and doubt, but the reader has no difficulty in ascertaining where Coetzee's heart lies" (*Story of South Africa*, 111).

8 For a similar analysis of the opening paragraph, see Penner, *Countries of the Mind*, 56. If analyzing one of Coetzee's paragraphs sentence by sentence seems like overkill, I can only say that he does exactly the same thing to Beckett. See "The Comedy of Point of View in Beckett's *Murphy*," *Critique: Studies in Modern Fiction* 12 (1970): 20–21, which documents Coetzee's acute awareness of Beckett's stylistic and narrative techniques.

9 Penner reports Coetzee as saying at a writer's workshop in 1984 that "realism is being subverted" in *In the Heart of the Country* by "an anti-realistic kind of game" (*Countries of the Mind*, 57).

10 The opening paragraph of *The Unnamable* is even more self-destroying than anything in *In the Heart of the Country*: "The fact would seem to be, if in my situation one may speak of facts, not only that I shall have to speak of things of which I cannot speak, but also, which is even more interesting, that I shall have to, I forget, no matter." I quote Beckett from *Three Novels* (New York, 1965), 291. In my discussion of Beckett's narrative techniques, I have been guided by Richard Begam's 1989 University of Virginia Ph.D. dissertation, "The World as Sam Made It: Phenomenology and Genre in Beckett's Novels."

11 I am adapting this idea to fiction from a more general point made by Jean-François Lyotard, who uses the term "metanarrative" in *The Postmodern Condition: A Report on Knowledge*, trans. Geoff Bennington and Brian Massumi (Minneapolis, 1984): "I define *postmodernism* as incredulity toward metanarratives" (xxiv). The term "master-narrative" comes from Fredric Jameson; see his foreword to this translation of Lyotard's book (xi–xii).

12 Coetzee, *Heart of the Country*, 122.

13 Ibid., 17. On the importance of "fictional models" for Magda, see Josephine Dodd, "Naming and Framing: Naturalization and Colonization in J. M. Coetzee's *In the Heart of the Country*," *World Literature Written in English* 27 (1987): 158.

14 Coetzee, *Heart of the Country*, 48.

15   Ibid., 79.

16   Ibid., 80. Compare what happens to the narrator in *The Unnamable*: "I think I must have blackouts, whole sentences lost, no, not whole" (368; see also 330). On the treatment of the convention of ellipsis in Beckett's trilogy, see Michael Valdez Moses, "The Sadly Rejoycing Slave: Beckett, Joyce, and Destructive Parody," *Modern Fiction Studies* 31 (1985): 664.

17   Coetzee, *Heart of the Country*, 93.

18   Ibid., 54, 47, 17; Beckett, *The Unnamable*, 399.

19   Coetzee, *Heart of the Country*, 62. For a similar moment in Beckett, see *The Unnamable*: "I'm all these words, all these strangers, this dust of words, with no ground for their settling" (386).

20   Coetzee, *Heart of the Country*, 62, 16. An essay by Coetzee on the confessional mode in fiction and autobiography sheds light on his first-person narratives. See "Confession and Double Thoughts: Tolstoy, Rousseau, Dostoevsky," *Comparative Literature* 37 (1985): 193–232.

21   Coetzee, *Heart of the Country*, 123–24. For Magda's own sense that her story may be already signed, sealed, and delivered, see 122: "Perhaps, therefore, my story has already had its end, the documents tied up with a ribbon and stored away, and only I do not know, for my own good."

22   For the implanting of memories in a character in Beckett, see *The Unnamable*, 324.

23   Coetzee, *Heart of the Country*, 72–73, 59, 26, 135, 48–49. On this point, see Lois Parkinson Zamora, "Allegories of Power in the Fiction of J. M. Coetzee," *Journal of Literary Studies* 2 (1986): 9.

24   Coetzee, *Heart of the Country*, 8. On this point, see Dodd, "Naming and Framing," 157: "[T]he self is constructed in language and not prior to it."

25   Coetzee explores this kind of paradox in his brief and enigmatic "A Note on Writing," in *Momentum: On Recent South African Writing*, ed. M. J. Daymond, J. U. Jacobs, and Margaret Lenta (Pietermaritzburg, 1984), 11–13, esp. 13, where Coetzee considers the case of "a particular kind of writing, writing in stereotyped forms and genres and characterological systems and narrative orderings, where the machine runs the operator."

26   Coetzee, *Heart of the Country*, 134; italics in original. See Hena Maes-Jelinek, "Ambivalent Clio: J. M. Coetzee's *In the Heart of the Country* and Wilson Harris's *Carnival*," *Journal of Commonwealth Literature* 22 (1987): 90, where she claims that Coetzee "comes very close to post-structuralist theories of language."

27   Coetzee, *White Writing*, 7–9, 62.

28   Ibid., 42.

29   Coetzee, *Heart of the Country*, 114; *White Writing*, 174.

30   Coetzee's critique of Wordsworth is evident in *In the Heart of the Country*: "What is there for me but dreary expansion to the limits of the universe? Is it any wonder that nothing is safe from me, that the lowliest veld-flower is likely to find itself raped in its being?" (74). "[T]he lowliest veld-flower" would seem to be the South African equivalent of "the meanest flower" that "can give / Thoughts that do often lie too deep for tears," in Wordsworth's "Ode: Intimations of Immortality."

31 Coetzee, *White Writing*, 173.

32 Ibid., 173, 81.

33 For the origin of this way of viewing the world in Nietzsche, see my "Friedrich Nietzsche: The Use and Abuse of Metaphor," in *Metaphor: Problems and Perspectives*, ed. David Miall (Brighton, 1982), 75–77.

34 Coetzee, *Heart of the Country*, 84.

35 Ibid., 34. For Magda's disgusted reaction to her father's conduct with Klein-Anna, see 35, 43.

36 Ibid., 97. The phrase "pathos of distance" (*Pathos der Distanz*) comes from *Beyond Good and Evil*, section 257, and *On the Genealogy of Morals*, First Essay, section 2.

37 Coetzee, *Heart of the Country*, 130.

38 Coetzee, *White Writing*: "Afrikaans . . . marks off whites from *anderskleuriges* (people of colour). For the concepts man/husband and woman/wife, Afrikaans uses *man* and *vrou* for whites, *jong* and *meid* for other people. For boy/son and girl/daughter it uses, for whites, *seun(tjie)* and *dogter(tije)* . . . but, for other people, *klong/klonkie* and *meid(jie)*. . . . What is significant about these racially defined distinctions—which inevitably convey hierarchy as well as separateness—is . . . that Coloured people use them among themselves. . . . This internalization of the inferior status prepared for [them] by the language [they] speak—a language which . . . declares itself to be the language of the other, the white and the master—is intimately linked to [their] . . . low self-esteem" (131).

39 Coetzee, *Heart of the Country*, 133, 126.

40 As, for example, Roland Smith claims: "The reader's feeling of unease grows when typical post-modernist conventions of authorial irony and ambiguity heighten the farcical element in the fictional events and throw into question the reality of all perceptions." See "The Seventies and After," in *Olive Schreiner and After: Essays on Southern African Literature in Honor of Guy Butler*, ed. Malvern Van Wyk Smith and Don Maclennan (Cape Town, 1983), 197. For other critiques of Coetzee's postmodernism, see Paul Rich, "Tradition and Revolt in South African Fiction: The Novels of André Brink, Nadine Gordimer and J. M. Coetzee"; and Michael Vaughan, "Literature and Politics: Currents in South African Writing in the Seventies," both in the *Journal of Southern African Studies* 9 (1982).

41 See Stephen Watson, "Colonialism and the Novels of J. M. Coetzee," *Research in African Literatures* 17 (1986): 374.

42 In the first South African edition of *In the Heart of the Country* (1977), the dialogue is given in Afrikaans.

43 For an example of this critical approach, see Edward Said, "Yeats and Decolonization," in *Nationalism, Colonialism, and Literature*, ed. Seamus Deane (Minneapolis, 1990), 69–95.

44 In that sense, *Foe* may be a more traditional novel than it first appears to be. In some ways, the relation of *Foe* to *Robinson Crusoe* resembles that of *Shamela* to *Pamela*, or even that of *Don Quixote* to *Amadis of Gaul*. As theorists such as Ortega y Gasset and Bakhtin have argued, the novel is a genre that is always seeking to correct false, incomplete, or biased views of reality embodied in prior

fiction. See José Ortega y Gasset, *Meditations on Quixote*, trans. Evelyn Rugg and Diego Marín (New York, 1961); and M. M. Bakhtin, *The Dialogic Imagination*, trans. Caryl Emerson and Michael Holquist (Austin, 1981).

45 Coetzee, *White Writing*, 58.

46 Ibid., 25. Appiah makes a similar argument that postcolonialism "is not an ally for Western postmodernism but an agonist, from which I believe postmodernism may have something to learn" (*In My Father's House*, 155).

47 Coetzee, *Heart of the Country*, 115.

48 Ibid., 6–7.

49 On the importance of childhood stories in *In the Heart of the Country*, see Maes-Jelinek, "Ambivalent Clio," 91.

Richard Begam

Silence and Mut(e)ilation: White Writing in J. M. Coetzee's *Foe*

Postmodernism and postcolonialism have often been treated as terms of opposition. In a recent article, which attempts to chart the definitional boundaries of these terms, Simon During argues that postcolonialism "name[s] and disclaim[s] postmodernism as neo-imperialist . . . by accepting and using those practices and concepts (representation, history, evaluation) which postmodernism most strenuously denies."[1] While some critics have quarreled with the strict division During draws between postmodernism and postcolonialism, most discussions of the subject nevertheless begin by assuming that these terms stand in significant tension with one another, that they represent, at some fundamental level, values and ideas which are essentially contradictory.[2] This antithetical approach to postmodernism and postcolonialism is especially evident in the case of J. M. Coetzee, whose work has frequently been criticized for promoting the interests of the former before the needs of the latter, for preferring the aesthetics of deconstruction

The *South Atlantic Quarterly* 93:1, Winter 1994.
Copyright © 1994 by Duke University Press.
CCC 0038-2876/94/$1.50.

to the politics of reconstruction. Paul Rich summarizes this critical view when he writes of the "failure of literary post-modernism" to grasp "the nature of class relationships in South Africa," and then goes on to argue that "[a]s an art form, [postmodernism] is probably destined to remain the vehicle for expressing the cultural and political dilemmas of a privileged class of white artists and intellectuals."[3] For critics like Rich, postmodernism and postcolonialism stand on either side of a great ideological divide, and writers are called upon— as a kind of litmus test of their political loyalties—to choose one or the other. Coetzee has consistently refused to choose. Or, more precisely, he has confounded the very logic of the choice by simultaneously choosing both options, by adopting postmodern strategies, which he has then used for postcolonial purposes.[4]

≡≡≡

In *Foe* the convergence of the postmodern and the postcolonial is most clearly evident in the way Coetzee deconstructs the traditional dichotomy between speech and writing. We might begin to explore that dichotomy and its deconstruction by considering a scene from one of his earlier novels, *Waiting for the Barbarians*. The Magistrate of a distant outpost of the Empire has excavated ruins where he discovered a number of poplar slips inscribed with an ancient and unknown script. Having unsuccessfully attempted to decipher the writing, the Magistrate returns to the ruins, hoping to discover there the voice which once animated the slips:

> One evening I lingered among the ruins after the children had run home to their suppers, into the violet of dusk and the first stars, the hour when, according to lore, ghosts awaken. I put my ear to the ground as the children had instructed me, to hear what they hear: thumps and groans under the earth, the deep irregular beat of drums. . . . For an hour I waited, wrapped in my cloak, with my back against the corner-post of a house in which people must once have talked and eaten and played music. I sat watching the moon rise, opening my senses to the night, waiting for a sign that what lay around me, what lay beneath my feet, was not only sand, the dust of bones, flakes of rust, shard, ash. The sign

did not come. I felt no tremor of ghostly fear. . . . Ridiculous, I thought: a greybeard sitting in the dark waiting for spirits from the byways of history to speak to him.[5]

The scene presents itself as a failed epiphany, one in which the Magistrate attempts to move from the dead body of writing to the living soul of speech. He believes that the writing will come alive, that it will repossess its lost meaning and incandesce into intelligibility, if only he can make it "speak." Standing behind this scene is, of course, an idea which has exercised considerable influence in the West. It is the idea that speech gives us pure meaning, a kind of semantic incarnation which requires no intercessor or substitute, while writing gives us a debased meaning, an imitation of the thing itself, existing as a second- or even third-order representation. When God speaks, or Adam names, meaning and being are identical. After the Fall, however, we are cast out of an Eden of transparent meaning and into a world of interpretive toil.

It is, of course, Jacques Derrida who has made the speech/writing dichotomy and its deconstruction most familiar to us. As is well known, Derrida attempts to purge speech of its theological and metaphysical ghosts, arguing that meaning is no more immediately present in speech than in writing. Indeed, for Derrida, speech may be regarded as simply another kind of writing insofar as all language is, in the Nietzschean sense, metaphoric and therefore a matter of substitution.[6] There are, in other words, no originary linguistic forms; all language functions as writing because all language involves supplements and simulacra.

Coetzee himself deconstructs the speech/writing dichotomy in the scene from *Waiting for the Barbarians*. The Magistrate's assumption that he can recover the lost "voice" of the poplar slips—and with it the "meaning" and "presence" which stand behind them—is here treated as nothing more than a myth, the kind of fiction children invent to frighten one another. When the Magistrate departs after an hour of sitting in the ruins, he is obviously embarrassed at his own credulity, and with good reason: he has been taken in, as it were, by a ghost story. Of course, *Waiting for the Barbarians* is not the only place where Coetzee explores the speech/writing dichotomy. Indeed, at one level or another, it informs all of his work.[7] However, nowhere does this dichotomy figure as prominently as it does in *Foe*, where it becomes the central focus of the story—in effect, what the novel is "about."

Foe begins as a piece of "writing" in the sense that it is a secondary or supplementary retelling of *Robinson Crusoe* from the perspective of Susan Barton, a female castaway who washes up on Cruso's island.[8] After a short and uneventful sojourn on the island, a rescue is effected. Cruso dies during the return passage, but Susan and Friday are safely delivered to England, where Susan seeks out the author Daniel Foe in the hope of having her story told. Yet, we soon learn, the only way to reconstruct what has happened on the island is with the help of Friday, whose tongue has been cut out. The very situation of the novel, then, grows out of a tension between *writing*—the book Foe has agreed to author—and an irrecoverable *speech*—the story Friday can no longer relate. As Susan puts it: "To tell my story and be silent on Friday's tongue is no better than offering a book for sale with pages in it quietly left empty. Yet the only tongue that can tell Friday's secret is the tongue he has lost."[9] Once again, Coetzee has deconstructed the speech/writing dichotomy, in this case by "cutting" his story off from the authorizing source and presence of Friday's speech. The missing tongue here functions not only as the necessary condition of writing—the "absence" out of which it generates itself—but also as the very subject of that writing, the theme around which the story builds itself. Coetzee's novel becomes, then, an exploration of *écriture*: a piece of writing which is about itself as a piece of writing.

Obviously, such an approach to Coetzee treats him primarily as a postmodern author, a writer concerned with problems of language and textuality. Yet what I am most interested in showing here is how Coetzee takes a postmodern notion—the deconstruction of the speech/writing dichotomy—and reconfigures it in terms which are essentially postcolonial. Coetzee accomplishes this by drawing out of the speech/writing dichotomy a colonialism that was always implicit in it: namely, the equation of speech with "savage man" and writing with "civilized man." Underlying these equations is an entire anthropological tradition that is largely defined by the work of two men: Jean-Jacques Rousseau and Claude Lévi-Strauss.[10]

The connection between Rousseau and Lévi-Strauss is not incidental. As Derrida writes, "Lévi-Strauss not only feels himself to be *in agreement* with Jean-Jacques, to be his heir at heart. . . . He also often presents himself as Rousseau's modern disciple; he reads Rousseau as the *founder*, not only the prophet, of modern anthropology." Rousseau's own proto-anthropology is implied in any number of his writings, but it is most unmistakably present in the *Second Discourse*, where he treats "Negroes," "Caribs," and "Hottentots" as the contemporary descendants of "natural man." In Derrida's view, Rousseau's primitivism represents a habit of mind characteristic of much, if not all, eighteenth-century thought:

> Non-European peoples were not only studied as the index to a hidden good Nature, as a native soil recovered, of a "zero degree" with reference to which one could outline the structure, the growth, and above all the degradation of our society and our culture.[11]

The introduction here of "zero degree" echoes Roland Barthes's *Le Degré zéro de l'écriture* and serves to remind us that writing is one of the defining terms in the nature/culture opposition, indeed *the* term most frequently used to distinguish the latter from the former. Hence, to remain at the "zero degree" of writing—which, ideally, is no writing at all—means to exist in a pre-civil condition where communication is exclusively oral and where words and things stand in close proximity to one another. Writing, on the other hand, is an invention of culture that alienates "savage man" from nature and enmeshes him in a corrupting logic of substitution or supplementarity. Derrida offers the following summary of this position:

> Rousseau considers writing as a dangerous means, a menacing aid, the critical response to a situation of distress. When Nature, as self-proximity, comes to be forbidden or interrupted, when

speech fails to protect presence, writing becomes necessary. It must *be added* to the word urgently. I have identified in advance one of the forms of this *addition*; speech being natural or at least the natural expression of thought, the most natural form of institution or convention for signifying thought, writing is added to it, is adjoined, as an image or representation. In that sense, it is not natural. It diverts the immediate presence of thought to speech into representation and the imagination. This recourse is not only "bizarre," but dangerous. It is the addition of a technique, a sort of artificial and artful ruse to make speech present when it is actually absent. It is a violence done to the natural destiny of the language.[12]

In *Tristes Tropiques*, Lévi-Strauss expands on this Rousseauistic view of speech and writing. In a chapter entitled "The Writing Lesson," he describes having passed out pencils and paper among the Nambikwaras, a people without a written language. To his surprise, the Nambikwaras were soon "drawing wavy, horizontal lines" in imitation of his own writing. Of particular interest was the Nambikwaran chief, who had "grasped the purpose of writing" and made a great show before his people of having mastered this new art. In reflecting on the "writing lesson," Lévi-Strauss takes the Rousseauistic position that writing has a corrupting influence, but he carries this view even further by explicitly linking writing to subjugation and oppression. As he sees it, writing among the Nambikwaras "had not been a question of acquiring knowledge or remembering or understanding, but rather of increasing the authority and prestige of one individual . . . at the expense of others." This observation then leads Lévi-Strauss to launch a wholesale attack on writing as one of the defining institutions of civilization: "The only phenomenon with which writing has always been concomitant is the creation of cities and empires. . . . [I]t seems to have favoured the exploitation of human beings rather than their enlightenment." Lévi-Strauss concludes by claiming that his "hypothesis, if correct, would oblige us to recognize the fact that the primary function of written communication is to facilitate slavery."[13]

While Lévi-Strauss takes Rousseau's arguments to their logical extreme, he nevertheless begins from an assumption which clearly underlies both the *Second Discourse* and *Essay on the Origin of Languages*: because speech is more "natural" than writing, it is in oral cultures that one is most likely to discover an anthropological "zero degree." As we have seen, Derrida deconstructs the speech/writing dichotomy on the grounds that we can never gain access to nature itself, to the world as it might speak in "its own voice." Like Derrida, Coetzee is also skeptical of the idea that speech functions as a kind of natural language, but while Derrida attacks the philosophical arguments that stand behind this idea, Coetzee attacks the anthropological elaborations that follow from it. In other words, if Derrida deconstructs an opposition between speech and writing, Coetzee deconstructs an opposition between black speech and white writing.

"White writing"—which provides the title of Coetzee's recent book on South African literature—is meant to resonate with Roland Barthes's *écriture blanche*. Barthes's term hypothesizes a "white" or transparently neutral language designed to register the world with clinical objectivity.[14] In a sense, *écriture blanche* functions as the scriptive equivalent of Derrida's *parole* or "speech": it is a form of discourse in which "writing" is at the "zero degree," in which communication "freed from all bondage to a pre-ordained state of language" becomes identical with nature itself.[15] Of course, for Barthes *écriture blanche* is, like Derridean speech, nothing more than a myth, the nostalgic longing for an Adamic language.

Coetzee has indicated that "there is an echo" of *écriture blanche* in "white writing," but the meaning he assigns to the phrase is, he says, "clearly set out" in *White Writing*.[16] Of course, what one finds in *White Writing* is not so much a definition of this term as a characterization, one which approaches it historically rather than theoretically: "Nor does the phrase *white writing* imply the existence of a body of writing different in nature from black writing. White writing is white only insofar as it is generated by the concerns of people no longer European, not yet African." Elsewhere, Coetzee has reinforced this historical conception of "white writing," insisting that he uses it "not with any theoretical intent but . . . as a catch-all term for a certain historically circumscribed point of departure in writing about (South) Africa, and perhaps about colonized worlds in general."[17]

Still, the concluding qualification ("perhaps about colonized worlds in general") raises the possibility that this term is not merely—or at least not narrowly—historical in its circumscription, that it might have a more general—if not universal—application. What is that application? It is here that the Barthesean echo becomes important. For as Coetzee himself uses "white writing," as he begins to fill out the term through example and elaboration, we see that it functions as a doubly ironic echo of *écriture blanche*: not only is "white writing" *not* linguistically "transparent" or neutral, it is, on the contrary, shot through with cultural preference and bias; it is, in other words, "white" in the racial sense.

This double irony leads, in turn, to a double deconstruction of the opposition between black speech and white writing. From a philosophical standpoint, there is no black speech because, as Derrida has argued, there is no "speech" at all, no transparent language in which nature utters itself. However, from a cultural standpoint, even if black speech were possible, we would not be able to "hear" it because white writing—despite its claims to objectivity—is racially motivated. In both cases, white writing confronts a form not of black speech, but of black silence. And it is for this reason that Coetzee repeatedly uses metaphors of silence to describe the way in which white writing apprehends blackness. Hence, black labor, black people, even the landscape of Africa are presented as stifled or mute:

> [T]he silences in the South African farm novel, particularly its silence about the place of the black man in the pastoral idyll, and the silence it creates when it puts into the mouth of the black countryman a white man's words . . . speak more loudly now than they did fifty years ago. Our ears today are finely attuned to modes of silence.

Black speech is manifested, then, as its own negation, as what is absent or lacking, and this means, in the final analysis, that "the black man becomes a *shadowy presence*." [18]

We may now return to *Foe,* bearing in mind what Coetzee has written about blackness as "silence" and "shadowy presence." Here is how Susan describes her story and Friday's place within it:

> [I]f the story seems stupid, that is only because it so doggedly
> holds its *silence*. The *shadow* whose lack you feel is there: it is
> the loss of Friday's tongue. . . . The story of Friday's tongue is a
> story unable to be told, or unable to be told by me. That is to say,
> many stories can be told of Friday's tongue, but the true story
> is buried within Friday, who is mute. The true story will not be
> heard till by art we have found a means of giving voice to Friday.[19]

In the situation Susan describes, the postmodern and the postcolonial
converge: Friday's mutilation, the sign of his status as a slave, produces his muteness or mut(e)-ilation, his inability to tell his "true"
story in his own "voice." That this mut(e)ilation cannot be heard,
that it can only be written, will become the pivotal point around
which Coetzee's entire novel turns. This means that the only way
Friday's story will be told is through Susan and Foe, which is to say,
through the intercession of white writing.

In large part, *Foe* becomes, then, an examination of the difficulties
that white writing encounters when it attempts to represent blackness. These difficulties arise in the first place because, as Derrida has
argued, individuals do not simply possess a language into which they
translate their conscious intentions, but are themselves possessed by
that language, and how they think, what they say, even the way they
perceive are all linguistically conditioned. In South Africa, one of
the languages which has historically possessed white writers is what
Coetzee calls the "Discourse of the Cape." This is a language that first
developed in the seventeenth century—roughly the period in which
Foe is set—out of the written reports of those "seamen, ships' doc-
tors, and Company officials" who were then colonizing South Africa.
In other words, the Discourse of the Cape grew out of that larger
genre of travel literature of which *Robinson Crusoe* is such a memorable and successful type. Many of the attitudes and ideas that were
derived from this travel literature provided, according to Coetzee, a
proto-anthropological vocabulary or conceptual scheme, which was
European in origin and which enabled whites to construct blacks
as "idle," "impure," and "savage."[20] As this conceptual scheme gradually gained acceptance, it became difficult for any white writer—
even the white writer working in good faith—to see or hear blackness
as anything other than a construction.

Susan herself recognizes how insidious and pervasive are the dangers of construction, especially when white writing confronts black silence:

> Friday has no command of words and therefore no defence against being re-shaped day by day in conformity with the desires of others. I say he is a cannibal and he becomes a cannibal; I say he is a laundryman and he becomes a laundryman.

In a book whose intertextuality is consciously anachronistic, one is tempted to read in these words an anticipatory echo of Marx's famous remark about the peasants of France: "They cannot represent themselves, they must be represented." Yet where Marx is confident that a material account of history will produce an accurate representation, Coetzee is deeply suspicious of those who purport to represent the unrepresented. We get some sense of the dangers involved in such "representation" when Susan decides, entirely on her own initiative, that Friday wants to return to Africa and almost delivers him into slavery as she attempts to negotiate his passage. We may also wonder how reliable a spokeswoman Susan is for Friday when she proclaims, "I am wasting my life on you, Friday, on you and your foolish story," or when she later concedes, "How are we ever to know what goes on in the heart of Friday?"[21] Indeed, as humane and well-motivated as Susan appears to be, she has fully assimilated the Discourse of the Cape and variously describes Friday as "superstitious," a "cannibal," a "child," an animal, and a "savage."

The relation of black silence to white writing reaches its crisis point when Foe remarks to Susan that they "must make Friday's silence speak" and Susan attempts to teach Friday how to write. There follows Coetzee's own version of "The Writing Lesson," one in which Susan plays Lévi-Strauss to Friday's chief of the Nambikwaras. Matters are further complicated by the fact that Susan's efforts at tutoring Friday are framed by a series of theoretical dialogues between Susan and Foe on the speech/writing dichotomy. During these dialogues—that literary form in which writing masquerades as speech—Foe plays Derrida to Susan's Lévi-Strauss. Not surprisingly, Susan takes a phonocentric position, arguing that because speech is prior to writing, the latter is impossible without the former: "How can

[Friday] write if he cannot speak? Letters are the mirror of words. Even when we seem to write in silence, our writing is the manifest of a speech spoken within ourselves." Foe, on the other hand, takes a grammatological position, insisting that writing is just as much a function of the body as speech is and, therefore, that it should not be treated as secondary or supplementary: "Nevertheless, Friday has fingers. If he has fingers he can form letters. Writing is not doomed to be the shadow of speech." For Susan, speech is in touch with the deep sources of language because it seems to inhere in consciousness itself, to whisper with all the undeniable authority of a voice from within: "How can he be taught to write if there are no words within him, in his heart, for writing to reflect?" Yet for Foe, Susan has fallen into a form of linguistic idealism that confuses the techniques of language with language itself: "Speech is but a means through which the word may be uttered, it is not the word itself. Friday has no speech, but he has fingers, and those fingers shall be his means."[22]

When the writing lesson finally occurs, what has functioned largely as a postmodern discussion of the speech/writing dichotomy again turns postcolonial. Here is how Susan describes the lesson:

> I drew a ship in full sail, and made him write *ship*, and then began to teach him *Africa*. Africa I represented as a row of palm trees with a lion roaming among them. Was my Africa the Africa whose memory Friday bore within him? I doubted it. Nevertheless, I wrote A-f-r-i-c-a and guided him in forming the letters.

The difficulties that arise when white writing attempts to represent blackness are tied to the linguistic conditioning that white writing and the Discourse of the Cape enforce on white writers. Here, that conditioning betrays itself in Susan's drawing of Africa, which is produced out of the clichés of colonial exoticism, clichés which assume that an entire continent can be represented by a lion and a row of palm trees. Coetzee connects this depopulated vision of Africa to the strategies of white writing and black silence:

> [T]he failure of the listening imagination to intuit the true language of Africa, the continued apprehension of silence (by the poet) or blankness (by the painter), stands for, or stands in the

place of, another failure, by no means inevitable: a failure to imagine a peopled landscape.

In other words, one of the effects of white writing, or the Discourse of the Cape, is to airbrush Africans out of Africa, to render them invisible to the European eye. So it is that when Susan wonders if Friday's poor scholarship might not be a form of mockery, she confesses her own blindness to what is African: "Somewhere in the deepest recesses of those black pupils was there a spark of mockery? I could not see it. But if it were there, would it not be an African spark, dark to my English eye?"[23]

On the basis of their one failed writing lesson, Susan concludes that Friday is incapable of learning and that any future tutelage is hopeless. From Susan's perspective, this has serious consequences, for until Friday is able to learn the language necessary to tell his story and acquire his freedom, Susan will not be able to bring her own narrative to a close. Foe argues that "[i]t is no great task to teach Friday such language as will serve his needs." Yet, for Susan—the linguistic essentialist—this is not enough. She feels that Friday must move beyond the outer forms of language to that transcendent realm associated with speech where words are shaped to meanings and meanings to words. Friday must understand the "true" nature of freedom—he must, in effect, possess it as a form of speech—before he will be able to experience it. Foe—the linguistic pragmatist—takes a very different view of the matter. As he tells Susan,

> If we devote ourselves to finding holes exactly shaped to house such great words as *Freedom, Honour, Bliss*, I agree, we shall spend a lifetime slipping and sliding and searching, and all in vain. They are words without a home, wanderers like the planets, and that is an end of it.

Where Susan would figuratively restore Friday to a condition of speech, Foe is content to help him cultivate the faculty of writing. Communication does not depend, in Foe's view, on discovering a final vocabulary, the "true" language in which nature speaks itself. Foe says to Susan, "[A]s there are many kinds of men, so there are many kinds of writing. Do not judge your pupil too hastily. He too may yet be visited by the Muse."[24]

The question of whether Friday is visited by the Muse, whether he does learn to write, constitutes one of the interpretive cruxes of the novel. How we answer this question depends on how we understand the word "writing." If, along with Susan, we understand it to mean a system of notation that is ancillary to an essentializing speech, then there can be only one kind of writing and Friday clearly has not acquired it. However, if, along with Foe, we understand it to mean a Derridean *écriture*, then there are (as Foe says) many kinds of writing and Friday may be said to practice at least some of these.[25] One that I would like to focus on occurs toward the end of the novel, when Susan comes upon Friday dressed in Foe's authorial guild robes and seated at Foe's writing table:

> In his hand, poised over Foe's papers, he held a quill with a drop of black ink glistening at its tip. I gave a cry and sprang forward to snatch it away. But at that moment Foe spoke from the bed where he lay. "Let him be, Susan," he said in a tired voice: "he is accustoming himself to his tools, it is part of learning to write."[26]

What Friday "writes" is row after row of the letter O. There is, I think, a strong tendency to interpret these redundant O's as zeros and to regard Friday's writing as a kind of self-consuming apostrophe in which he addresses himself as a textual gap or lacuna. According to this reading, Friday has written himself into Coetzee's novel, but as a "shadowy presence" that white writing cannot apprehend, the hole at the center of Susan's story, the open and empty mouth which no longer contains a tongue. Friday exists, but he exists as a narrative absence.

Within its limits, such an interpretation is perfectly plausible, but there is a second interpretation that I would like to propose, one which functions as the precise opposite of the first. In *Robinson Crusoe*, we learn that before Friday converted to Christianity, he believed in his peoples' God, the great Benamuckee. When a bemused Crusoe asks why, if Benamuckee is the creator of the universe, all things do not worship him, Friday replies, quite disarmingly, that all things do worship him, "All things . . . say O to him."[27] This passage has the effect of opening up an entirely new, and strikingly different, perspective on Friday's writing: the O represents not an empty cipher but a divine circle, and by repeating it, much as he would a mantra, Friday expresses not his own nullity, his sense of isolation and self-alienation, but a fundamental unity with all of creation, here achieved through the worship of Benamuckee.

What happens as we move between these two interpretations is not unlike the gestalt shift that occurs when Chinua Achebe quotes Yeats in the title of his novel, *Things Fall Apart*. The object before us—Friday's writing or Yeats's poetic phrase—remains constant, but the terms of its signification are transposed, reversed, turned upside down. Hence, within the context of Yeats's white writing, "things fall apart" refers to the *demise* of Christianity; whereas, within the context of Achebe's black writing, "things fall apart" refers to the *rise* of Christianity. The two interpretations of Friday's redundant O's function in much the same way. Viewed from the standpoint of white writing, Friday remains at the periphery—he is, in effect, nothing; viewed from the standpoint of black writing, Friday occupies the center—he is, in effect, everything.

And yet, it might be objected, how can Friday's worship of Bena-muckee, his prayerful O, his sense of atonement with the world—how can this be considered an example of black writing when it de-rives from one of the most powerful examples of white writing we have—namely, *Robinson Crusoe*? Such an objection carries consider-able weight. Given the stern logic of white writing, Coetzee can do little more than communicate Friday's incommunicability, even as he hints at the possibility of an alternative form of writing that is black. Does this mean that Friday is, in the final analysis, excluded from the novel, that Friday's mutilation effectively condemns him to a condition of muteness?

Foe's much discussed concluding section proposes at least one way of addressing this difficult problem. By writing this section in a delib-erately fantastic manner, Coetzee marks it as an exercise in the hypo-thetical, a kind of thought experiment, which poses the following question: If black speech were possible, if white writing could ap-prehend it, what would it look like, what would it sound like, how would it express itself? Part four of the novel appears to be set many years after the events described in the first three parts. An unnamed narrator enters the rooms of "Daniel Defoe, Author," now identified by the blue and white plaque which designates houses of historical interest. Inside the rooms, the narrator encounters what we imagine to be the corpses of Susan and Foe, lying side by side in bed. Their skin, "dry as paper, is stretched tight over their bones" and "their lips have receded, uncovering their teeth, so that they seem to be smiling." Apparently "three hundred years" have passed, almost exactly the length of time that has transpired between Susan's arrival in England and Coetzee's publication of *Foe*.[28] Since the time frame places the novel in a contemporary setting, and since the novel itself represents Coetzee's own confrontation with *Robinson Crusoe*, there is good reason to draw a connection between the narrator and Coetzee.[29]

Part four of the novel presents what are, in effect, two separate endings, in both of which the narrator approaches Friday, opens his mouth, and attempts to "make his silence speak." However, in the first ending, the approach is direct and unmediated: no writing interposes itself between Friday and the narrator, who finds Friday, presses his ear to the recumbent man's mouth, and listens. What he hears are the "sounds of the island," but nothing identifiable with Friday himself. The attempt to reclaim black speech has failed. The island speaks, but Friday remains silent.

The second version of the ending replays the first, taking us once more up the stairs, over the body on the landing, and into the room with Susan and Foe in bed, Friday in the adjacent alcove. In other words, the second ending functions as a simulacrum of the first, but a simulacrum in which the approach to Friday is mediated by writing. Hence, this time, the narrator goes not to Friday's mouth, but to Susan's manuscript, from which he reads the first sentence (". . . At last I could row no further"). What had appeared to be a lived experience, the vividly narrated opening of the novel, has now curled and yellowed into a piece of writing. And this, in turn, becomes the occasion for another instance of textual redoubling, as the narrator takes up the opening words of Susan's narrative ("With a sigh, making barely a splash, I slipped overboard"), but then alters them ("With a sigh, with barely a splash, I duck my head under the water"), thereby acknowledging their supplementary status.

Having deliberately framed this second ending as a piece of writing, the narrator now descends into the submerged shipwreck, which, described as a "hole" or "black space," is compared to Friday's mouth. In this submarine setting we discover "the home of Friday," a place which is "not a place of words" but "a place where bodies are their own signs."[30] We have entered into a prelinguistic Eden, a world in which meaning has grown so luminously transparent that words themselves have become superfluous, the mere filmy excrescences that pure signification sloughs off. It is as though the Magistrate's hour in the ruins has finally been redeemed, as though the poplar slips have stirred into consciousness and begun to whisper their secret. What do the poplar slips tell us? What does Friday communicate? Here is the final paragraph of *Foe*:

> His mouth opens. From inside him comes a slow stream, without breath, without interruption. It flows up through his body and out upon me; it passes through the cabin, through the wreck; washing the cliffs and shores of the island, it runs northward and southward to the ends of the earth. Soft and cold, dark and unending, it beats against my eyelids, against the skin of my face.

When Friday opens his mouth at the end of *Foe*, the whole tradition of colonial discourse, of white writing, is forced to confront the object of its colonization, here epitomized in the fugitive identity of a tongueless slave. We who have grown up in the tradition of white writing cannot "read" what Friday "says," but we can relate it to his earlier piece of writing—his prayer to Benamuckee. For the breathless stream that now emerges from Friday functions precisely as did his devotional O: it washes over the island; it runs to the ends of the earth; it connects him to all of creation. The result is a "muted" epiphany. White writing continues to be unable to read blackness, to construe it into some specifiable and paraphrasable meaning. But as it encounters Friday's wordless speech, as it confronts and registers the unassimilable otherness of his mut(e)ilation, white writing is compelled to acknowledge, perhaps for the first time in its long and melancholy history, that there might be a form of writing, a form of speaking, a form of being, different from itself.

What finally emerges from Friday's sunken home is neither black speech nor black writing, but something that occupies an undefined middle ground, a form of expression that, quite simply, resists classification.[31] It is, of course, no accident that Friday's language is exorbitant, that it stands outside all available categories. For, given his position within white writing, Coetzee can neither speak for nor write for Friday. This does not mean, however, that Coetzee has enclosed himself within an aestheticized postmodernism where he narcissistically meditates "the dilemmas of a privileged class of white artists and intellectuals."[32] We should remember Foe's remark to Susan: "[A]s it was a slaver's stratagem to rob Friday of his tongue, may it not be a slaver's stratagem to hold him in subjection while we cavil over words in a dispute we know to be endless?"[33] Coetzee certainly does "cavil over words"—words which are, after all, our medium of cultural exchange—but at the same time, he insists, in terms which are unmistakable, that the subjection end.

Earlier, I quoted Marx's dictum: "They cannot represent themselves, they must be represented." If Marx sought to speak and write for the subjected, to represent the unrepresented, Coetzee seeks something that is both less presumptuous and more liberating: he seeks to represent the unrepresented *as unrepresented*, to show precisely the necessity of enabling them to represent themselves. *Foe* is, then, a novel whose postmodernism is ultimately pressed into the service of its postcolonialism, a novel that deconstructs its own white writing to clear a space for someone else's black writing. In the end, we feel certain, Friday will represent himself. But he will represent himself after his own fashion, and in his own words.

Notes

1   Simon During, "Postmodernism or Postcolonialism?" *Landfall* 39 (1985): 369.
2   See, for example, Diana Brydon, "The Myths That Write Us: Decolonizing the Mind," *Commonwealth* 10 (1987): 1–14; and Helen Tiffin, "Post-Colonialism, Post-Modernism, and the Rehabilitation of Post-Colonial History," *Journal of Commonwealth Literature* 23 (1988): 169–81.

I use "postmodernism" to indicate a series of related phenomena, including the end of philosophical foundationalism, the "legitimation crisis," the culture of the simulacrum, pastiche, and "depthlessness." I use "postcolonialism" in the historically and geographically restricted sense (i.e., literature written after colonialism), but I am aware that the term also suggests a heightened interest in social, political, and historical issues related to colonization and its aftermath.

3 Paul Rich, "Tradition and Revolt in South African Fiction: The Novels of André Brink, Nadine Gordimer, and J. M. Coetzee," *Journal of Southern African Studies* 9 (1982): 73.

4 While Coetzee himself has questioned the utility of the term "postmodernism," he is not averse to using it. See my "Interview with J. M. Coetzee," *Contemporary Literature* 33 (1992): 427; and J. M. Coetzee, "A Note on Writing," in *Momentum: On Recent South African Writing*, ed. M. J. Daymond, J. U. Jacobs, and M. Lenta (Pietermaritzburg, 1984), 11.

5 J. M. Coetzee, *Waiting for the Barbarians* (New York, 1982 [1980]), 16.

6 See Friedrich Nietzsche, *Philosophy and Truth: Selections from Nietzsche's Notebooks of the Early 1870s*, ed. and trans. Daniel Breazeale (New Jersey and London, 1979), where he writes, "What then is truth? A movable host of metaphors, metonymies, and anthropomorphisms: in short, a sum of human relations which have been poetically and rhetorically intensified, transferred, and embellished, and which, after long usage, seem to people to be fixed, canonical, and binding" (84).

7 With the exception of *Life & Times of Michael K* (1983), all of Coetzee's fiction is written in the first-person singular voice (suggesting a speaker), but is deliberately and unmistakably represented as a textual object (indicating a piece of writing).

8 Coetzee alters "Crusoe" to "Cruso"; for an interesting discussion of the significance of the omitted "e," see Brian Macaskill and Jeanne Colleran, "Reading History, Writing Heresy: The Resistance of Representation and the Representation of Resistance in J. M. Coetzee's *Foe*," *Contemporary Literature* 33 (1992): 432–57.

9 J. M. Coetzee, *Foe* (New York, 1987 [1986]), 67.

10 This argument is developed in Jacques Derrida, *Of Grammatology*, trans. Gayatri Chakravorty Spivak (Baltimore, 1974), which Coetzee cites in "Confession and Double Thoughts: Tolstoy, Rousseau, Dostoevsky," *Comparative Literature* 37 (1985): 213; see also his discussion of Rousseau and the relation of anthropology to the "Discourse of the Cape," in *White Writing* (New Haven, 1988), 24–25.

11 Derrida, *Of Grammatology*, 105, 114–15.

12 Ibid., 144; emphases in original. While Derrida's reading of Rousseau is largely based on the *Essay on the Origin of Languages*, Rousseau makes it clear in the *Second Discourse* that "natural man" is prelinguistic. Speech comes into being only in primitive society, which Rousseau identifies with "savage man." See *The First and Second Discourses*, ed. Roger D. Masters, trans. Roger D. and Judith R. Masters (New York, 1964), 119–23.

13 Claude Lévi-Strauss, *Tristes Tropiques*, trans. John and Doreen Weightman (New York, 1974), 296, 298, 299.

14 Roland Barthes, *Writing Degree Zero*, trans. Annette Lavers and Colin Smith (New York, 1968). Barthes writes that "this transparent form of speech, initiated by Camus's *Outsider*, achieves a style of absence which is almost an ideal absence of style; writing is then reduced to a sort of negative mood in which the social

or mythical characters of a language are abolished in favour of a neutral or inert state of form" (77). Neutral writing, or *écriture blanche*, presents itself as pure "instrumentality" (78). In an attempt to emphasize the transparence of *écriture blanche*, the English translation renders it as "colorless writing."

15 Ibid., 76.
16 Personal communication (letter of 15 November 1991).
17 Coetzee, *White Writing*, 11; and Begam, "Interview," 423.
18 Coetzee, *White Writing*, 81, 5; emphasis mine.
19 Coetzee, *Foe*, 117–18; emphases mine.
20 Coetzee, *White Writing*, 12–17.
21 Coetzee, *Foe*, 121, 109–11, 70, 115.
22 Ibid., 142, 143.
23 Ibid., 146; Coetzee, *White Writing*, 9; Coetzee, *Foe*, 146.
24 Ibid., 149–50, 147. I use the term "pragmatist" quite deliberately; see Richard Rorty, *Contingency, Irony and Solidarity* (Cambridge, 1989), especially the first chapter, "The Contingency of Language."
25 Both the flute-playing and the dancing may be regarded as forms of writing in the expanded Derridean sense.
26 Coetzee, *Foe*, 151.
27 Daniel Defoe, *Robinson Crusoe* (Harmondsworth, 1981 [1719]), 218.
28 Crusoe is shipwrecked in 1659 and rescued twenty-eight years later, in 1687. *Foe* was published in 1986, 299 years after the rescue.
29 I do not mean to suggest that we should literally read the narrator of part four as Coetzee. However, insofar as this part stages a confrontation between white writing and Friday, and insofar as Coetzee himself practices white writing (however subversively), we may draw a generic connection between Coetzee and this narrator.
30 Coetzee, *Foe*, 155–56, 141–42, 157.
31 See Coetzee's fascinating discussion of the "middle voice" in "A Note on Writing."
32 Rich, "Tradition and Revolt," 73.
33 Coetzee, *Foe*, 150.

Michael Valdez Moses

Solitary Walkers: Rousseau and Coetzee's
Life & Times of Michael K

> The man who is isolated—who is unable to share in the benefits of political association, or has no need to share because he is already self-sufficient —is no part of the polis, and must therefore be either a beast or a god.
> —Aristotle, *The Politics*

> Everything is finished for me on earth. People can no longer do good or evil to me here. I have nothing more to hope for or to fear in this world; and here I am, tranquil at the bottom of the abyss, a poor unfortunate mortal, but unperturbed, like God Himself.
>
> Everything external is henceforth foreign to me. I no longer have neighbors, fellow creatures, or brothers in this world. I am on earth as though on a foreign planet onto which I have fallen from the one I inhabited.
> —Rousseau, *The Reveries of the Solitary Walker*

He remains always just beyond our grasp, perpetually in retreat, a refugee from history and a living repudiation of political life: Michael K. And though he might be received as "a spirit invisible, a visitor on our planet,

The *South Atlantic Quarterly* 93:1, Winter 1994.
Copyright © 1994 by Duke University Press.
CCC 0038-2876/94/$1.50.

a creature beyond the reach of the laws of nations," he is not without earthly ancestors and distant kin.[1] For Michael K follows in a long and distinguished line of isolates whose radical challenge to the political order consists not in their resistance to the laws of any particular regime, but in their refusal to accept the limits of politics per se. Among modern thinkers, Jean-Jacques Rousseau, especially in his last work, *The Reveries of the Solitary Walker* (1782), is perhaps the most influential and persuasive advocate of an apolitical or antipolitical existence.[2] Considered in light of Rousseau's work, the scandal that is Michael K, and that has provoked the moral and political criticism of engagé writers such as Nadine Gordimer, assumes a philosophic importance that demands our attention.[3]

There are few immediately recognizable parallels between the "lives" of Rousseau and Michael K. While the former moved for a time in the most fashionable and socially privileged circles of eighteenth-century European society (guest of the French court, literary and musical celebrity of Paris, friend of Diderot and Hume), the latter is an obscure assistant gardener working for the City of Cape Town, who sinks into a life of vagabondage and near-starvation, a penniless "colored," adrift in the Karoo during a time of civil war. Whereas Rousseau's writings brought him first fame and then infamy, Michael K's laconic and inarticulate manner barely gains him the passing attention of low-level bureaucrats, hospital workers, common soldiers, and labor camp administrators nearly as obscure as he. However, after 1762, Rousseau was forced to assume a way of life that in a few essentials was strikingly similar to that of Michael K. Having alienated his many influential friends and patrons, and scandalized European society with the publication of such works as *Emile* and the *Social Contract*, Rousseau was repeatedly forced to flee his place of residence. His books publicly burned in Paris, Geneva, and The Hague, himself subject to arrest and exile by several governments and to persecution by religious authorities, his home in Môtiers stoned by an angry mob in 1765, the destitute Rousseau increasingly sought obscurity and isolation. The *Reveries* offers Rousseau's autobiographical account of this period of his life, which lasted until his return to Paris in 1770. It is in this highly idiosyncratic work that one encounters a genuinely personal but ultimately philosophic defense of solitude, of a complete withdrawal from all social and political life. Rousseau's apology for his repudiation of all civic ties and obligations can both illuminate the nature of Michael K's increasingly asocial existence and provide a serious response to the charge of political irresponsibility and moral evasiveness that has been brought against Michael K and his creator.[4]

≡≡≡

Central to both Michael K's and Rousseau's solitary existence are the experiences of idleness and reverie. Having fled the Visagie farm in order to escape being pressed into service by the Visagie grandson, Michael K hides in the mountains of the Swartberg. At the mouth of a cave he temporarily occupies, Michael K recaptures a mode of being he was first compelled to experience at the orphanage, Huis Norenius:

> One of the teachers used to make his class sit with their hands on their heads, their lips pressed tightly together and their eyes closed, while he patrolled the rows with his long ruler. In time, to K, the posture grew to lose its meaning as punishment and became an avenue of *reverie*; he remembered sitting, hands on head, through hot afternoons with doves cooing in the gum trees and the chant of the tables coming from other classrooms, struggling with a delicious drowsiness. Now, in front of his cave, he sometimes locked his fingers behind his head, closed his eyes, and emptied his mind, wanting nothing, looking forward to nothing.[5]

Rousseau's idyll on St. Peter's Island in Lake Bienne, recounted in the crucial Fifth Walk of the *Reveries*, anticipates in several key details Michael K's experience in the Swartberg. Rousseau comes to St. Peter's not of his own free will, but because he is forced to flee civilized society. The involuntary solitude he endures following the assault on his home in Môtiers is a "destiny . . . imposed . . . on him as a law." However, like K, Rousseau discovers that his punishment provides a new and unexpected form of joy: "Of all the places I have lived . . . none has made me so truly happy."[6] Rousseau speculates that this form of contentment—an extended reverie of sorts—would be available even were he imprisoned in the Bastille. So complete is his happiness that Rousseau comes to regard his prison as a paradise where he hopes to end his days:

> I wanted them to make this refuge a perpetual prison for me, to confine me to it for life, and—removing every possibility and hope of getting off it—to forbid me any kind of communication with the mainland so that being unaware of all that went on in the world I might forget its existence and that it might also forget mine.

The seductiveness of life on the island for Rousseau consists in no particular activity or enterprise, but rather in the utter lack of content in or purpose to his existence: "The precious *far niente* was the first and the principal enjoyment I wanted to savor in all its sweetness, and all I did during my sojourn was in effect only the delicious and necessary pursuit of a man who has devoted himself to idleness."[7]

In his eloquent defense of what Rousseau calls "luxurious idleness,"[8] Coetzee offers an appreciative critique of the legendary sloth of those Hottentots (Khoikhoi) first encountered by Europeans in the Cape during the seventeenth century, as well as of those Boer settlers who came to share the lassitude of the native peoples. Coetzee makes his own sympathies clear: "The luxurious idleness of the settler is still denounced from Europe, the idleness of the native still deplored by his master. I hope that it is clear that I by no means add my voice to the chorus of moralizing disapproval."[9]

The idleness of Rousseau and Michael K is thus characterized largely by what it is not—that is, by what the idler avoids or escapes. Chief among these is the obligation to work. Rousseau refuses to unpack his books on St. Peter's Island and takes up his pen only with the greatest reluctance and distaste. Michael K flees to the Swartberg rather than become the body-servant of the Visagie grandson; he refuses to labor for the latter on "his" farm. To be sure, both Rousseau and Michael K voluntarily engage in activities that might, if performed in a different social context, be credited as forms of economically productive labor. Rousseau takes up the study of botany on St. Peter's Island, while K practices gardening on the Visagie farm before the arrival and after the departure of the grandson. But in both cases, these physical "labors" are characterized by their economic and social purposelessness. Rousseau contrasts his purely contemplative botanical research with the debilitating and alienated labor of those who work in industrial mines and with the pharmacological toil of a barber-surgeon's assistant. Rousseau refrains from making use of plants for any economic or medical end, seeking neither "profit" nor bodily "remedies."[10] In a similar fashion, K's gardening in the Karoo stands in marked contrast both to the paid employment he performs for the Parks and Gardens division of Cape Town's municipal services and to his forced labor at the Jakkalsdrif work camp. He does not grow pumpkins under compulsion, nor for hourly wages, nor for sale on the open market. And because he grows more food than his ever-dwindling body can consume, K's gardening is not even classifiable as a form of subsistence farming, but rather as an activity aimed at some other, apparently asocial end: keeping the earth alive.

The relative poverty of Rousseau and Michael K, and their apparent indifference to money (K goes so far as to bury all the cash in his possession), signals a symbolic, if not actual, return to the "state of nature" before the invention of private property. In his *Discourse on the Origin and Foundations of Inequality among Men*, Rousseau describes his now-famous concept of the transition between the state of nature and civil society:

> The first person who, having fenced off a plot of ground, took it into his head to say *this is mine* and found people simple enough to believe him, was the true founder of civil society. What crimes, wars, murders, what miseries and horror would the human race have been spared by someone who, uprooting the stakes or filling in the ditch, had shouted to his fellow-men: Beware of listening to this impostor; you are lost if you forget that the fruits belong to all and the earth to no one![11]

This passage resonates throughout Coetzee's novel, most audibly when Michael K wanders among the fenced-off farms of the Karoo, looking for some uninhabited refuge: "he wondered whether there were not forgotten corners and angles and corridors between the fences, land that belonged to no one yet."[12] During his imprisonment in the Jakkalsdrif camp, K works for a short time repairing fences, an occupation at which he excels but soon rejects for the sake of his freedom. He feels most at home in a pristine natural landscape that shows no sign of human habitation, one free of the marks of civilized, propertied existence: "The landscape was so empty that it was not hard to believe at times that his was the first foot ever to tread a particular inch of earth or disturb a particular pebble. But every mile or two there was a fence to remind him that he was a trespasser as well as a runaway." K comes to articulate Rousseau's claim that the fruits of the earth belong to all. During his interrogation at the Kenilworth rehabilitation camp, he insists to the medical officer and Major van Rensburg that the pumpkins he grew on the Visagie farm were not his own: "What grows is for all of us. We are all the children of the earth."[13]

The fantasy of the uninhabited place, the untouched and unmarked refuge lost to history and civil society, plays a prominent role in both Rousseau's and Coetzee's works. Rousseau begins the Fifth Walk of the *Reveries* with the following description of St. Peter's: "This small island, which is called Hillock Island in Neuchâtel, is quite unknown, even in Switzerland. As far as I know, no traveler mentions it."[14] In a similar vein, the allure of the unsettled island comes to haunt the first-person narration of the medical officer who encounters K at the Kenilworth camp:

> Yet I am convinced there are areas that lie between the camps and belong to no camp . . . certain mountaintops, for example, certain islands in the middle of swamps, certain arid strips where human beings may not find it worth their while to live. I am looking for such a place in order to settle there, perhaps only till things improve, perhaps forever.[15]

The seductive call of the desert island returns in Coetzee's *Foe*. When Susan Barton washes ashore she discovers not the indefatigable and industrious Crusoe of Defoe's novel, but an indolent pair, Cruso and Friday, who have built nothing, farmed little, and lazed in the sun, sinking ever deeper into a slothful state that shocks and horrifies the resourceful European heroine.

And yet, however alluring this fantastic state of nature, both Coetzee and Rousseau acknowledge the historical impossibility of ever rediscovering it. Playing upon the meaning of the Greek root of "utopia" (a good place, a no-place), the medical officer recognizes the illusory character of Michael K's Edenic garden: "Let me tell you the meaning of the sacred and alluring garden that blooms in the heart of the desert and produces the food of life. The garden for which you are presently heading is nowhere and everywhere except in the camps. . . . It is off every map, no road leads to it that is merely a road, and only you know the way."[16] In a similar vein, Rousseau notes that St. Peter's Island is not, after all, quite uninhabited or unknown: it is occupied not only by Rousseau and his "help-mate" Thérèse, but also by a "tax-collector, his wife, and his servants."[17] Although he chooses to gloss over this inconvenient fact, the irony of an official representative of the Bernese government—a tax-collector, no less— sharing this unknown island paradise with the solitary walker cannot have escaped Rousseau's notice.

═══

If the reality of the uninhabited island, the recovered state of nature, remains in doubt, its nevertheless persistent attractiveness may be explained in terms of the freedoms it promises. For Rousseau and Michael K seek not only liberation from the bonds of work and private property, but also freedom from all social obligations and civic duties. Although both Rousseau and Michael K agree that the fruits of the earth belong to all, the ultimate aim of their solitary lives is not to benefit human society as a whole. Their withdrawal from the market economy, though a radical gesture, fulfills no Marxist imperative, and their "communistic" (in the strict sense of the word) attitude toward food and property serves no communal end. For what defines their moments of greatest happiness is extreme solitude and self-absorption. Rousseau is quite explicit on this point: "Alone for the rest of my life—since I find consolation, hope, and peace only in myself—I no longer ought nor want to concern myself with anything but me."[18] In contrast to material goods, which by nature belong to everyone, a reverie remains an essentially private experience that by definition cannot be shared. Although Michael K first communes with himself amidst the other beleaguered students at Huis Norenius, the highly subjective character of his reverie isolates him from his peers.

Rousseau's and Michael K's rejection of social ties and civic duties manifests itself in a number of ways, including a common aversion to familial and especially patriarchal responsibilities. Rousseau was notorious in his day for placing his children in a foundling home. If, as some critics have speculated, Rousseau fabricated this piece of gossip about himself, it is all the more likely that he intended his dramatic rejection of the responsibilities of fatherhood as part of a more general critique of the onerous demands of civil society. Rousseau certainly knew that Aristotle regarded the family as the necessary and natural basis for the establishment of the polis—that is, of political life in general.[19] By refusing to accept the most elementary responsibilities of fatherhood, Rousseau implicitly denies his willingness to participate in civic life; instead he returns, at least symbolically, to a precivilized state in which solitary natural man forms no domestic attachments and no families exist.[20] Following in Rousseau's path, Michael K neither knows the identity of his father nor believes in his own fitness as a father:

> How fortunate that I have no children. . . . [H]ow fortunate that I have no desire to father. I would not know what to do with a child out here in the heart of the country, who would need milk and clothes and friends and schooling. I would fail in my duties, I would be the worst of fathers. Whereas it is not hard to live a life that consists merely of passing time.[21]

What K avoids by rejecting fatherhood is the entire web of relationships from which he has momentarily escaped—economic ties (milk, clothes), social obligations (friends), and civic duties (schooling). Michael K's only sexual encounter in the novel is a purely passive one—a prostitute engages him in oral sex—and involves no risk that he might father a child. Even so, this brief episode leaves K ashamed and incommunicative, signaling his anxiety over an act, however furtive and trivial, that has the potential of ensnaring him in a network of social conventions and obligations.

Given their thoroughgoing rejection of civic and social ties, it comes as no surprise that Rousseau and Michael K should be viewed by others as irresponsible and untrustworthy citizens. This is clear enough in Rousseau's case, given the real political and religious persecution he suffered for much of his life. In that of K, his vagabondage and destitution function as outward marks of his tenuous relation to the South African regime. Harried by police, hospital workers, army patrols, petty government officials, and camp officers, K is as much an object of general suspicion and hostility as Rousseau claimed to be.

Of course, for the vast majority of politically attuned readers of *Life & Times of Michael K*, the uncompromising rejection of civil life that K embodies poses few moral or political difficulties so long as he is seen in relation to an oppressive racist regime. Much more problematic, however, is Michael K's ultimate refusal to assist actively the guerrillas fighting against South African apartheid.[22] Coetzee himself openly acknowledges that K is no hero. In effect endorsing—though perhaps with considerable irony—Gordimer's quasi-revolutionary criticism of his novel, Coetzee suggests that *Michael K* "is just one fancy evasion after another of an overriding political question: how shall the tyranny of apartheid be ended?"[23]

But it is not only those who sympathize with the revolutionary demands of the ANC that are likely to find Michael K wanting. For like Rousseau, K exemplifies a mode of existence inimical to the humanitarian ethos of an old-fashioned, if still powerful, liberalism. In particular, Michael K increasingly shrinks from the charitable impulses of those who are prepared to pity him. Although he seems slow-witted to others, he eventually penetrates to the insidious and unappealing core of a liberal generosity that implicitly requires subservience and verbal acts of self-abasement from its recipients:

> I have become an object of charity. . . . Everywhere I go there are people waiting to exercise their forms of charity on me. . . . They treat me like the children of Jakkalsdrif, whom they were prepared to feed because they were still too young to be guilty of anything. From the children they expected only a stammer of thanks in return. From me they want more. . . . They want me to open my heart and tell them the story of a life lived in cages. They want to hear about all the cages I have lived in, as if I were a budgie or a white mouse or a monkey.[24]

In exchange for charity, Michael K must spin tales of his own victimization and subhuman degradation; the more debased he presents himself in the eyes of his patrons, the greater their sense of superiority and social importance.

Rousseau is no less hostile to the liberal prejudice in favor of charity, although he criticizes it from the perspective of one who gives rather than receives. Having prided himself on his extraordinary sympathy for others and his surpassing generosity to the poor, Rousseau comes to the conclusion in the *Reveries* that he must finally avoid indulging in all acts of charity to others:

> I have often felt the burden of my own good deeds by the chain of duties they later entailed. Then the pleasure disappeared, and the continuation of the very attentiveness which had charmed me at first no longer struck me as anything but an almost unbearable annoyance. During my brief moments of prosperity, many people appealed to me; and despite the multitude of favors they asked of me, none of them was ever turned away. But from these first good deeds, which my heart poured out effusively, were forged chains of subsequent liabilities I had not foreseen and whose yoke I could no longer shake off. In the eyes of those who received them, my first favors were only a pledge for those which were supposed to follow; and as soon as some unfortunate man had hooked me with my own good deed, that was it from then on. This first free and voluntary good deed became an unlimited right to all those he might need afterward, without even my lack of power being enough to release me from his claim. That is how very delightful enjoyments were transformed into onerous subjections for me ever afterward.[25]

Rousseau and Michael K reject not only the particular vices and virtues of their respective societies, but also, and more fundamentally, socialization itself. They understand all civilization, all social life to be based on mutual dependence and obligation, which they feel as an objectionable burden, a severe restriction on their personal freedom and individual autonomy. When Coetzee admits to having evaded an "overriding political question," he is perhaps implying that the secret aim of his work is the evasion of politics itself. Like Rousseau, Coetzee is interested in exploring a territory free of political and social commitments in which a *truly radical* form of freedom is possible. Such a freedom is incompatible not only with apartheid, but also with a liberal democratic or socialist regime. For Gordimer to find in Michael K an unheroic and politically irresponsible character is both perfectly correct and also beside the point, since what is at issue is the unsatisfactory character of social life in general.

━━━━━
━━━━━

The key to understanding Rousseau's fundamental objection to civil society is to be found in his *Second Discourse*, in which the fall of natural man into civil society is said to entail the endless creation of new and unquenchable desires. For Rousseau, in his natural state man has limited, in fact subhuman needs that are easily and immediately met. The peculiar characteristic of man's civilized existence, however, is the acquisition of mediated or socially refracted desires. The form that these mediated desires most visibly assume is vanity or *amour-propre*. As Rousseau succinctly puts it: "[T]he savage lives within himself; the sociable man, always outside of himself, knows how to live only in the opinion of others; and it is, so to speak, from their judgment alone that he draws the sentiment of his own existence."[26] Hegel, in his *Phenomenology*, was to take this insight from Rousseau and reevaluate and transform it into the motivating engine of all human progress. For Hegel what distinguishes human from merely animal desire is that only the former can be directed at another's desire. That is, human beings are distinguished by their unique concern for recognition. And it is their willingness to risk their lives in a fight for recognition that makes possible the dialectical unfolding of history.[27] But whereas Hegel understands the end of history as the realization of the idea of universal recognition and therefore of human freedom, Rousseau regards such a progressive historical attainment of human freedom as an illusion. Rousseau believes that once man begins to see himself in the eyes of others, to desire their good opinion, to desire what others desire as a means to increase one's own sense of importance and well-being, the unmediated happiness and complete freedom of man's natural state is forever lost. Rousseau agrees with Hegel insofar as he understands the desire for recognition, or vanity, as the basis for civil society and the engine of its subsequent development; but unlike Hegel, Rousseau sees this to be the fatal, inherent, and irremediable flaw of civilized life. Although Rousseau's analysis of civilization may seem on first reflection to be merely the result of his negative reaction to the artificiality of eighteenth-century aristocratic and bourgeois society, his critical view of mediated desire forms the basis of much contemporary analysis of modern and postmodern society. From René Girard's sweeping critique of "triangular" or "mimetic desire" to Jean Baudrillard's analysis of a postmodern culture of circulating "simulacra" in which exchange-value completely displaces use-value, Rousseau's philosophic legacy remains powerful and influential.

What distinguishes K from those he encounters both in and out of the camps is his relative lack of social vanity, or to employ Hegelian terminology, his unusually weak desire for recognition.[28] The anonymity of Coetzee's protagonist is in fact inscribed in the title of the novel that bears his enigmatic name—*Michael K.* Coetzee steadfastly refuses to divulge the last name or public identity of its principal character. K himself consistently fails to correct those who arbitrarily impose an apparently erroneous name upon him: the medical officer, for example, who calls K "Michaels." What paradoxically distinguishes K is his extraordinary and voluntary obscurity. The medical officer who falls under his sway describes K in the following manner: "No papers, no money; no family, no friends, no sense of who you are. The obscurest of the obscure, so obscure as to be a prodigy."[29] In fact, K increasingly seems motivated by a desire opposed to that which Hegel credits to human beings: he wishes to go unrecognized, to leave absolutely no mark on the face of the earth. He thinks of himself "not as something heavy that left tracks behind it, but if anything as a speck upon the surface of an earth too deeply asleep to notice the scratch of ant-feet, the rasp of butterfly teeth, the tumbling of dust." On the abandoned farm of the Visagies, K assumes the life of one who "must live so that he leaves no trace of his living."[30] In effect, K embarks on the remarkable and difficult enterprise of complete self-obliteration, a task that he conceives as the obverse of civilizing the wilderness, taming the land, establishing a new dynasty:

> The worst mistake, he told himself, would be to try to found a new house, a rival line. . . . Even his tools should be of wood and leather and gut, materials the insects would eat when one day he no longer needed them.[31]

Like Rousseau on St. Peter's Island, K wishes to leave as little impression of his own existence as possible on the face of nature.

Regarded by others as a "simpleton," K nevertheless powerfully attracts the medical officer at the Kenilworth camp, who marvels at the
complete freedom of his patient from mediated desire. Like the characters who surround another "idiot," Dostoevsky's Prince Myshkin,
the medical officer finds that the individual who is indifferent to
social opinion becomes the object of obsessive fascination for others.
The very lack of vanity and amour propre in K and Myshkin excites
and inflames the envy and desire of those who surround them.[32] In
Hegelian terms, the less K desires the recognition of the other, the
more the other desires the recognition of K. The ultimate irony of
K's disinterest in social recognition becomes evident in the medical
officer's unsent letter to K: the writer imagines himself vainly chasing
after the fleeing K, desperately seeking his notice, wishing to join K
in his flight from the camp and all civilization.[33]

But if K's lack of desire for recognition paradoxically provokes that
very recognition in another, it cannot by its very nature produce a
political alteration in the regime. For without a strong desire for
recognition, which takes the form of the demand to have one's human
dignity publicly acknowledged, K cannot take political activity very
seriously. That is, the demand to be treated by others with dignity and
justice, which for Hegel provides the basis of all politically revolutionary activity, is essentially a socially mediated desire. To be sure,
K does not wish to be imprisoned or enslaved, but he is not willing
to fight for his freedom—only to run away whenever he can manage
it. On the whole, K simply does not much care what others think of
him, and, having no concern for his public reputation or dignity, he
is finally indifferent to social and political demands for justice.

Although Rousseau spent much of his life writing about the nature
of political justice, by the time he came to compose the *Reveries*
he had reached a comparable state of detachment. He characterizes
his attitude toward his own persecution as that of resignation rather
than resistance: "I have found compensation for all my hurts in this
resignation through the tranquility it provides me, tranquility which
could not be united with the continual toil of a resistance as painful as it was fruitless." Rousseau considers that his only "duty" is to
"abstain" altogether from social activity. The only moral good that
he is any longer capable of doing is refusing to act: "I know that the
only good which might henceforth be within my power is to abstain

from acting, from fear of doing evil without wanting to and without knowing it." Rousseau's detachment from society, his indifference to political concerns for justice, is precisely what makes him, in his own eyes, a divinity: he is "unperturbed, like God himself." From the perspective of those still immersed in the struggle for recognition and political justice, such a god is indistinguishable from a beast. Accordingly, Rousseau recognizes that society sees him as "a monster, a poisoner, an assassin."[34] This double and divided image of the solitary walker as both lower and higher than civilized man, a beast and a god, finds its way unobtrusively into the medical officer's characterization of Rousseau's heir, Michael K: "I am the only one who sees you for the original soul you are. . . . I alone see you as neither a soft case for a soft camp nor a hard case for a hard camp but a human soul above and beneath classification, a soul blessedly untouched by doctrine, untouched by history."[35]

≡≡≡≡≡

But what, one may well ask, is an unperturbed god to do? What, finally, is so attractive about the life of a solitary walker besides the negative freedom from social responsibility that he finds so onerous and burdensome? The answers to these questions lead us to a phenomenological analysis of the reverie itself; for it is the subjective experiential character of the reverie that ultimately provides both Rousseau and Michael K with a form of contentment that is inaccessible to those enmeshed in social relationships. First and foremost, the reverie is a release from the passions—socially created or inculcated passions—that are at the root of the perpetual discontent of civilized man. Rousseau repeatedly stresses the calm and tranquility he experiences, sensations that also characterize Michael K, who "wants nothing" at the mouth of the cave in the Swartberg.

This release from the passions opens up the solitary walker to a new (or renewed) relationship to nature. Whereas civilized man comes to regard nature as something to be conquered, controlled, and manipulated for the sake of an ever-expanding range of desires, the solitary walker reverts to an unmediated relationship with nature, in which the subject/object distinction between human consciousness and the natural world is overcome.[36] When a reverie is brought on by a violent collision with a Great Dane that knocks him nearly senseless, Rousseau remarks: "[I]t seemed to me that I filled all the objects I perceived with my frail existence. . . . I had no distinct notion of my person nor the least idea of what had just happened to me; I knew neither who I was nor where I was." Later, on St. Peter's Island, when reviewing the "trees, shrubs, and plants" that form the objects of his botanical observations, Rousseau notes that as he gradually sinks into reverie he feels himself swallowed up in the immensity of the natural world:

> The more sensitive a soul a contemplator has, the more he gives himself up to the ecstasies this harmony arouses in him. A sweet and deep reverie takes possession of his senses then, and through a delicious intoxication he loses himself in the immensity of this beautiful system with which he feels himself one. Then, all particular objects elude him; he sees and feels nothing except in the whole.[37]

In Michael K's case, the merging of self and nature takes the form of a radical askesis: self-imposed and nearly total starvation. As his bodily appetites dwindle and K sinks into a physical stupor, he increasingly imagines himself, in the form of his decayed body, slowly merging with the organic world about him: "It came home to him that he might die, he or his body, it was the same thing, that he might lie here till the moss on the roof grew dark before his eyes, that his story might end with his bones growing white in this faroff place."[38]

This gradual erosion of the boundary between the ego and the natural world also induces in the self a new experience of time. Whereas man in civil society must observe "clock-time," the publicly agreed upon measure of marking duration into objectively equivalent quantifiable units, natural man of the *Second Discourse* is "given over to the sole sentiment of its present existence without any idea of the future."[39] Likewise, Rousseau in his reverie is "entirely absorbed in the present moment." The reverie offers Rousseau an opportunity to lose himself in a state in which neither a sense of the past nor of the future encroaches upon him, in which "time is nothing," in which the "present lasts forever without, however, making its duration noticed and without any trace of time's passage." "As long as this state lasts," he confesses, "we are sufficient unto ourselves, like God." In this experience, Rousseau finds "supreme felicity."[40]

Michael K's reveries on the Visagie farm involve a similar detachment from the regulated and structured clock-time of civilized existence:

> He had kept no tally of the days nor recorded the changes of the moon. . . . [H]e was learning to love idleness, idleness no longer as stretches of freedom reclaimed by stealth here and there from involuntary labour, surreptitious thefts to be enjoyed sitting on his heels before a flowerbed with the fork dangling from his fingers, but as a yielding up of himself to time, to a time flowing slowly like oil from horizon to horizon over the face of the world, washing over his body, circulating in his armpits and his groin, stirring his eyelids. . . . [A]ll that was moving was time, bearing him onward in its flow. . . . [H]e was living beyond the reach of calendar and clock in a blessedly neglected corner, half awake, half asleep.[41]

Like Rousseau, K finds that his existential submersion in the cycle of the days and seasons, his sense of an endlessly repeating present, produces in him a feeling of utter contentment:

> He did not turn his cave into a home or keep a record of the passage of the days. There was nothing to look forward to but the sight, every morning, of the shadow of the rim of the mountain chasing faster and faster towards him till all of a sudden he was bathed in sunlight. . . . He wondered if he were living in what was known as bliss.[42]

In this atemporal state, the solitary walker finds that he can enjoy a primordial experience which is covered over and hidden from him when he lives in society: the pure and rarified sensation of merely existing. What Rousseau calls the "sentiment" of "existence" reappears in Michael K as a "deep joy in his physical being."

This cancellation of the socialized experience of time, of chronology, helps to explain the central role that memory and recollection play for both Rousseau and Michael K. Precisely because the reverie consists of an immersion in an eternal present, the gulf that separates one reverie from another over time is annihilated in the reverie itself. A "present" reverie is in a fundamental sense indistinguishable from a "past" or "future" one. Thus Rousseau can take as much or even more joy in the recollection of a past reverie as he does in his initial experience of it. In a similar fashion, Michael K can enter his reverie at the mouth of the cave in the Swartberg via a recollected reverie from his days at Huis Norenius; in turn, the reverie in the Swartberg is almost identical to that which he experiences later in his burrow on the Visagie farm.

This series of atemporal reveries ultimately offers Rousseau and Michael K the closest approximation they are likely to experience of an unmediated existence. For a time, they seem immersed in *being* itself. Befitting those who elect to return to the condition of natural man, such a state is, quite literally, subhuman and pre- or nonlinguistic.[43] Not only is there no communication with others, there is no discourse with the self. Rousseau insists that his reveries are different from and opposed to "thought" or even "meditation." Thinking requires labor and an engagement with the social world; it therefore threatens to rob Rousseau of the deep pleasure of the reverie.[44] In Coetzee's essay on René Girard and triangular desire, he makes explicit the connection between an unmediated world of existence and silence: "the contrast is between an unmediated original and a fallen, mediated modern [world]; and the hidden yearning is for an unmediated world, that is, a world without language."[45] What troubles some critics about Michael K, his apparent simplicity or stupidity, his lack of linguistic facility (marked by his cleft palate), and his inclination toward silence can be understood less as social liabilities (which they are) than as "natural" advantages that facilitate K's return to an unmediated and nonlinguistic state of being.

———

The primordial existential state of the solitary walker is not equivalent to that which Heidegger describes in *Being and Time*. For Heidegger, the overcoming of the tyranny of clock-time and the uncovering of the existential experience of temporality actually heighten rather than diminish *Dasein*'s sense of the past and the future. *Dasein* is acutely aware of its finitude, of its inevitable impending death. By

contrast, for Rousseau, the reverie offers a momentary sense of immortality, of living in an eternal present in which the self's anxiety
concerning the future is removed. Nevertheless, this immersion in
the present, for both Rousseau and Michael K, serves as a means
of addressing the question of one's mortality. For the reverie grants
to both a remarkable detachment from and disinterest in their own
mortal bodies.

In the Second Walk, when Rousseau is violently up-ended by a
Great Dane and hurled into his first reverie, he finds himself surprisingly indifferent to his own rather considerable injuries:

> I watched my blood flow as I would have watched a brook flow,
> without even suspecting that this blood belonged to me in any
> way. I felt a rapturous calm in my whole being; and each time I
> remember it, I find nothing comparable to it in all the activity of
> known pleasures.[46]

In his state of perpetual somnolence, Michael K experiences an analogous detachment from his bodily needs: he must constantly remind
himself to eat, although he can hardly muster the will to perform this
vitally necessary task. The most basic physiological functions suddenly seem dispensable to K: "You are forgetting to breathe, he would
say to himself, and yet lie without breathing." One might say that
Michael K, like Rousseau, overcomes the fear of death only by ap-
proximating a condition of lifelessness; by asymptotically approaching a state of nonexistence, the solitary walker blurs the boundary
that demarcates life from death. As the medical officer puts it, K approaches "as near to a state of life in death or death in life . . . as is
humanly possible."[47]

But the natural limits placed upon the solitary walker by the physical demands of the body frustrate his quest for absolute freedom and
ultimately compel him to enter civil society once more. For though
the reverie at its deepest and most satisfying level may approximate
death, the experience itself is possible only if the solitary walker is
literally alive. In fact, a somewhat less idealistic interpretation of
the phenomenological experience of the reverie would suggest a material cause for many of its most peculiar characteristics. Rousseau's

indifference to his own injuries might be understood by a physician as a symptom of shock (Rousseau himself offers this explanation as a possibility), while the delirium and listlessness of Michael K can be interpreted as the effects of a lowered metabolic rate brought on by malnutrition or starvation. By introducing the medical officer as a commentator on K's life in the second part of his novel, Coetzee recognizes the cogency, if not the authority, of this physiological interpretation of the reverie.

Although Rousseau praises detachment from the body and elevates spiritual needs over material ones, the organization of the ten chapters of the *Reveries* implicitly acknowledges that bodily needs cannot ever be fully overcome. Whereas the most extended and detailed description of a reverie comes in the central Fifth Walk, the opening two chapters deal with the pains of old age and bodily injury, and the last two touch upon the attractions of food and physical love. The body, it seems, is both the entrance to and the exit from the spiritual ecstasy of the reverie. Michael K's reveries are similarly bounded by the demands of the body; K cannot sustain himself in the Swartberg or on the veld. Were it not for his retreat down the mountainside to the city of Prince Albert and the arrival of the army patrol at the Visagie farm, it seems clear that K would simply die of hunger. At the most basic level of human existence, the body provides an undeniable link between the life of the most solitary individual and the social existence of civilized humanity. In his interviews with David Attwell, Coetzee has explicitly recognized the power of the body, most particularly the body in pain, as the ultimate ontological standard and authority that cannot be ignored, the thing that necessarily leads us back to politics and political life:

> I see a simple (simple-minded?) standard erected. That standard is the body. Whatever else, the body is not "that which is not," and the proof that it *is* is the pain it feels. The body with its pain becomes a counter to the endless trials of doubt. . . . Let me put it baldly: in South Africa it is not possible to deny the authority of suffering and therefore of the body. It is not possible, not for logical reasons, not for ethical reasons, . . . but for political reasons, for reasons of power. And let me again be unambiguous: it

is not that one *grants* the authority of the suffering body: the suffering body *takes* this authority: that is its power. To use other words: its power is undeniable.[48]

And although the pain of the body is the ultimate compulsory authority that forces Michael K back into the camps, the pleasures of the body, even the most innocent, pure, and intense, can exercise the same effect upon the solitary walker. In one of the most tactile and beautiful scenes in the novel, K relishes a bite of the first fruits of his private garden:

> Such pumpkin, he thought, such pumpkin I could eat every day of my life and never want anything else. And what perfection it would be with a pinch of salt—with a pinch of salt, and a dab of butter, and a sprinkling of sugar, and a little cinnamon scattered over the top![49]

Thus in the moment of greatest contentment and self-sufficiency, K discovers or recollects a taste for salt, butter, sugar, and cinnamon. Need we add that salt is mined, butter requires the domestication of cattle, sugar calls forth the entire modern industrial process of refining, with its unsavory links to the colonial slave plantations of the Caribbean, and that cinnamon was at the center of Dutch imperial ventures to control the spice trade in Ceylon (Sri Lanka) and the Moluccas at the beginning of the seventeenth century?[50] In one bite, Michael K, in all his innocence, summons up the history of civilization, with its attendant wars of imperial conquest and relentless industrial development.

Lest we think that Rousseau somehow shares Michael K's naiveté and lacks Coetzee's sense of irony, we should note that one of Rousseau's great pleasures on St. Peter's Island is the "founding of [a] little colony" of rabbits. Although Rousseau seems free of the vice of vanity and the ambitions that motivate his socialized fellows, he hints that even his apolitical botanical pursuits conceal a desire to rule over the earth, for he reminds us that the plants he studies form a *Regnum vegetabile*. And it is clear that the undisputed ruler of this kingdom is Rousseau himself, who, in the same passage in which he praises the disinterestedness of botanical studies, confesses to his impotent hatred of those who persecute him and on whom he would revenge himself.[51] Even the relatively simple Michael K develops a proprietary interest in his pumpkins, worrying that wild animals are preying on his crops. Although the fruits of the earth ideally belong to all, Michael K briefly considers building "a fence of stout wire mesh with its bottom edge staked a foot underground to stop the burrowers."[52] We are reminded immediately of the pivotal role that the fence-builder plays in the foundation of civilization in the *Second Discourse*. It would seem that gardening is neither so innocent nor so free of social and political consequences as it first appears. The simplest needs of the body and the most apolitical and solitary occupations contain the seeds of civilization, with all its burdens and sorrows.

═════

If the brute physical existence of the body supplies the material link between the solitary walker and civilization, then writing provides the ideological or discursive bond that is never completely broken. We have noted that the reverie is essentially nonlinguistic, a dwelling in silence. But whatever the supreme felicity offered to the solitary walker by the "unmediated world, the world without language," the reverie comes to us only via the medium of writing—the works called the *Reveries* and *Life & Times of Michael K*. This critical paradox— the inescapability of the mediated representation of unmediated experience—is recognized by both Rousseau and Coetzee, but never overcome. The acknowledgment of this, shall we say, logical contradiction, takes the form of a heightened self-consciousness of presentation and a deliberate disruption of conventional (unselfcritical) forms of narrative representation. In the Fourth Walk, Rousseau confesses to "concocting fables," while maintaining that a deeper truth is contained in his "fictions."[53] I cannot pause here to analyze in detail Rousseau's reflections on the esoteric form of writing he employs, one in which the deepest truths are concealed from the majority of his readers and revealed only to a select few. I would merely note that Rousseau demonstrates an acute consciousness of the fictive status of his *Reveries*, while insisting that it is possible to employ such fables as a means of pointing obliquely to a higher truth that cannot be stated openly or directly.

I take this hint as a partial explanation of the peculiarly achrono-
logical character of the *Reveries*; Rousseau's discourse proceeds pro-
leptically and analeptically, with apparent disregard for the strict
order of the events represented. The fictive effect produced is of spontaneously generated reveries that lie outside the conventional narrative flow of biographical chronology, and of an elliptical "life" with
an extraordinary number of gaps for which Rousseau fails to account.
For although Rousseau claims that the *Reveries* are a continuation of
his *Confessions*, he reveals remarkably little of his life from 1765 (the
last period covered by the *Confessions*) to 1778 (the year in which
he began writing the *Reveries*). To call Rousseau's narrative "postmodern" must surely seem anachronistic; nevertheless, the narrative
techniques he employs are analogous to those that Coetzee uses in
Life & Times of Michael K.

These self-reflexive and self-critical features signal Coetzee's
awareness of the contradictory aims of representing in his publicly
available writing the unmediated nonlinguistic and asocial experiences of his solitary walker. Most notably, this textual self-reflexivity
manifests itself in K's inability to tell his own story; like Beckett's
vagabonds, K finds that his life contains unaccountable "gaps":

> Always, when he tried to explain himself to himself, there re-
> mained a gap, a hole, a darkness before which his understanding
> baulked, into which it was useless to put words. The words were
> eaten up, the gap remained. His was always a story with a hole
> in it: a wrong story, always wrong.[54]

The reason K can never give a full or satisfying account of his life
to himself, or for that matter to anyone else, is that the most important moments of his existence—his reveries—are precisely those
that cannot fully or finally be expressed in and through language. In
effect, language can only provide a social context for something that
cannot be represented.

The other characters K encounters demand a complete account
from the protagonist, one he is unable to provide. Unwilling to grant
him a right to silence, even those who come closest to appreciating
K, such as the medical officer, ultimately resort to imposing on him
or inventing for him a story.[55] They compel K to reenter the world of

recorded history, the world of politics and written laws. By providing an official account of his life, the medical officer and Major van Rensburg, however well-motivated and humane they may be, once more shackle Michael K with the "iron" "laws of nations."[56] But if writing is a tool of state power, an iron manacle of history, what are we to make of Coetzee's own writing?

The self-critical features of Coetzee's postmodern narrative are his limited, but nevertheless significant response to this aporia. The self-conscious fictiveness of *Michael K* is finally intended as the admittedly weak, but only available counter to the power of history. In his interviews with David Attwell, Coetzee speaks of the external authority of history and the force of politics.[57] Just as K must ultimately acknowledge the hold that society has upon him, and the transitory and effectively powerless state of the solitary reverie, so too must Coetzee acknowledge that the world of fiction is not fully autonomous or immune to external forces. Yet it is fair to say that Coetzee's fiction forms an intermediate state halfway between the nonlinguistic world of the unmediated reverie and the authoritative world of politics and history. In his little-known essay, "The Novel Today," Coetzee looks to storytelling, to the world of the novel as a "rival to history," a kind of discursive space that provides a limited autonomy to those who dwell there; such a world offers "an other mode of thinking," and, one is tempted to say, an *other* mode of being as well.[58]

Neither Rousseau nor Coetzee would deny the ultimate power of the political world, and yet they also understand that its very oppressiveness may provoke a quest for an alternative realm of radical freedom and autonomous solitude. The epigraph to *Michael K*, taken from Heraclitus's *The Cosmic Fragments*, hints at a paradoxical relationship between the freedom of the self and the tyranny of political life:

> War is the father of all and the king of all.
> Some he shows as gods, others as men.
> Some he makes slaves, and others free.

It is war that makes possible K's transitory freedom and compels him toward the world—however ephemeral, insubstantial, and parasitical—of the reverie. In a similar fashion, it is Rousseau's political and religious persecution that drives him to St. Peter's Island and to the composition of the *Reveries*. If war—the most terrible form that the overweening authority of politics can assume—is king, then its power, at the very least, creates the desire for a realm outside of history: a life on the island of fiction.

Notes

1   J. M. Coetzee, *Life & Times of Michael K* (New York, 1985 [1983]), 151.
2   Of course, not all of Rousseau's major works articulate this apolitical or antipolitical critique of politics. In such works as the *Social Contract, Discourse on the Sciences and the Arts, Discourse on the Origin and Foundations of Inequality, Discourse on Political Economy,* the *Letter to d'Alembert on the Theatre,* and *Considerations on the Government in Poland,* Rousseau engages in the elaboration of what he regards as the best regime possible in the modern age. As opposed to these explicitly political writings, the *Reveries,* along with such works as the *Confessions,* form an important countercurrent in Rousseau's thought. Although it is possible to argue for the overall coherence of these two distinct strains in Rousseau's work, I shall not make such an attempt in this essay.
3   See Nadine Gordimer, "The Idea of Gardening," *New York Review of Books,* 2 February 1984, 3, 6.
4   Coetzee's familiarity with Rousseau's work is evident in his many critical essays, most notably in "Confession and Double Thoughts: Tolstoy, Rousseau, Dostoevsky," where he makes particular mention of the *Reveries.* See his *Doubling the Point: Essays and Interviews,* ed. David Attwell (Cambridge, MA, 1992), 251–93.
5   Coetzee, *Michael K,* 68–69; emphasis mine.
6   Jean-Jacques Rousseau, *The Reveries of the Solitary Walker,* trans. Charles E. Butterworth (New York, 1979), 62.
7   Ibid., 63, 64.
8   Ibid., 70. The phrase in the original French is "la plus molle oisiveté." See *Les Rêveries du promeneur solitaire* (Paris, 1960), 73.
9   J. M. Coetzee, "Idleness in South Africa," in *White Writing: On the Culture of Letters in South Africa* (New Haven, 1988), 35.
10 Rousseau, *Reveries,* 93, 96, 94. For a more complete analysis of the philosophic and political status of botany in the *Reveries,* see Paul A. Cantor, "The Metaphysics of Botany: Rousseau and the New Criticism of Plants," *Southwest Review* 70 (1985): 362–80.
11 Jean-Jacques Rousseau, *The First and Second Discourses,* trans. Roger D. and Judith R. Masters (New York, 1964), 141–42.
12 Coetzee, *Michael K,* 47.

13 Ibid., 97, 139.

14 Rousseau, *Reveries*, 62.

15 Coetzee, *Michael K*, 162–63.

16 Ibid., 166.

17 Rousseau, *Reveries*, 64.

18 Ibid., 5.

19 See Aristotle, *The Politics*, 1252a–b.

20 See Rousseau, *First and Second Discourses*, 134–37.

21 Coetzee, *Michael K*, 104.

22 Ibid., 109.

23 Coetzee, *Doubling the Point*, 207.

24 Coetzee, *Michael K*, 181.

25 Rousseau, *Reveries*, 75–76.

26 Rousseau, *First and Second Discourses*, 179; see also 116, 129, 135–37, and 148–49.

27 Coetzee's knowledge of and interest in Hegel's *Phenomenology* are evident in his interviews with David Attwell; see *Doubling the Point*, 58, 131, 378.

28 There are isolated instances, especially in the beginning of the novel, in which Michael K exhibits a much more conventional attachment to his person, property, and dignity: for example, he repels the thieves who attempt to rob him and his mother on their way to Prince Albert. Over the course of the novel, however, K increasingly abstains from such aggressive acts, slipping into an ever more passive state.

29 Coetzee, *Michael K*, 142.

30 Ibid., 97, 99.

31 Ibid., 104.

32 My reading of both Dostoevsky's and Coetzee's novels is indebted to René Girard's *Deceit, Desire, and the Novel*, trans. Yvonne Freccero (Baltimore, 1965), esp. 163–64. Girard's work is a direct influence on Coetzee; see the latter's "Triangular Structures of Desire in Advertising," in *Doubling the Point*, 127–38.

33 Coetzee, *Michael K*, 167.

34 Rousseau, *Reveries*, 2, 6, 75, 5.

35 Coetzee, *Michael K*, 151.

36 One form this disavowal of man's power over nature takes is the vegetarianism of natural man in the *Second Discourse* and of Michael K. No doubt the latter's dietary habits in some respects reflect those of his creator, but reference to this biographical detail finally begs the question of the thematic and philosophic importance of vegetarianism in *Michael K*.

37 Rousseau, *Reveries*, 16, 92.

38 Coetzee, *Michael K*, 69.

39 Rousseau, *First and Second Discourses*, 117.

40 Rousseau, *Reveries*, 16, 68, 69.

41 Coetzee, *Michael K*, 115–16.

42 Ibid., 68.

43   For Rousseau's observation in his *Second Discourse* that natural man lacks language, see 119–26.

44   Rousseau, *Reveries*, 91.

45   Coetzee, *Doubling the Point*, 138.

46   Rousseau, *Reveries*, 16.

47   Coetzee, *Michael K*, 118, 159.

48   Coetzee, *Doubling the Point*, 248.

49   Coetzee, *Michael K*, 114.

50   On the histories of sugar production and the spice trade, see Sidney W. Mintz, *Sweetness and Power: The Place of Sugar in Modern History* (Harmondsworth, 1985); and Holden Furber, *Rival Empires of Trade in the Orient, 1600–1800* (Minneapolis, 1976), 6, 52, 54–57.

51   Rousseau, *Reveries*, 66, 90.

52   Coetzee, *Michael K*, 117.

53   Rousseau, *Reveries*, 57, 48.

54   Coetzee, *Michael K*, 110.

55   Ibid.; see 140, 149–50, 155.

56   For an account of the connection between writing, history, and the power of the state in Coetzee's work, see Michael Valdez Moses, "The Mark of Empire: Writing, History, and Torture in Coetzee's *Waiting for the Barbarians*," *Kenyon Review* 15 (1993): 115–27.

57   Coetzee, *Doubling the Point*, 64–68.

58   J. M. Coetzee, "The Novel Today," *Upstream* 6 (1988): 3–4.

Caroline Rody

The Mad Colonial Daughter's Revolt:
J. M. Coetzee's *In the Heart of the Country*

In the annals of English imperial literature, perhaps no white female character plays a more unfortunate or predictable role than the deluded Adela Quested, she who hallucinates the "insult" to her person by Dr. Aziz in the Marabar Caves, in Forster's *A Passage to India*. Standing in for her entire people and its Orientalist projections, Miss Quested, by imagining the dark man's touch, creates the crisis on which the whole plot turns. But when the incident that begins at the Marabar Caves has been closed, she is quickly dropped from the plot, while her companion Mrs. Moore dies, a mad nihilist, at sea. Concerned primarily with the (im)possibilities of a cross-cultural relationship between his male characters, Forster spends little time envisioning transcendent "connection" in the female. It is upon these "good" English *women*, however, that Forster places most of the weight of the novel's psychological quest. Arriving in India as naifs, Miss Quested and Mrs. Moore hope to meet Indians on a more or less equal basis, but are defeated by

The *South Atlantic Quarterly* 93:1, Winter 1994.
Copyright © 1994 by Duke University Press.
CCC 0038-2876/94/$1.50.

the class distinctions and social prohibitions of a colonial society. And at the Marabar Caves both suffer incapacitating sexual and spiritual experiences, after which they exit the plot, poignant casualties of the (sub-military) imperialist wars.

What does *A Passage to India* tell us about the white woman's burden? At the novel's opening an Indian character wagers that he will "give any Englishman two years" in India before he loses his liberal values and becomes a racist imperial martinet; "and," he adds, "I give any Englishwoman six months." Indeed, the women of Forster's Anglo-Indian club society do exhibit a bigotry and pettiness surpassing that of their husbands. But the fate of his "good" Englishwomen reveals an insight more subtle than the misogyny of which Forster is sometimes capable: that women tend to be particularly vulnerable to, particularly disturbed by, the experience of being colonizers, part of an oppressive white European presence in someone else's land. They tend to get nasty, the novel suggests, or to start asking themselves deep and painful questions, and even, with some regularity, to go mad.

In the Anglo-Indian world of *A Passage to India* several explanations for these behaviors can be noted—chief among them the lack of anything at all for white women to do. Further, the text suggests, as do many other anti- and postcolonial novels, that in their position in the colonial power hierarchy, below white men and above native/black men and native/black women, white women are uncomfortably situated as inferior members of the dominant but deracinated group. What is in the colonial lives of white men a simpler experience of occupying the high side of every binary opposition is in the lives of white women more complex. Forster's women must at all times obey the men in charge—who may be their sons or their fiancés. They must give orders to native male servants all day long at home, but elsewhere avoid the danger of finding themselves unescorted—thus disempowered—in their presence. The native women decline to offer themselves as subjects of real encounters for the English women; too much embarrassment ensues when conversation is attempted.

Central to the white women's problem and to their plot, inevitably, is the threat that Forster exploits to the fullest: the sexual encounter between white woman and dark man, in the danger zone between the middle rungs of the social scale. This opposition is by no means "binary," but rather is multiply determined; the power dynamics within it are unusually vulnerable to circumstance and personality, with the slightest encounter between a white woman and a native or black man threatening to develop into a sexual crisis capable of toppling the whole shaky ladder. In *A Passage to India* Forster relies upon the pivotal position of white women to advance a homosocial colonial romance; just as the incautious friendliness of the grandmotherly Mrs. Moore is needed to initiate the novel's flirtation with Dr. Aziz, so Adela Quested is, as Sara Suleri observes, "a conduit or passageway for the aborted eroticism between the European Fielding and the Indian Aziz."[1] An English virgin brought to India to consider marriage with a British officer, she is a character designed to enact the psychosexual fantasy of her race and thus to embody the failure of English liberal humanism.

But after all, what kind of hope can Miss Quested really have? I have long wondered why no one remarks on the absurdity of her name: What kind of hero's chance can one have with the name quest-*ed*? The contradictions of Adela's existence are wonderfully encapsulated right there; an individual marked as the *object* of a quest is unlikely to *find* much of anything. And indeed, in her appalling moment of truth inside the cave, Adela's fearful insight is that she is not, as she had thought herself, an explorer, a seeker of knowledge, but rather just what she had always heard herself called: *quested*.

More recent anticolonial literature has begun to imagine an Adela who rebels against her own passive construction, as it were. An emerging body of texts by women writers, including Jean Rhys, Nadine Gordimer, Doris Lessing, and Caryl Churchill, reinvestigates the subjectivity of the white colonial woman.[2] But it is in the work of a male writer that the literature of the white colonial daughter produces its most defiant heroine yet. J. M. Coetzee's 1977 novel *In the Heart of the Country* presents a woman whose furious rebellion, in words and violent action, against the patriarchal, imperialist structure of her world reinflects the conventional "madness" of her literary kind. Uniting sociopolitical subversion and literary-historical revision, Coetzee's heroine voices opposition not only to earlier characterizations of white colonial women, but to characterization itself, to her very imprisonment in literary discourse. She thus stages a metaphoric revolt against, simultaneously, the regimes of language and literature, and of patriarchy and colonialism, inscribing a degree of alienation and rage within the upper echelons of the colonial system far beyond what texts by white writers had shown in the past. The voice of a white colonial daughter—like Miss Quested, both victimized and compromised, heir to both halves of her family name—proves an apt medium for this complex critique.

—————

"There was a time when I imagined that if I talked long enough," says Coetzee's narrator, "it would be revealed to me what it means to be an angry spinster in the heart of nowhere."[3] Such is the discourse of a colonial heroine who has made the postmodern turn, glimpsing at once the surface of her writtenness and the oppressive structure of her social world while elaborating a tragicomic deconstruction of both. In this rambling, female voice Coetzee creates a tour de force of postmodern lyricism, compressed yet expansive, by turns farcical and poignant, in which a woman attempts to write herself into being while struggling against the exigencies of novelistic plot. With devastating irony and artful comic delivery, this speaker narrates her life in a succession of numbered paragraphs, the diary entries of a self-fabulating consciousness.

But this is also the voice of a woman, a white woman named at one point "Magda," who is firmly situated on a remote farm of the South African veld, where her isolated and unhappy life with an "angry, loveless" father and her paltry communications with the other two people in her world, a black servant couple, make her "a poetess of interiority," seeking in writing the uneasy solace of self-creation. In the narration of *In the Heart of the Country* Coetzee explores a liminal territory between mimesis and self-reflection, life and language, in which a narrative presence oscillates, turns back upon itself, rises to awareness of its own entrapment, and revolts. This volatile speaking position Coetzee assigns to a white daughter of the colonies, and in her effusive, subversive *écriture féminine* she demonstrates that the attribution of this extreme degree of alienation in language to her particular narrative voice is no accident. If we are uncertain whether we are confronted with a character in a realist plot or with a paper-thin literary trope, so is Magda, whose angst derives from being "written" into both a conventional narrative and the colonial social order. She asks the page before her:

> Am I an angry yet somehow after all complacent farmyard spinster . . . ? The story of my rage and its dire sequel: am I going to climb into this vehicle and close my eyes and be carried downstream . . . ? What automatism is this, what liberation is it going to bring me, and without liberation what is the point of my story? Do I feel rich outrage at my spinster fate? Who is behind my oppression? . . . Am I . . . to be crucified head downward as a warning to those who love their rage and lack all vision of another tale? But what other tale is there for me? Marriage to the neighbour's second son? I am not a happy peasant. I am a miserable black virgin, and my story is my story, even if it is a dull black blind stupid miserable story, ignorant of its meaning and of all its many possible untapped happy variants. I am I. Character is fate. History is God. Pique, pique, pique.[4]

The complaint of this text-obsessed, text-dependent voice against the tyranny of literary plot is also a protest against a confining social position. Magda's characterization thus operates on several levels: she is in some sense a woman with a plight and a plot; at the same time she is a garrulous talking head straight out of Beckett; and, in the confluence of the postcolonial and the postmodern, she is also gender-, race-, and class-marked language itself, given a body from which to lament its own self-entrapment. She is perhaps the best spokesperson we have for a person's—or a text's—entrapment in language:

> Words are coin. Words alienate. Language is no medium for desire. Desire is rapture, not exchange. It is only by alienating the desired that language masters it. Hendrik's bride, her sly doe-eyes, her narrow hips, are beyond the grope of words until desire consents to mutate into the curiosity of the watcher. The frenzy of desire in the medium of words yields the mania of the catalogue. I struggle with the proverbs of hell.[5]

Contextualizing a Beckettian consciousness in colonial history and the politics of gender and race, Coetzee fuses two kinds of alienation: this white colonial woman is extremely well situated to voice the frustrations of life in language, and this paper-thin narrator, unwillingly speaking a language she did not create, protests the oppressions and divisions in human life more loudly and effectively than many a more conventionally realized literary soul.

Among the most daring experimenters with a white postcolonial literature, Coetzee's characteristic mode might be described in a phrase that Linda Hutcheon applies not to postcolonial but to postmodern discourse: "complicitous critique."[6] That is to say, his postcolonial novels, scrutinizing the implication of whites in colonial power systems, are saturated with the self-reflexive irony and parody that have come to be most closely associated with white, male European and American "postmodern" writers. Because the term "postmodern" tends not to be applied to black and native postcolonial texts that—unsurprisingly—lack this tone of "complicity," its usefulness as a master term for our literary era is limited. But in his tragicomic fables of the complicitous white soul, Coetzee bridges this divide, demonstrating the link between postmodern "complicitous critique" and the nexus of race and power characteristic of postcolonial texts.

In the vehicle of a mad, white colonial daughter's revolt, Coetzee fuses the postmodern and the postcolonial with a feminist aesthetic, finding in feminist critique a subversive way into the heart of the colonial conundrum and the postmodern condition. Both *In the Heart of the Country* and his 1986 novel *Foe* use the voices of white women to create a complex, contradictory discourse coextensive with their author's postcolonial postmodernity. Like the Magistrate at the scene of his public humiliation in *Waiting for the Barbarians*, Coetzee is dressed "in a woman's clothes" in *In the Heart of the Country* and *Foe* and, thus freed of a certain entitlement, can "roar" in something a bit closer to "barbarian language." While the black characters in Coetzee's oeuvre, notably, the barbarian girl in *Waiting for the Barbarians* and Friday in *Foe*, remain resolutely silent, their self-understandings inaccessible to "white writing" (as Coetzee titled his collection of essays on white South African literature), the more accessible voice of a white woman makes available to the white, male postcolonial writer a speaking position of less authority but more credible pain, of simultaneous power and subjection, complicity and subversion.[7] By developing in Magda a feminist voice equal to any produced by women writers of recent fiction, Coetzee is also able to exploit, as fertile discursive resources for his postcolonial critique, the final refuge of the stubbornly resistant female literary mind— madness and its corollary: rich reserves of female anger.

The subversions enacted by Coetzee's Magda begin with her re- sistance to the laws of realist characterization. Combating the very writing that gives her breath, Magda struggles from beginning to end to emerge out of text and into life:

> Am I, I wonder, a thing among things, a body propelled along a track by sinews and bony levers, or am I a monologue moving through time, approximately five feet above the ground, if the ground does not turn out to be just another word, in which case I am indeed lost?[8]

She worries that between the numbered entries she may not exist: "A day must have intervened here. Where there is a blank there must have been a day." But at other times she insists, "I am sure that I am real. This is my hand, bone and flesh." Oddly enough for a mere trope, Magda has a passionate love for nature. "I am corrupted to the bone with the beauty of this forsaken world," she says, and be- lieves that the world intends communication with humanity: "[W]hy these glorious sunsets, I ask myself, if nature does not speak to us with tongues of fire?" But her desire for communion with nature is unrequited, returning her to her fundamental alienation:

> [F]rom me only do these flowers draw the energy that enables them to commune with themselves, with each other, in their ecstasy of pure being, just as the stones and bushes of the veld hum with life, with such happiness that happiness is not the word, because I am here to set them vibrating with their own variety of material awareness that I am forever not they, and they not I, that I can never be the rapture of pure self that they are but am alas forever set off from them by the babble of words

within me. . . . The farm, the desert, the whole world as far as
the horizon is in an ecstasy of communion with itself, exalted
by the vain urge of my consciousness to inhabit it. Such are the
thoughts I think looking at the wallpaper. . . . Would that I had
never learned to read.[9]

Magda's desire to join the life of nature is inevitably frustrated by
the problem of words, the coin in her pocket that keeps her impli-
cated in the alienating economy of human discourse. If she could
escape from words, it seems to her, she would really be entering life:

I wish only to be at home in the world as the merest beast is at
home. Much, much less than all would satisfy me: to begin with,
a life unmediated by words: these stones, these bushes, this sky
experienced and known without question.

Although a self-consciously "written" narrator, Magda expresses a
striking desire to be a real person in a world outside of a book. She
does not want to be a mere trope, though her author gives her reason
to fear she is one. She chides herself for lacking the assertiveness of
"a woman with red blood in her veins (what color is mine? a watery
pink? an inky violet?)" or, on the other hand, of "a woman determined to be the author of her own life." If she is, indeed, written, a
woman with ink in her veins, then she will preferably do the writing herself. She alternates between the desire to be in life and the
desire to "write" or create her own life; "life" thus becomes conflated
with escape from male prose. For it is *as a woman* that Magda resists
her postmodern characterization:

I was not, after all, made to live alone. If I had been set down by
fate in the middle of the veld in the middle of nowhere, buried to
my waist and commanded to live a life, I could not have done it.
I am not a philosopher. Women are not philosophers, and I am a
woman. . . . I am not a principle, a rule of discourse, a machine
planted by a being from another planet on this desolate earth beneath the Southern Cross to generate sentiments day after day,
night after night, keeping count of them as I go. . . . I need
people to talk to, brothers and sisters or fathers and mothers,
I need a history and a culture, I need hopes and aspirations, I

need a moral sense and a teleology before I will be happy, not to mention food and drink.

She does not want to be the Beckett persona she resembles because a woman needs life, not just words. Voicing in the female a desire for connection to people, to nature, to life itself, Coetzee's text uses feminism to challenge the limits of the postmodern. It represents a female subjectivity "written" into patriarchy and postmodern self-reflexivity at once, which yet expresses a vision of community and conversation beyond these categories:

> For the day will come when I must have another human being, must hear another voice, even if it speaks only abuse. This monologue of the self is a maze of words out of which I shall not find a way until someone else gives me a lead.[10]

A similar protest against writtenness and an affirmation of life are made by Susan Barton in Coetzee's *Foe*, who, in many ways a sister character to Magda, engages in a power struggle over the text with the famous author Daniel Foe, announcing, "I am not a story, Mr. Foe." Both of these female characters, in effect, talk back to male authors, constituting moments when a text acknowledges in a female voice that it has not gotten hold of life, that something real and breathing has eluded it. Like Shakespeare's Cleopatra defying both her Roman conquerors and her author, declaring (in the voice of the boy actor who portrays her) that she would rather die than "see some squeaking Cleopatra boy my greatness" in Rome, these women rage against their captivity in the male writing that gives them voice. When, rebelling against his designs on them, Coetzee's literate, white female characters oppose writtenness to life itself and declare themselves to be as uncontainable in white male prose as are black characters like the illiterate, tongueless Friday, Coetzee evokes a degree of white, female alienation in Western discourse analogous to the experience of colonization. This rebellion against writtenness, and insistence on life, by the female characters who rage at the confines of Coetzee's fiction adds a "complicitous critique" of gender relations to those of race and power.

But Magda's feminist revolt against writing also performs a postcolonial literary revision. *In the Heart of the Country* revises a colonial literary type: the woman of the South African farm novel, discussed by Coetzee in *White Writing*. Magda seems derived particularly from the feminist heroine of Olive Schreiner's *The Story of an African Farm* (1883), which itself criticizes the farm novel convention.[11] Coetzee's text aggressively rejects that genre's idealization of the South African farm as a locus of distinct spiritual unity between humanity and nature: a mystical "marriage" between a lineage and a farm that Coetzee describes as "available only to landowners." Living in such a valorized landscape, the prototypical (male) South African farmer in this tradition is empowered by learning to "read nature" and thus to understand his place in it. He progresses beyond individual consciousness to "lineal consciousness" and, eventually, "towards the revelation of the farm as a source of meaning."[12]

In the Heart of the Country wickedly parodies the figure of the good descendant in Magda, who revolts most emphatically against "lineal consciousness" by killing her father, and who spends the rest of the novel trying (but failing) to read nature on a farm where she despairs of finding meaning and feels utterly unmarried to any person, place, or thing. Rejecting the ideologies that justify white South African rule, she asserts, "No one is ancestral to the stone desert" in which she lives, and indeed:

> I do not think it was ever intended that people should live here. This is a land made for insects who eat sand and lay eggs in each other's corpses and have no voices with which to scream when they die.

She extends this bleak view of her land to its colonial history, committing the heresy of imagining it from the point of view of conquered Africans, and concluding with a singularly uncelebratory portrait of her own family's entrance onto the scene:

> . . . my father and myself in this lonely house where we kick our heels waiting for the wool to grow and gather about ourselves the remnants of the lost tribes of the Hottentots to be hewers of wood and drawers of water and shepherds and body-servants in perpetuity and where we are devoured by boredom and pull the wings off flies.

In place of the revelations of unity offered in the conventional farm novel, Magda situates herself in the farm landscape as "the one who stays in her room reading or writing or fighting migraines. The colonies are full of girls like that, but none, I think, so extreme as I." In the farm novel tradition no Afrikaner feels alienated on his or her own land; the very construction of Magda as a self-conscious textual presence who, after eliminating her father, decides to "give up the fiction of farming," undermines the colonialist ideal of natural, hereditary connectedness to the colonized land.[13]

Coetzee's narrator also vehemently rejects the conventional plot of the colonial farm woman, representing farm wife- and motherhood in the ghastliest of terms:

> I can imagine . . . giving birth to a child, with no midwife and my husband blind drunk in the next room, gnawing through the umbilical cord, clapping the livid babyface to my flat sour breast; and then, after a decade of closeted breeding, emerging into the light of day at the head of a litter of ratlike, runty girls, all the spit image of myself, scowling into the sun.

Determined "not to have to figure in a bucolic comedy like the above," Magda ceaselessly fantasizes other plots, giving in the novel's opening pages a compelling account of her axe-murder of her father and new stepmother, which then appears to have been an afternoon's fancy. Having muddied the distinction between imagination and reality at the outset, the novel never allows its readers to be certain of what really happens. If, for example, Magda actually does later shoot her father dead, we do not know which horrifying variation on his final hours is the "real" one, or even whether such distinctions matter. Magda remains a distanced, ironic observer of all the dramas she narrates, for "[w]hich is the more plausible," she asks, "the story of my life as lived by me or the story of the good daughter humming the psalms as she bastes the Sunday roast in a Dutch kitchen in the dead centre of the stone desert?" Disdaining the stifling roles available to her, she rejects plot in the abstract and cultivates a sort of Emily Dickinson pose: as the "poetess of interiority," she writes obsessively in her room, wearing long black or white dresses, claiming a sense of "election" and refusing to go "trotting from room to room performing realistic tasks." "My talent is all for immanence," she says, "for the fire or ice of identity at the heart of things. Lyric is my medium, not chronicle." But while her disdain for the plot of a colonial daughter motivates her flight from "chronicle" to "lyric," Magda desperately wants to enter a story of her own, one with "a beginning, middle and end, not the yawning middle" of her Beckettian narrative stasis.[14] In the act of shooting her father—a most decisive departure from the conventional colonial heroine's plot—Magda makes a dramatic entrance into the plot, breaking free of both her role as "good daughter" and her static condition. But upon entering this plot, Magda must face the power relations into which she was born and that structure any drama in which she can participate.

=====

In the Heart of the Country further revises the Afrikaner farm novel by intensively exploring the operations of race and gender in the heroine's life, most notably in the inclusion of black characters, who, Coetzee notes, are virtually nonexistent in the traditional South African genre.[15] Coetzee fashions, in his crazed white heroine, a subversive persona who overthrows the rule of the white father and openly expresses a desire and need for blacks, placing them not at the margins but at the very center of her life. Magda claims that she "grew up with the servants' children, . . . spoke like one of them before [she] learned to speak like this," and "sat at the feet of their blind old grandfather while he [told] . . . a long tale of dead heroes in a language I have not unlearned." But with childhood long past, she admits, "[W]e might as well be on separate planets, we on ours, they on theirs." Over the course of the novel her wistful attraction to the black servants deepens into strong desire, but her attempts at intimacy only reveal an insurmountable distance:

> Reading the brown folk I grope, as they grope reading me: for they too hear my words only dully, listening for those overtones of the voice, those subtleties of the eyebrows that tell them my true meaning: "Beware, do not cross me," "What I say does not come from me." Across valleys of space and time we strain ourselves to catch the pale smoke of each other's signals. . . . Alone

in my room . . . I creak into rhythms that are my own, stumble over the rocks of words that I have never heard on another tongue. I, who . . . have never beheld myself in the equal regard of another's eye, have never held another in the equal regard of mine. . . . [My] voice . . . cracks and oozes the peevish loony sentiments that belong to the dead of night when the censor snores, to the crazy hornpipe I dance with myself.

The failure of her communication with blacks, Magda suggests, has helped to make her a mad, reclusive writer; in her estrangement from them lies the genesis of her obsessive monologue. All attempts to break out of monologue and into real interchange with black people are defeated by the very language she speaks:

I cannot carry on with these idiot dialogues. The language that should pass between myself and these people was subverted by my father and cannot be recovered. What passes between us now is a parody. I was born into a language of hierarchy, of distance and perspective. It was my father-tongue. I do not say it is the language my heart wants to speak, I feel too much the pathos of its distances, but it is all we have. I can believe there is a language lovers speak but cannot imagine how it goes.[16]

Wishing to exchange the father's tongue for a lover's in order to speak her heart to black people, Coetzee's mad heroine transgresses the race barrier in the desire for love and community. She thus demonstrates, contrary to the psychological apartheid in conventional colonial fictions, that the binary racial structure of colonialism can profoundly and painfully infect a white person's sense of identity and contribute substantially to the madness that is the white colonial woman's conventional fate.

In its revision of the figure of the mad, white colonial daughter, Coetzee's text bears striking similarities to a novel that is vastly different in tone and degree of postmodern experimentation: Jean Rhys's *Wide Sargasso Sea* (1966). Rhys more overtly rewrites a white female character with a prior literary incarnation: Bertha Mason/Rochester, the Creole madwoman in the attic of Charlotte Bronte's *Jane Eyre* (1847). As Gayatri Spivak has argued, Bronte's Bertha is "a figure produced by the axiomatics of imperialism," who must marry the English colonist, become a raging madwoman, "set fire to the house and kill herself, so Jane Eyre can become the feminist individualist heroine of British fiction."[17] In her postcolonial revision, Rhys grants her West Indian countrywoman a narrating voice, a history, a mother, and a maternal name. And as I have argued elsewhere, when at the end of *Wide Sargasso Sea* Rhys's reimagined Antoinette/Bertha is brought, a raving madwoman, to England and is last seen stalking the corridors of Rochester's house with a flaming torch, about to do her notorious incendiary deed, she seems to rebel against her own previous literary characterization. She thus embodies her author's feminist, anticolonialist assault on the Great House of English prose and is revitalized as a potent figure for the "resisting" feminist re-reader of her literary heritage.[18]

Coetzee's Magda and Rhys's Antoinette/Bertha go mad within similar social worlds: both occupy Miss Quested's position in a tightly constrained social hierarchy; both have the tyrannical father and the lost mother that seem endemic to white colonial life; both attempt to cross racial barriers to pursue relationships with black men and women. The white colonial daughter's path toward madness and revolt in both texts passes through a distinctive kind of existential crisis generated by the racist structures of their societies. Each heroine's acute awareness that she is alien in real, geopolitical terms to the people around her makes her feel uncertain about her identity and her place in the world. Antoinette says:

> Did you hear what that girl was singing? . . . It was a song about a white cockroach. That's me. That's what they call all of us who were here before their own people in Africa sold them to the slave traders. And I've heard English women call us white niggers. So between you I often wonder who I am and where is my country and where do I belong and why was I ever born at all.

Her racial alienation further estranges the heroine from her very surroundings, the land that is her only home. Rochester recounts a conversation with Antoinette:

"I feel very much a stranger here," I said. "I feel that this place is my enemy and on your side." "You are quite mistaken," she said. "It is not for you and not for me. It has nothing to do with either of us. That is why you are afraid of it, because it is something else. I found that out long ago when I was a child. I loved it because I had nothing else to love, but it is indifferent as this God you call on so often."[19]

Isak Dinesen muses on this subject in *Out of Africa*, a 1938 colonialist text, with as much sense of personal pain (though without political scruple): Could it be that, despite the intensity of her feelings for the life of her African farm, she would always remain an alien there?

If I know a song of Africa . . . of the Giraffe, and the African new moon lying on her back, of the ploughs in the fields, and the sweaty faces of the coffee-pickers, does Africa know a song of me? Would the air over the plain quiver with a colour that I had had on, or the children invent a game in which my name was, or the full moon throw a shadow over the gravel of the drive that was like me, or would the eagles of Ngong look out for me?[20]

Coetzee's Magda also experiences racial alienation as an estrangement from the landscape of her home. This passage from *In the Heart of the Country* bears a strong family resemblance to the "naive" one by Dinesen:

I stand at the window. . . . The massed twitter of birds in the riverbed rises and wanes. . . . What are pain, jealousy, loneliness doing in the African night? Does a woman looking through a window into the dark mean anything? I place all ten fingertips on the cool glass. The wound in my chest slides open. If I am an emblem then I am an emblem. I am incomplete, I am a being with a hole inside me, I signify something, I do not know what, I am dumb, I stare out through a sheet of glass into a darkness that is complete, that lives in itself, bats, bushes, predators and all, that does not regard me, that is blind, that does not signify but merely is. . . . I live inside a skin inside a house. There is no act I know of that will liberate me into the world. There is no act I know of that will bring the world into me.

When Magda looks out her window she sees a natural world that has nothing to do with her and cannot meet her desire. Like others in her position, she expresses an existential homelessness in specifically racial terms. Although she was born on the farm, while Hendrik has merely labored there for some years, Magda says in her thoughts to the black man: "You can sleep here all day, and at night you can walk about in the moonlight saying to yourself whatever it is that men say to themselves on a piece of earth that is their own." Magda sees Hendrik as at home on his own "piece of earth," but sees herself as utterly alien in terms of both gender and race. Although she lives on property that is hers by law, she repeatedly refers to herself (perhaps anticipating *Foe*) as a "castaway."[21] Her alienation from the land, which causes her to reject the sentimental vision of the Afrikaner farm novel, derives from a racial alienation so profound that it makes her feel shipwrecked on her own farm. Her character strongly marked by the rule of apartheid under which she was invented, this mad heroine demonstrates what a postcolonial sensibility brings to a postmodern revolt against language: insight into tyrannical systems of binary division.

Both *In the Heart of the Country* and *Wide Sargasso Sea* treat madness as the exclusive province of white colonial women, who progress from isolation to insanity amidst catastrophic exchanges of money and love in an interracial context. Anticipating Coetzee's novel, *Wide Sargasso Sea* situates the white colonial woman in an economy of race and power about which its precursor text pretends innocence, representing a white, female colonial subjectivity that relates intensely to blacks. Rhys rewrites what *Jane Eyre* depicts as Bertha's genetic insanity, characterizing it as the result of male exploitation and turbulent interracial relationships, including acts of revenge both public and intimate: house-burnings, transgressive sexual relationships, and emotional betrayals. Coetzee pares things down so that Magda's world contains a single representative of each hierarchical position, whose range of interactions with the others is a parody of plot. Having lost the mother and killed the father, Magda faces the dangerous, power-testing sexual game with the black man, while seeking an impossible emotional/sexual fulfillment with the black woman. All of these efforts end disastrously, of course; a series of sexual and violent interactions with black people sends Magda, too, deeper into isolation and madness. Like Antoinette's, Magda's growing rage eventually becomes murderous, as she envisions "building a great bonfire," then "screaming with wild glee as the flames soar into the night sky," and burning down the house (she apparently does burn her dead father's clothing and mattress).[22]

Both of these feminist postcolonial texts rewrite the white woman's madness to inscribe racial conflict. But if both could be said to subvert colonialist ideology simply by representing a white woman's intimate relationships with blacks, as well as black anger and resistance, both might also be said to use blackness as a metaphor for resistance, drawing energy from it for the white heroine's rebellion against patriarchal control—just as Coetzee might be said to borrow feminist anger in his exploration of colonial repression. In both novels the psychosexual desire of whites for blacks is double-edged, at once exploitative and genuine. In white colonial and postcolonial texts such desires, however subordinated to more "proper" ones in the plot, are often the most powerful desires expressed: witness the crises of passion for Aziz in *A Passage to India*, or Antoinette's love for Sandi, Tia, and Christophine in *Wide Sargasso Sea*. Based inevitably on racist erotic projections and the thrill of taboo contact, these desires often also signify an impulse to overcome an unjust and deeply felt separation. If Magda's desire for Hendrik and Klein-Anna shares certain elements of Adela Quested's projections, and if she shares with Antoinette/Bertha her contradictory attitudes toward blacks, still Magda does make it possible for Coetzee to suggest, as do Forster and Rhys, that a white person can become imprisoned by privilege and wish for relationships of equality across the hierarchical divisions of her world.

The figure of the colonial woman who deposes the white father enables Coetzee to experiment with other possible reversals throughout the ranks of colonial society; if parricide brings such a woman new freedom, it also brings her a degree of vulnerability to which she is unaccustomed. After her father's death, the resulting unfamiliar power balance allows Magda to hope for a new comradeship with "the brown folk," as she tends to call her father's hired help, a term at once affectionate (softening the absolute otherness of "black") and appropriative (in that she retains for herself the adjective "black").[23] But in this complicated, power-tainted matrix of relationships, Coetzee shows all well-intentioned desire to backfire or merely to dead-end. Magda, wanting the threesome to start over as equals, suggests that Klein-Anna call her "Magda," not "Miss." But Anna will not do so. Magda invites the couple to live in her house, but she cannot say, in the uncomfortable new arrangement, "whether Hendrik and Anna are guests or invaders or prisoners." At one moment she fantasizes joining the servants in symbolic collective labor, Hendrik the expert and she the eager apprentice, as they carve her father's bedroom completely off the house and send it floating skyward. But at another moment, she hurls "torrents of mean-spirited resentment on" Anna for her adultery, trying out a pose that "comes of itself, one needs no lessons, only meek folk around one and a grudge against them for not speaking back . . . and evidence in these bowed faces of limitless power."[24]

Her power evaporates, however, when the servants realize that it all stems from her relationship to the white man and his money. Without either (for she has no idea where her father kept his money, has never in her life "had to touch a coin larger than sixpence"), she is suddenly vulnerable to their mockery, their anger, and their revenge. The two dress up and prance about in her parents' clothing, a scene she finds "grotesque." "What can I do against the two of them," she thinks; "I am so alone, and a woman!" When Hendrik demands his pay, Magda must for the first time consider the economic basis of her social relations, a subject about which she, as a daughter, has been kept ignorant. Her awkwardness in the new role of employer is comically demonstrated when she has Hendrik make a two-day journey to the post office with a note requesting a withdrawal of cash, and he returns not with money but with a withdrawal slip requiring the "[s]ignature of depositor."[25] The dead father's hand (the text notes that "signature" is "handtekening" in Afrikaans) still controls the gold. The idea of forging her father's signature, interestingly enough, never occurs to Magda.

It is at this moment, when her economic disempowerment is revealed, that Hendrik enacts the stereotypical black man's revenge, attacking and raping the white woman. But by repeatedly restaging the event in successive entries, Magda undercuts our belief in the reality of the rape and implicates her own projections, even her desires—like those of Miss Quested—in the assault upon her. Imagined or experienced, this inevitable crisis finally reverses the power relations of the black man and the white woman. With the white master absent, Hendrik's gender superiority overrides Magda's racial superiority, a reversal that allows his anger free rein to cause her pain. In this new situation, Magda speaks words unlikely to come from a white character in possession of power:

> I am not simply one of the whites, I am *I*! I am I, not a people. Why have *I* to pay for other peoples' sins? . . . Why should I side with them against you? . . . Can't you see that you and Anna are the only people in the world I am attached to?

In one version of her descriptions of the rape that follows, Magda tries pathetically to interpret Hendrik's act of hatred as an act of love, but realizes finally that this violent conclusion represents the failure of all her earlier attempts at human connection. She wonders "whether there is not something to do with desire other than striving to possess the desired in a project which must be vain, since its end can only be the annihilation of the desired."[26]

As she muses over her failure with Hendrik, she focuses her corrupt desire on Klein-Anna, imagining a more fulfilling connection with her. Magda's feeling for Klein-Anna is at times sisterly:

> I would like to stroll arm in arm with her of a Saturday night dressed in my gayest clothes, whispering and giggling like a girl, showing myself off to the country beaux. I would like to hear from her, in a quiet corner, the great secrets of life, how to be beautiful, how to win a husband, how to please a man. I would like to be her little sister.

At other times Magda regards Anna's body with explicitly sexual interest, as when she can find no words for the beauty of the light on Anna's "bronze flanks and breasts," or when she actually caresses her.

Ultimately, Magda seems to want to become the black woman. But the passage in which she envisions their fusion recalls an earlier one, in which Magda describes the invasion of her body by patriarchal, imperialist law:

> The law has gripped my throat . . . it invades my larynx, its one hand on my tongue, its other hand on my lips. . . . How can I say that the law does not stand fullgrown inside my shell, its feet in my feet, its hands in my hands, its sex drooping through my hole?

A similar image occurs to her after Hendrik rapes her:

> What is this man trying to find in me? . . . What deeper invasion . . . does he plot? . . . That one day all his bony frame shall lie packed inside me, his skull inside my skull, his limbs along my limbs, the rest of him crammed into my belly? What will he leave me of myself?

It is a sad irony that Magda should imagine a cohabitation in Anna's body, picturing herself as invader/lover:

> I would like to climb into Klein-Anna's body, I would like to climb down her throat while she sleeps and spread myself gently inside her, my hands in her hands, my feet in her feet, my skull in the benign quiet of her skull where images of soap and flour and milk revolve, the holes of my body sliding into place over the holes of hers.

At once identifying with and imaginatively colonizing Anna, Magda attempts to blur their difference by an exchange of colors across the race barrier: she imagines Anna to have a head full of white things (soap, flour, milk), whereas she frequently describes herself as black. But the gentle invasion of this fantasy later gives way to an acknowledgment that their relationship contains the potential for explosive conflict: "And what of Anna? . . . Will she and I one day be sisters and sleep in the same bed? Or will she, when she finds herself, scratch my eyes out?"[27]

Magda's desire for the black woman also recalls the strong attachments of Rhys's heroine to her nurse, Christophine, and her childhood friend, Tia, both of whom she loses to racial conflict (and to the higher demands of the romance plot). Magda's attraction to Anna, who may be sister or enemy, finds a parallel in Antoinette's attachment to Tia, to whom she runs when a crowd of blacks burns her family's house down, deciding, "I will live with Tia and I will be like her."[28] Tia throws a stone at her, yet she still sees them as mirroring each other: the blood on her own face reflected by the tears on Tia's. Like the image of Tia-as-mirror for Antoinette, the image of female, interracial identification with Klein-Anna arises for Magda at a moment of crisis, representing a desired resolution of the moment's tensions. These motherless, white colonial heroines, like innumerable slave mistresses and other white women in American literature, look to black women for emotional refuge from their more threatening relationships. But whereas the desire for black women is sacrificed to the romance with the white man in the plot of *Wide Sargasso Sea* and most other narratives about white women, Coetzee's novel, which rules out rescue or defeat by a white romance plot, gives the black woman the opportunity to refuse this desire of her own accord.

Like Rhys's heroine, Magda sinks to her lowest point when she is bereft of all possibility of receiving the love of black people. When Hendrik and Anna leave her, she asks:

> Why will no one speak to me in the true language of the heart? The medium, the median—that is what I wanted to be! Neither master nor slave, neither parent nor child, but the bridge between, so that in me the contraries should be reconciled!

If Coetzee created this white female speaker to experiment with a "median" position in postcolonial discourse, he did not create her to succeed in reconciling racial contraries, but rather to be a "medium" of undying desire—of attempt, failure, and repeated attempt. Unlike Antoinette/Bertha, whose narrative must end in its prewritten apotheosis, Magda, having lost everything, resourcefully renews her hope for communication. Although she fails to reach across the racial divide and enter into a dialogue with blacks, in her utter loneliness she invents a whole new cast of characters with whom to desire conversation. To attract the voices in the "machines" that traverse her sky, she eagerly constructs messages in stone, hoping, as she puts it, that the "sky gods" will "descend and live with me here in paradise, making up with their ambrosial breath for all that I lost when the ghostly brown figures of the last people I knew crept away from me in the night." The voices speak to her only in bland, Hegelian master/slave dichotomies, but she attempts to bypass the language barrier with a "Spanish of pure meanings" (Esperanto?) in a poignant, comic quest to overcome all previous obstacles to communication by means of a universal discourse. "ES MI," she shouts first to the invisible men; "VENE!" "ISOLADO!" she cries, voicing the simple conviction that others *ought* to respond to her personal appeal. Maintaining an unflaggingly hopeful view to the end of her story, she writes "CINDRLA ES MI" and "FEMM—AMOR POR TU" in stone letters twelve feet high, and builds a stone "sketch" of a woman's body in an openly inviting pose, but receives no response.[29]

In this final, lovely, loony stage, before she crawls off to the death that she has anticipated from the novel's opening pages, Magda exhibits a willingness to do anything at all to win interlocutors. "It is not speech that makes man man," she declares in what is perhaps a quintessential Coetzee line, "but the speech of others." The desire to hear others speak is what most drives Coetzee's white narrators, including the Magistrate of *Barbarians* and Susan Barton of *Foe*. But it is exactly the desire that writing cannot fulfill. In the throes of this desperate desire, Magda allows the italicized words of the sky-gods to enter and change the surface of her prose, and she even changes the very language she speaks—about as big a change as a narrator can make. Even the failure of Magda's attempts to communicate with these mysterious aeronauts does not lead her to despair, but rather, to doubt her methods: human language, which has confounded all of her relationships, must be primitive, she thinks, "paltry," "a stone-moving, word-building intelligence," while the flying men may communicate by means beyond what she can even imagine.[30]

"The land is full of melancholy spinsters like me, lost to history," says Magda.[31] Coetzee's recuperation of one of their voices allows him not only to examine the tragic world of patriarchal, colonial race and gender relations from a "median" position, but to articulate a furious resistance to the systems—political, social, linguistic—that define both Magda's existence and his own. Reimagining the madness of the white colonial woman so as to inscribe the pain of life in a racist society, Coetzee discovers in that madness a fertile vocabulary for the horror and the absurdity of his own postcolonial condition.

But, finally, it is to the credit of Coetzee's art that, despite Magda's entrapment in a paper existence, the hell of her human relationships, and her failure to reach others through language, she becomes in the end as humane a voice as we have heard in recent literature. Dancing about, lighting signal fires (and transforming the fire of destruction to a fire of hope), and "proclaiming [her] uniqueness" in wild isolation, Magda still believes that beings who fly overhead in machines might want to be her friends, and she is even capable of imagining that as they fly they look down and see, "from horizon to horizon," that "the world is dense with dancing folk signalling out of their private fires."[32] In the mad vision of Coetzee's rebellious, compromised, white colonial heroine, others, like herself, are madly signalling too.

Notes

The author wishes to thank Paul Cantor, to whose lectures on Coetzee this essay is greatly indebted, and Jahan Ramazani, a gifted and willing reader.

1   Sara Suleri, "The Geography of *A Passage to India*," in *E. M. Forster's A Passage to India: Modern Critical Interpretations*, ed. Harold Bloom (New Haven, 1987), 112.

2   Notable in this regard, of course, is the heroine of Lessing's Children of Violence series, Martha Quest.

3   J. M. Coetzee, *In the Heart of the Country* (New York, 1982 [1977]), 4.

4   Ibid., 4–5.

5   Ibid., 26.

6   Linda Hutcheon, *The Politics of Postmodernism* (London, 1989), 2.

7   See J. M. Coetzee, *White Writing: On the Culture of Letters in South Africa* (New Haven, 1988).

8   Coetzee, *Heart of the Country*, 62.

9   Ibid., 79, 127, 139, 14, 48–49.

10   Ibid., 135, 62, 119–20, 16.

11   See Olive Schreiner, *The Story of an African Farm* (New York, 1979 [1883]). Teresa Dovey elaborates the connection to Schreiner's novel in her Lacanian reading of Magda's relationship to imperial, patriarchal language. See *The Novels of J. M. Coetzee: Lacanian Allegories* (Johannesburg, 1988).

12   Coetzee, *White Writing*, 87, 113, 90, 88.

13   Coetzee, *Heart of the Country*, 18, 108, 19, 1, 116.

14   Ibid., 42, 129, 72, 71, 42–43.

15   Coetzee, *White Writing*, 71–72.

16   Coetzee, *Heart of the Country*, 6–7, 28, 7–8, 97.

17   Gayatri Chakravorty Spivak, "Three Women's Texts and a Critique of Imperialism," in *"Race," Writing, and Difference*, ed. Henry Louis Gates, Jr. (Chicago, 1986), 266, 270.

18   On the portrayal of the white colonial woman and the revisionary aesthetic in *Wide Sargasso Sea*, see my "Burning Down the House: The Revisionary Paradigm of Jean Rhys's *Wide Sargasso Sea*," in *Famous Last Words: Changes in Gender and Narrative Closure*, ed. Alison Booth (Charlottesville, 1993), 300–325.

19   Jean Rhys, *Wide Sargasso Sea* (New York, 1982 [1966]), 102, 129–30.

20   Isak Dinesen, *Out of Africa and Shadows on the Grass* (New York, 1985 [1938, 1961]), 82–83.

21   Coetzee, *Heart of the Country*, 9–10, 123, 131, 135.

22   Ibid., 45, 82.

23   Ibid., 5, 40, 96.

24   Ibid., 102, 112, 74.

25   Ibid., 94, 98, 103.

26   Ibid., 118, 114.

27   Ibid., 87, 85, 114–15, 84, 108–9, 119.

28   Rhys, *Wide Sargasso Sea*, 45.

29   Coetzee, *Heart of the Country*, 133, 139, 132–34.

30   Ibid., 126, 134.

31   Ibid., 3.

32   Ibid., 132.

Philip R. Wood

Aporias of the Postcolonial Subject: Correspondence with J. M. Coetzee

The following correspondence took place in 1991. It will be observed that there is a marked disproportion between the length of my questions and that of J. M. Coetzee's answers. Questions of this length were submitted in order to make them as clear as possible to Coetzee, with a view to cutting them for publication. Contrary to my expectations, the result may well have been to make it *more* difficult to respond, rather than less so, for an author who has always made a virtue of concision. It is not without some diffidence that, despite some subsequent trimming of my questions and comments, I have retained passages that may seem prolix. But I trust that a question's going almost unanswered can be as interesting and revealing as a question that provokes a copious response.

Question 1. It is possible to deduce from your first book, *Dusklands*, what one might call a metaphysical indictment of the West (the "evening lands" or "dusklands" of the title) — that is, a critical evocation of our most funda-

The *South Atlantic Quarterly* 93:1, Winter 1994.
Copyright © 1994 by Duke University Press.
CCC 0038-2876/94/$1.50.

mental collective existential modes, which, the work suggests, are intrinsically inimical to life. Thus Eugene Dawn, in a moment of breakdown and panic, inflicts a nearly fatal wound on the child he believes he loves, not so much because—as his wife and psychologists believe—he has been brutalized by his work on the Vietnam Project, as because, at a more fundamental level, his distinctly modern, Cartesian consciousness is such as to dispose him to try to master the world by dissolving it into an image or projection of his own subjectivity. Anything that resists this process, anything distinct from Dawn's subjectivity (including his own body), is consequently a source of exasperation, anxiety, and loathing. Hence his sexual fastidiousness, the failure of his marriage, and his unhappy relations with his child; hence, too, the satisfaction he derives from the photograph of the North Vietnamese prisoner, which on close examination reveals that the glint in the prisoner's eye—denoting intelligence, humanity, *another* center of consciousness—has been reduced to a composite pattern of white and black, a *res extensa*, in short, that can be represented and thereby tamed. The book implies that this pathology characterizes not only Dawn but the United States in general, especially in its relations with Vietnam. The solipsism attendant upon such a way of being in the world, by a classic dialectical inversion, turns into its opposite: the Other, whose independent existence as a center of consciousness has been denied, or demeaned, or impotently raged at, is now appealed to in order to affirm my own existence, which has come to feel increasingly and worryingly oneiric: love me, damn you! And when your response does not conform to my desires, when it does not affirm me in my conception of myself, why, then I shall kill you. If I do this, then I shall *know* I exist. Given this basis for his relations with all other people, there is a sense in which Dawn's participation in the Vietnam War is the continuation of his relations with his family by other means, and vice versa. (Clearly, something very similar to much of this is happening in *The Narrative of Jacobus Coetzee*.)

Eugene Dawn's story concludes with the following declaration: "I have high hopes of finding whose fault I am." We know that neither he ("in the heart of America, with my private toilet") nor his psychologists will ever fathom his disorder; but, by the end of the book, we, the readers, attribute his pathology to a cultural order that, from the United States to South Africa, across two centuries, from classic settler colonialism to the neocolonial order in whose name the Vietnam War was fought, has exhibited a distinct continuity. My question is: How does one come to grope one's way toward that fateful confrontation with a world-historical epoch that is the successful creation of a great work of art? How does one come to recognize that one's own pathology is no merely singular aberration but a universal cultural phenomenon? For one does often sense that, in creating Eugene Dawn and Jacobus Coetzee, you have knowingly drawn on something within yourself (or, at least, some place that has been easy for you to occupy in the imagination, or some place you perhaps feel to have been one of your intimate possibilities, albeit rejected). This seems evident even if only at the level of the obvious, although grim, relish with which you have so successfully crafted the vicious, horribly funny, repulsive, pedantic inner writhings of Dawn, or the magniloquent, terrifying, crazed conquistadorial phrases of bronze of Jacobus Coetzee. (We, too, feel this ambivalent relish as we recognize ourselves in these characters—at least, such was my experience.) So, the interesting question is not what your/our secret monsters are, or what their etiology is, but how one comes to recognize the collective nature of one's own pathology.

Answer 1. To me the question is not how the pathology emerges as representative (or collective, to use your term), but whether the pathology can be made to seem representative, in other words, whether the writing is convincing enough (has enough power) to evoke the response you express here.

Those, anyhow, are the terms on which I prefer to take your question. I don't see that there is any profit—least of all for me—in using this occasion to grub any "deeper" than I do in the book.

Question 2. Let me refine the first question further and give it a particular focus in the course of another example that, it seems to me, merits separate treatment. Is it true that what we might swiftly summarize as death-dealing Cartesian paranoia—which you denounce in *Dusklands*—infects the very aesthetic tradition that has made your own work possible and upon which you draw? Might one also suggest that, at some level, you knew this even as you wrote *Dusklands*? Recall, for example, the calmly lucid and yet demented, chilling, somber imperial grandeur of Jacobus Coetzee's last words, which perfectly summarize and enact a judgment upon the world order he stands for: "[W]hether I am alive or dead, whether I ever lived or never was born, has never been of real concern to me. I have other things to think about." It is not hard to find resonances of this kind of thinking—and of Jacobus Coetzee's "worldview" as a whole—throughout that literary tradition, from Flaubert through Henry James and Joyce to (early) Sartre, to which you are heir (that is, in one shape or another the positing of the deontological primacy of art over life and the distortions and mutilations entailed thereby). Again, Jacobus's brief fantasy of dying at the sacrificial stake is motivated by a classically modernist preference for "having belonged to a satisfying aesthetic whole" rather than the mortifyingly contingent, merely biological end with which he is threatened from "a putrefying backside." Flaubert certainly would have sympathized with Jacobus's wish to die of fevers, "wasted in body but on fire to the end with omnipotent fantasies." The writer as sacrificial victim, or object of self-immolation, in the name of the higher reality of the "aesthetic whole" is also a familiar fantasy among modern writers. And, of course, the assimilation of the writer to God is a constant feature of the tradition (in the passage just quoted, Jacobus goes on to express irritation at the Hottentots' failure really to believe in a Creator). Do you recognize the affinities between Jacobus and the modern artist, and if so, were you, do you think, conscious of them at the time of writing? Or is this something that is simply easy to read retroactively into this first novel once one has assimilated your growing concern with that nexus of language, power, representation, authorship/authority, etc., which becomes so prominent in subsequent works like *Life & Times of Michael K* or, especially, *Foe*?

Answer 2. Yes, of course I was conscious of the line of affiliation going from imperial artists like Flaubert to Jacobus Coetzee. *Dusklands*, after all, has an epigraph taken from *Bouvard et Pécuchet*.

Question 3. Still pursuing this same line of thinking, how does one, indeed, find the means to subvert a tradition to which one belongs? (Or is it perhaps that subversion—the ritual slaying of the father—*is* our modern tradition?) Obviously, a sine qua non for universalizing one's singularity is the assimilation of "influences": one plugs oneself into a general system of meaning that progressively enables one to intertwine the culture and what one had originally believed was unique to oneself, such that one recognizes each of these two components—intensely lived personal or "individual" life, and a tradition—in the other. In your own case, one guesses at the influence of such figures as Sartre, Heidegger, or Marcuse, who may have served you in turning yourself into this critic of the West. But, of course, this does not really answer the question, unless one simply assumes that subversion and interrogation are the privileged loci of personal identity in the modern West—at least, among its significant artificers of ideology and culture—which somehow suggests too smooth a functioning total machine. Because, after all, one *chooses* one's influences—at least in some measure.

Answer 3. The tradition to which you refer is a supremely self-confident one, to the extent of making the critique—the self-devouring—of itself into one of its procedures. That self-confidence is part of the paradox of skepticism: skepticism has never feared that it will destroy philosophizing, reduce it to silence. Thus, to return to your question, one does not have to look far to find the means to subvert the tradition, because subversion is part of the tradition.

Question 4. So, what is it in you (in any of us) that resists death-dealing modernity? Can we simply answer "life"? Although we are all, supposedly, alive, not all of us resist. What is it that rises up against Eugene Dawn, against Jacobus Coetzee? What resists a dominant social order? Or must one conclude that, to need to answer this question, one is somehow already doomed, already one of those who is inside or stands at the gates of the camps? (In the latter vein, one could, of course, point to Michael K as an eloquent evocation of resistance, "of how outrageously a meaning can take up residence in a system without becoming a term in it.") But his degree of downtroddenness and then his abnegation and self-destitution, the purity of his absolute rejection of the "system" you mention, are so extreme as to operate or apply only in a realm that is beyond the existential (but not imaginative) reach of those of us who have some stake in the prevailing dispensation of power (including perhaps even those who are just getting by) as an archetype or monitory ideal form. And yet the medical officer in the Kenilworth camp also resists, albeit with nothing like the persistent resolve or extremism of Michael K.

Answer 4. What resists "death-dealing modernity" is the body and its undeniable life.

Question 5. What does the ineluctable intertwining of unconscious/ subconscious complicity with and resistance to oppressive power mean for the novelist and for the novel in formal terms? What kinds of vigilance does one practice to avoid being lured into a bind? The question clearly preoccupies you—most obviously in *Foe*, but also in *Life & Times of Michael K.* One thinks, for example, of that scene of pointed high comedy in which the medical officer imagines himself pursuing a fugitive Michael K across the Cape Flats with a tormented, highly intelligent, decent, and altogether legitimate interpretation and interrogation of Michael that is nonetheless condemned— by what separates the two men (the history of the country)—to being meddlesome and aggressive. (To his credit, the medical officer knows this.) One senses here an echo of a danger consciously skirted by the novelist—almost a case of Freudian *Verneinung*: "I am going to show you, in someone else, what *I* cannot be accused of doing!" A fear, perhaps, of doing to Michael K what the Magistrate had done to the barbarian girl: indulging a subtle hunger for some fresh, albeit deeply convoluted and opaque, form of dominion. Actually, in both cases, what seems to be involved is a form of selfishness—the Magistrate hopes to redeem himself (his complicity with the crimes of the Empire) through his relationship with the barbarian girl (with no thought of the cost to her); and, similarly, the medical officer wants to clarify his understanding of the challenge that Michael represents for him instead of simply rising to the challenge (he wants knowledge, but not in order to act upon it). In a sense, the Magistrate gets what he deserves: he has hoped to redeem himself at no cost to himself and ends up having to pay the atrocious price of what solidarity with the barbarians really entails (a solidarity of which he is unjustly accused and for which he is tortured and utterly humiliated).

This concern has taken the form of *Foe*, a rewriting of one of the founding texts of the modern novel—*Robinson Crusoe*. The rewriting makes possible an interrogation of what this classic text of colonialism had suppressed or distorted in the interests of commercial success, of what the novelist had fed upon parasitically (the life stories of prisoners awaiting execution), and so on. A significant change entails the story's being narrated by a woman. While her story gets told, Friday's emphatically does not. Or, more accurately, *he* does not recount the small part of it that we get (unlike Michael K, who gives us the definitive summation of his life and times—"I am a gardener"). Significantly, too, Friday's disfigurement (his tongue has been cut out) is more pronounced and a greater obstacle to communication than Michael K's cleft palate. Does all of this indicate a greater diffidence on your part toward Friday than toward Michael K? A deepened wariness (in this subsequent work) with regard to the potential violence entailed in representation? And if so, does this mean that you perhaps have your own reservations, now, about the earlier work?

Answer 5. The crude answer is that, just because the erstwhile oppressor has had a change of heart and wishes to take sides with the oppressed, there is no guarantee that he will be welcomed by the oppressed. This goes not only for fictional personages like the Magistrate and the medical officer, but for the writer who sees his work as calculated disloyalty to the class that gave him birth.

As for your question about Michael K and Friday, does the fact that Friday's oral wound is worse than Michael's necessarily imply greater diffidence about representation on my part? *Michael K* is about Michael, after all, while *Foe* is about Susan Barton, not Friday.

Question 6. The Magistrate and Elizabeth Curren [*Age of Iron*] are fundamentally decent people. Indeed, they are exceptionally so, even at the outset. And yet they do not escape the infection of the subtle forms of ugliness and brutality they inherit from their societies, and which they will unthinkingly mobilize themselves, until they have passed through the purification of utter desolation. We have discussed the Magistrate earlier; in the case of Curren, she is liberated by the knowledge of impending death and is thus able to order her priorities with a purity of motive to which most of us are generally incapable of rising. One can only guess at the similar kind of long *askesis* that one assumes the novelist to have practiced. To the extent that many of us have recognized your works as significant interventions within the South African tragedy, it seems to me that we effectively assume your work to float free of what it denounces. Is this a delusion (albeit one that a novelist perhaps has to strive to sustain)? Do you in fact ever find yourself, like Lady Macbeth, as it were, pacing the corridors of your books at night, wringing your hands over indelible spots of gore, secret complicities with monumental crimes? How much real control, mastery, can (should?) a novelist expect to attain in this area?

How far should we take Walter Benjamin's assertion that every document of civilization is always also a "document of barbarism"—fatally compromised by the social cost of its production in terms of oppression? Could we perhaps distinguish between what it has taken (socially) to produce the work (a life of relative privilege for the author, injustice, atrocities committed in his or her name, etc.) and what the work *does*? Is this merely what some Marxists denounce as idealism? Or what poststructuralists would denounce as logocentrism (a belief that one can get outside of the text as an absolute cultural horizon)? How else could a work be "for all time," that is, transcend—at least in some measure—its own conditions of possibility, its own epoch? Or is there some merciless, unforgiving, economy of blood and taint that always haunts the secret interstices of the greatest of works?

The question is especially interesting in the case of an author such as yourself who has been more preoccupied by it, and addressed it more carefully, than perhaps anyone else. Your novels, and some of your essays, implicitly answer the question, and yet in contradictory ways (this is not a complaint). Thus, in your article for *Le Nouvel Observateur*, you talk about the necessary "mutilation" and loss of freedom entailed in being a South African writer. It is no less true, however, that one of the marks of your fiction is its successful struggle to avoid at least some of those historically constituted positions of complicity with the prevailing dispensation of power that can ambush the writer's best intentions. So something can indeed be achieved; it is possible to create a significant critical distance from the dominant discursive formation. Freedom does exist, despite everything. You suggest, however, in the same article, that this freedom is marginal and ineffective (or only minimally effective) in terms of its impact. Has this not been true for the vast majority of agents at all times (not just writers, and not just in South Africa)?

Answer 6. I would be the last person in the world to claim that writing rids one of complicity. As for your question about how a work transcends its epoch, maybe the answer is simply that as time goes on, we (inevitably) care less about the epoch and therefore less about what you call the "taint" carried by the work.

Question 7. Foe strikes me as your most difficult work (at least in terms of certain readerly expectations). It has also provoked some hostility from that constituency devoted to the notion that the function of literature in a postcolonial context is to call a spade a spade. I do not share this view of *Foe* (or, indeed, the assumption that only realism can constitute a significant gesture in the South African context). The greatest strength of your work, it seems to me, has been that it resolutely avoids allowing your (mostly white, educated) readers to feel good about themselves. You deny us the comfortable satisfaction of sharing in an outraged, self-righteous denunciation of an easily identifiable evil (out there, not in us), which plunges us still deeper into the complacent stupor we have never left in the first place.

But it must be said that the conclusion to *Foe* (part 4) is especially difficult, for here the book turns its back on realism more decisively than at any prior point. Part 4 opens with the abrupt introduction of a new narrator, never identified, who inspects the bodies (which, in dreamlike fashion, are not quite corpses) of the main characters (including that of our narrator up to this point), peacefully disposed within the house of "Daniel Defoe, Author." The narrator stoops over a comatose Friday, trying to hear the sounds of the island issuing from his mouth. One feels this to be a meditative inspection by the author, a valedictory examination of his handiwork. Apparently dissatisfied, however, this "I" returns to the house a second time and starts to read the manuscript of Barton's narrative, with which *Foe* itself opens: ". . . At last I could row no further. . . ." Our mysterious narrator/author then takes over the Barton narrative as it had continued at the beginning of the novel: "With a sigh, making barely a splash, I slip overboard." With this flagrant contravention of realism, a classic *mise en abyme*, one senses, if not a repudiation of everything that has preceded this point in the book, at least a dissatisfaction with it, an impulse to try again, from the beginning. With the two (perhaps even three) rapid switches in narrating voice, one has a distinct impression of telescoped gestures of renunciation, of something being discarded. What then follows is the exploration, by this final narrator, of the submerged wreck of Cruso's ship, the vessel that had brought him to the island.

This passage presents difficulties not unlike those we experience in reading one of the more elusive French symbolist poets. Indeed, the passage is powerfully reminiscent of Mallarmé's "Un coup de dès jamais n'abolira le hasard"—even in terms of "content": a wreck (more specifically, "du fond d'un naufrage"), a storm-tossed mariner, corpses, the dominance of white and black, stars, profound silence, the cold, a cosmic resonance, above all, the flat impossibility of synthesizing the details in a realist narrative. If I mention the similarities, it is not so much to establish a lineage or an influence as it is to point to a literary-historical situation and to a practice that is common to yourself and Mallarmé: perseverance in a form that—because of the extraordinary challenges to it posed by a sociohistorical crisis—can continue to be practiced (authentically) only if subjected to substantial formal innovation and defamiliarization.

The underwater wreck is a special, fabulous (in the original sense of the term) place. It is preternaturally "huge, greater than the leviathan," so much so that it may well house the kraken, made famous by Tennyson—which was so enormous as sometimes to be taken for an island by unfortunate mariners—that most exotic and fearsome of monsters, incarnation of everything alien to be faced by the wandering seafarer (a nightmare inversion of the enchanted isle in the colonial imagination). The wreck is also a hallowed place: Friday once cast sacramental white petals on the waves above it like an officiating priest; the wreck is also an oracle: Friday "speaks," albeit silently, from it—or passes judgment in suitably enigmatic and oracular fashion on the preceding text and on our world; it has a mysterious "guardian" (the mummified shark or human corpse); one enters the wreck with a "talisman" (the stub of an unlit candle); it is the tomb not only of Barton, Friday, and the captain (whose bodies, magically, have not decomposed after "three hundred years"), but also perhaps of many immemorial others, surrounded as it is by slime, which "is like the mud of Flanders, in which generations of grenadiers now lie dead." Grenadiers in Flanders were among Foe's inventions: so is this perhaps not just a fictional, fabulous tomb but a tomb of fiction ("But this is not a place of words") in the sense that here words not only have no currency but must perish? Most strikingly of all, "this is a place where bodies are their own signs."

Now, this assertion *is* fiction; not just, as the French say, to the power of two (as in *mise en abyme*), but to the power of three. It leaves one puzzled. After all, your work is marked by an understanding of what is exemplified by Derrida's notorious statement that "there is no outside to the text," which does not mean—as some have read it—that the world is constituted by words or concepts, that there are only words or texts (a kind of semiotic idealism, if you will, or Cartesian doubt in the guise of a dictionary). What it does mean is that the world—the real world "of flesh and blood," as we say—is always textualized. That is, that the meanings, the signs, the significations, the ontological identities of things—the unique quality of their thingness here and now as *this* or *that* thing—all this comes to each and every entity from somewhere else as the outcome of an endlessly deferred process. Thus, the table is the table because it is not the chair, or the Andromeda constellation, or, ultimately, the rest of the universe. If chairs suddenly ceased to exist, tables would no longer be quite what they are—qua tables—in a world where chairs do exist. This sounds like Hegel, but for Derrida, or Heidegger, these differences are not the result of subject-centered negation ("the table is not the chair, and vice versa"), but a system of "différance" that "precedes" subjectivity and mere difference and that one might call *pre*human were there not the risk that it might be taken to mean *in*human (in the sense of taking place without human beings).

Enough said. You know all this. But this is precisely what makes the end of *Foe* such a significant and powerful gesture on your part: for what textuality entails is precisely that there is no such place as one "where bodies are their own signs," where identity is immanent. Which makes the wreck a nowhere, an *ou topos*, or utopia. Which is why, presumably, you have conspicuously advertised its extraordinary or fabulous status. The only way I have been able to interpret all of this is in terms of a diffidence on your part toward Friday— an unwillingness to commit the violation of telling Friday's story for him, which would be the literary equivalent of *bestowing* freedom upon him, as opposed to his *taking* it. You have sought to avoid the liberal gesture, or literary affirmative action, as it were. It seems important, for example, that the narrator—in a suitably humble posture, on hands and knees—asks Friday not, "What is your story?" as we might have expected given everything else that has preceded this moment (the frantic attempts to get Friday to tell his tale, Foe's insistence that the book will be incomplete as long as they do not have his story, etc.), but, "What is this ship?"

While nothing justifies reading this narrator as the author, I would argue that everything up to this point has been designed to encourage the reader to do so. For the voice of summation, for the author (to whom all is presumably known) to ask, on hands and knees, of the mute Friday, "What is this ship?" and to be told that "this is not a place of words," that the moment for tales and texts has come and gone, can strike one only as an act of abdication, a gesture of renunciation of authorial power.

This gesture concludes and brings to fulfillment a steadily evolving interrogation in your work of your literary function and powers. In our postcolonial era, such an interrogation has never been more valid. All the more so to the extent that it can be argued that at some proto-metaphorical level the underwater wreck is the wrack of the West. Not just in the literal sense that the vessel in this originally colonial narrative *is* imperialism and the island *is* the third world, but in the sense that it is also the West's collective cultural ethos that has foundered upon the rock of the third world, weighed down by the guilt-sedimented history of its phantasms, its literary-historical props, and its crimes. (Indeed, were Friday to answer verbally, he might reply, "This ship is another one of your fictions, another one of those stories that people like you keep telling yourselves about people like me.") Thus, for the narrator to ask of Friday, "What is this ship?" is in part to ask, "Who am I? *You* tell *me* who I am." This desire for self-knowledge is not vouchsafed. (Still *our* desire: as for the Magistrate, the medical officer, or Eugene Dawn in your other novels—the Other is a mirror, or instrument, for our self-delectation.) It is appropriate, under these circumstances, that the answer the narrator receives is a great stream of cold, indifferent silence, vomited over him after he has, in a final violation, pried open Friday's teeth.

Nevertheless, something in all of this leaves me slightly uncomfortable. That the wreck should not be a place of words is necessary and integral to your project. But how does one interpret "This is a place where bodies are their own signs. It is the home of Friday"? These two sentences can be taken in two ways: in a strong "theoretical" sense— that is, in a utopian sense, as denoting somewhere outside of the play of the world, of the text. This interpretation is troubling because, of course, it rehearses one of the classic moves of colonialism, which is to project a space of desire from the metropolitan culture (in which that space cannot be found) onto the colonized culture, a fantasy/projection that ultimately becomes one more ploy in the panoply of instruments of oppression. The noble savage is the most notorious example of this phenomenon. In my own case, this was how I initially read these sentences. Indeed, it was my being reminded of a particularly striking example in Heidegger of this kind of thinking that determined my reading. Speaking of fetishism and magic, Heidegger declares that "for primitive man, the sign coincides with that which is indicated . . . the sign itself always *is* what it indicates."[1]

But it then occured to me that perhaps I was simply leaning too heavily on these sentences (this is what happens when one brings too much "theory" to bear) and that there was a weak or colloquial sense in which the sentences could be read: "At this point, words are no longer appropriate, bodies too can be eloquent, and Friday's silence says it all." I'm now convinced by this interpretation. But I leave my first one above (as well as my perplexed meandering through it) because I think it is one that will have occurred to many readers (the question it raises is a fair one to ask), because it needs to be pondered.

Answer 7. I find your meditation on the last section of *Foe* interesting at every level. More I cannot say. I have always resisted being nudged into the role of interpreter of my own books. In this case, moreover, you do it more fluently and convincingly than I can imagine myself doing.

Question 8. It used to be, when we were all still modernists, that when we asked what constituted the value or beauty of those canonically tragic or "depressing" works—*King Lear, Madame Bovary*—we were told that it resided in the recuperation of the meaningless pain of life by the mastered totality of the work of art. The latter transfigured brute meaninglessness into meaning: because every element in the work was essential to the whole (and vice versa), mere meaningless contingency was transformed into meaningful necessity (even if the meaning which resulted was simply the beauty of perfected horror, as in Flaubert, for example). Meaning and purpose came to reside in the work of art as they had once permeated the older premodern cosmos (itself a totality). Art redeemed life and the artist (well, just a little!). Small wonder that art came to fulfill for secularized modernity the functions religion had once served. Another word for this, of course, is humanism. Your work, however, appears to eschew notions of mastery, of totality or redemption, or any suggestion that there might be an angle that one could get on history, or "discourse," such that one could escape being already constructed within their contaminating, transindividual ramifications. It seems to me that one ought to reiterate the point made by others that this "postmodern" turn is not the outcome of a turn *from* history—as postmodernity, literary or philosophical, is regularly represented—but rather the product of a head-on confrontation with an exceptionally problematic historical situation.[2] One thinks, for example, of Elizabeth Curren in *Age of Iron*. She has nothing to say that her servant, Florence, or Bheki, John, or Mr. Thabane can respond to, that can stir them out of their indifference to her and her plight as an exceptionally decent person horrified by what she has been condemned to be guilty of. ("What times these are when to be a good person is not enough.") While one cannot conflate you and Curren, one inevitably feels that this is close to your assessment of the white writer's predicament: "I have no voice. . . . The rest should be silence. But with this—whatever it is—this voice that is no voice, I go on. On and on."

And yet you have a voice. If there is no redemption for you or your readers (and yet we salute the product), if there is no mastery (and yet there is clearly achievement), what is it you have done? When you have come to the end of a book and, at last, after all the revisions, you say to yourself, "Enough," can you articulate the criteria you mobilize at that point? While life may well be a matter of "biting the dust"—by the end of *Age of Iron*, who could gainsay that?—there are nonetheless dark victories, and *Age of Iron* is one of them.

Apart from the important difference that you must grapple with the issue of complicity between literary representation and political oppression, and the greater degree of self-reflexivity that this has entailed as an aesthetic distancing device, how is all of this really different for you than it was for the great modernists, for Flaubert? *Is your situation different from Flaubert's, or Henry James's?*

Answer 8. How am I different from Flaubert? All I can say is that I do not expect my countrymen to devote many pages to me when in a hundred years' time they sit down to write the history of writing in this country.

Notes

1   Martin Heidegger, *Being & Time*, trans. John Macquarrie and Edward Robinson (Oxford, 1973), 113.
2   David Attwell has made this case most compellingly in his excellent *J. M. Coetzee and South Africa: Contemporary History and the Politics of Writing* (Berkeley, 1993).

Notes on Contributors

DEREK ATTRIDGE, Professor of English at Rutgers University, New Brunswick, has published books and articles on poetic form and literary theory as well as on Renaissance, Romantic, and modernist writers. He is currently coediting a collection of essays on recent South African writing.

RITA BARNARD, a South African expatriate, is Assistant Professor of English at the University of Pennsylvania. She has previously written about the work of J. M. Coetzee in *Postmodern Culture* (September 1993). Her first book, *The Great Depression and the Culture of Abundance*, is forthcoming from Cambridge University Press.

RICHARD BEGAM, Assistant Professor of English at the University of Wisconsin-Madison, has just completed a book, *Samuel Beckett and the End of Modernity*. His interview with J. M. Coetzee appeared in *Contemporary Literature* (1992).

PAUL A. CANTOR is Professor of English at the University of Virginia, where he also teaches comparative literature. He has published principally on Shakespeare, including the *Hamlet* volume in the Cambridge Landmarks of World Literature series and the forthcoming *Macbeth und die Evangelisierung von Schottland*.

J. M. COETZEE, Professor of General Literature at the University of Cape Town, is the author of *White Writing: On the Culture of Letters in South Africa* (1988) and *Doubling the Point: Essays and Interviews* (1992). His novels include *Dusklands* (1974), *In the Heart of the Country* (1977), *Waiting for the Barbarians* (1980), *Life & Times of Michael K* (1983), *Foe* (1986), and *Age of Iron* (1990).

IAN GLENN is Associate Professor of English at the University of Cape Town. He is currently writing a study of the portrayal of interracial sexual relationships in South African novels in English.

MICHAEL VALDEZ MOSES is Andrew W. Mellon Assistant Professor of English at Duke University. He has published essays on contemporary postcolonial and third world literature, most recently "The Mark of Empire: Writing, History, and Torture in Coetzee's *Waiting for the Barbarians*," *Kenyon Review* (Winter 1993). His book, *The Novel and the Globalization of Culture*, will be published by Oxford University Press in 1994.

CAROLINE RODY, who teaches English at Yale, is working on a study of recent historical fiction by African-American and Caribbean women. Her essay on Toni Morrison's *Beloved* is forthcoming in *American Literary History*, and her article on Jean Rhys's *Wide Sargasso Sea* appears in *Famous Last Words: Changes in Gender and Narrative Closure*, ed. Alison Booth (1993).

PHILIP R. WOOD, a South African expatriate, is Associate Professor of French Studies at Rice University. He is the author of *Jean-Paul Sartre* (1990) and *From Existentialism to Poststructuralism and the Third Industrial Revolution* (forthcoming, Stanford University Press).

differences

A Journal of Feminist Cultural Studies

QUEER THEORY: LESBIAN AND GAY SEXUALITIES
Edited by Teresa de Lauretis
With essays by Teresa de Lauretis, Sue-Ellen Case,
Samuel R. Delany, Elizabeth A. Grosz, Jennifer Terry,
Tomás Almaguer, Ekua Omosupe, Earl Jackson, Jr., and
Julia Creet
Vol. 3, No. 2 $14.70

THE PHALLUS ISSUE
Edited by Naomi Schor and Elizabeth Weed
With essays by Maria Torok, Jean-Joseph Goux,
Parveen Adams, Kaja Silverman, Charles Bernheimer,
Judith Butler, Jonathan Goldberg, Emily Apter
Vol. 4, No. 1 $14.70

ON ADDICTION
Edited by Naomi Schor and Elizabeth Weed
With essays by Jacques Derrida, Leslie Camhi,
Richard Klein, Lynne Joyrich, and Mark Seltzer
Vol. 5, No. 1 $14.70

Subscription (3 issues); $28.00 individual; $60.00 institution; foreign surface
postage add $10.00; foreign air mail postage add $20.00
Send orders to: Journals Division, Indiana University Press, 601 N. Morton,
Bloomington, IN 47404. Phone: (812)855-9449. FAX: (812)855-7931.